CROSSBILL NATUR

Spanish Pyrenees

Spain

WILDLIFE
LANDSCAPE
FLORA AND FAUNA
ROUTES AND SITES
BIRD WATCHING

Dirk Hilbers – Kees Woutersen

Crossbill Guides: Spanish Pyrenees – Spain
First print: 2012
Second print: 2016
Third, fully revised print: 2025

Initiative, text and research: Dirk Hilbers, Kees Woutersen
Editing: John Cantelo, Brian Clews, Cees Hilbers, Riet Hilbers, Niels de Haan, Kim Lotterman, Gino Smeulders, Albert Vliegenthart
Illustrations: Chris Braat
Maps: Dirk Hilbers / mapy.com
Type and image setting: Oscar Lourens
Print: ORO grafic projectmanagement / PNB Letland

ISBN 978-94-91648-39-7

This book is made with FSC-certified paper. Instead of compensating the CO_2-emissions of the printing process, as we usually do when making a Crossbill Guide, we've chosen to invest that money in nature conservation. You can find details of the project we're supporting on our website, under 'Downloads' on the Spanish Pyrenees guidebook page.

Published by Crossbill Guides in association with KNNV Publishing.

FSC
www.fsc.org
MIX
Paper | Supporting responsible forestry
FSC® C084698

KNNV Publishing

KNNV vereniging voor veldbiologie

SAXIFRAGA foundation

MAPY.COM

crossbillguides.org
knnvpublishing.nl
saxifraga.nl

CROSSBILL
GUIDES
FOUNDATION

This guidebook is a product of the non-profit foundation Crossbill Guides. By publishing these books we want to introduce more people to the joys of Europe's beautiful natural heritage and to increase the understanding of the ecological values that underlie conservation efforts. Most of this heritage is protected for ecological reasons and we want to provide insight into these reasons to the public at large. By doing so we hope that more people support the ideas behind nature conservation. For more information about us and our guides you can visit our website at: crossbillguides.org

Highlights of the Pyrenees and steppes of Huesca

1 Walk the dramatic glacial gorge of Ordesa – one of the most awe-inspiring landscapes of Europe (route 15).

2 Search for the special birdlife of the high Pyrenees starring such avian delights as Wallcreepers, Lammergeiers and Citril Finches (routes 9, 13, 15, 16 and site C on page 203).

3 Take long walks through pristine Pyrenean meadows and along glacial lakes and marvel at the wealth of wildflowers and butterflies (e.g. routes 18, 19).

4 Watch wild vultures fight over a carcass at one of the *comederos* or vulture feeding stations in the Sierra de Guara (D on page 162).

5 Go south into the Monegros and watch flocks of sandgrouse before a rising sun with a supporting choir of the rare Dupont's Lark (routes 2 – 5).

6 Embrace Huesca's alternative nightlife and see Foxes, Beech Martens, Red-necked Nightjars and owls along the minor roads in *Dépresion del Ebro*.

7 Be surprised at how many ways the earth's surface can be sculpted into the oddest towers, pillars, cliffs and caves (e.g. routes 5, 6, 15 and 17).

8 Examine the endemic flora of the cliffs and rock faces of Añisclo and Alquézar (routes 8 and 17).

About this guide

This guide is meant for all those who enjoy being in and learning about nature, whether you already know all about it or not. It is set up a little differently from most guides. We focus on explaining the natural and ecological features of an area rather than merely describing the site. We choose this approach because the nature of an area is more interesting, enjoyable and valuable when seen in the context of its complex relationships. The interplay of different species with each other and with their environment is astonishing. The clever tricks and gimmicks that are put to use to beat life's challenges are as fascinating as they are countless.

Take our namesake the Crossbill: at first glance it's just a big finch with an awkward bill. But there is more to the Crossbill than meets the eye. This bill is beautifully adapted for life in coniferous forests. It is used like scissors to cut open pinecones and eat the seeds that are unobtainable for other birds. In the Scandinavian countries where Pine and Spruce take up the greater part of the forests, several Crossbill species have each managed to answer two of life's most pressing questions: how to get food and avoid direct competition. By evolving crossed bills, each differing subtly, they have secured a monopoly of the seeds produced by cones of varying sizes. So complex is this relationship that scientists are still debating exactly how many different species of Crossbill actually exist. Now this should heighten the appreciation of what at first glance was merely an odd bird with a beak that doesn't seem to close properly. Once its interrelationships are seen, nature comes alive, wherever you are.

To some, impressed by the 'virtual' familiarity that television has granted to the wilderness of the Amazon, the vastness of the Serengeti or the sublimity of Yellowstone, European nature may seem a puny surrogate, good merely for the casual stroll. In short, the argument seems to be that if you haven't seen a Jaguar, Lion or Grizzly Bear, then you haven't seen the 'real thing'. Nonsense, of course.

But where to go? And how? What is there to see? That is where this guide comes in. We describe the how, the why, the when, the where and the how come of Europe's most beautiful areas. In clear and accessible language, we explain the nature of Pyrenees and refer extensively to routes where the area's features can be observed best. We try to make Pyrenees come alive. We hope that we succeed.

How to use this guide

This guidebook contains a descriptive and a practical section. The descriptive part comes first and gives you insight into the most striking and interesting natural features of the area. It provides an understanding of what you will see when you go out exploring. The descriptive part consists of a landscape section (marked with a red bar), describing the habitats, the history and the landscape in general, and of a flora and fauna section (marked with a green bar), which discusses the plants and animals that occur in the region.
The second part offers the practical information (marked with a purple bar). A series of routes (walks and car drives) are carefully selected to give you a good flavour of all the habitats, flora and fauna that Pyrenees have to offer. At the start of each route description, a number of icons give a quick overview of the characteristics of each route. These icons are explained in the margin of this page. The final part of the book (marked with blue squares) provides some basic tourist information and some tips on finding plants, birds and other animals.
There is no need to read the book from cover to cover. Instead, each small chapter stands on its own and refers to the routes most suitable for viewing the particular features described in it. Conversely, descriptions of each route refer to the chapters that explain more in depth the most typical features that can be seen along the way.
In the back of the guide we have included a list of all the mentioned plant and animal species, with their scientific names and translations into German and Dutch. Some species names have an asterix (*) following them. This indicates that there is no official English name for this species and that we have taken the liberty of coining one. We realise this will meet with some reservations by those who are familiar with scientific names. For the sake of readability however, we have decided to translate the scientific name, or, when this made no sense, we gave a name that best describes the species' appearance or distribution. Please note that we do not want to claim these as the official names. We merely want to make the text easier to follow for those not familiar with scientific names. An overview of the area described in this book is given on the map on page 15. For your convenience we have also turned the inner side of the back flap into a map of the area indicating all the described routes. Descriptions in the explanatory text refer to these routes.

Icons used to charactarise the routes and to show the key interest:

- 1 Waypoint
- Walk
- Ticket
- Photo spot
- History
- Scenery
- Geology
- Ecology
- Flora
- Mammals
- Birds
- Reptiles / amphibians
- Butterflies
- Dragonflies
- Invertebrates

Table of contents

*The names and locations of the additional sites are shown in the map in the back cover.

LANDSCAPE

Introduction

The Pyrenees are both lush and bleak, dramatic and gentle. The mountainous character of the landscape is sharpened and thrown into relief by its stark desert-like southern hinterland. It is this combination that makes this region such a popular destination for naturalists. You will immediately understand why this is so from the first moment you set foot here. The lofty cliffs are overwhelming and the distant snow-covered peaks add a mysterious allure.

The wildest and most scenic parts of the Spanish Pyrenees are found in the Province of Huesca, the area of this guidebook. This region is characterised by its abrupt landscape with countless cliffs of several hundreds of metres high, which make large parts quiet and inaccessible – one of the reasons that there is so much wildlife here.

If one had to summarise the area in a single word, it would be 'variability'. Climate, landscape, flora and fauna change dramatically over short distances. It is only a little over 100 km from the snow-capped mountains on the border with France to the arid, semi-desert lowlands of the basin of the river Ebro. From cold, barren conditions at 3,000 metres, you can move down through fresh Alpine meadows, then on into dense mountain woodlands then further down into Mediterranean evergreen oak woods and scrub and eventually, onto steppe and desert-like terrain (around Zaragoza). From the city of Huesca, each of these habitats can be reached within an hour – an exceptionally swift transition of the landscape.

This varied landscape translates into a rich flora and fauna. And since most areas, including those without any protection, are still in good condition, you can expect to find interesting things just about anywhere. However, for a more focused and informed exploration of the Pyrenees and steppes of Huesca, you need a little background knowledge. And that is where this guide comes in.

Massive Beech trees grow deep down in the damp gorges of the Pyrenees.

Geographical overview

The area described in this book covers the province of Huesca and a few sites directly adjacent in the province of Zaragoza. Both provinces form, together with Teruel province, the autonomous region of Aragón. Our region can be divided in three parts of about the same size. Each of these areas are strikingly different in landscape, ambiance, climate, flora and fauna.

The Ebro basin: Somontano and Monegros

The relatively flat and low land surrounding the Ebro and its tributaries is known as the Ebro basin. In Huesca, it is divided in the *Somontano* and *Los Monegros*. Route 2 to 6 cover territory in this area.
Somontano, literally means 'land under the mountains', and is the green and picturesque strip just south of the *Sierras Exteriores*. The important cities of Huesca and Barbastro are situated in the *Somontano*. Travelling south from here (as route 5 does), the landscape gradually becomes more arid as one enters the Monegros. The Ebro river is the life line in this dry region and supports the large city of Zaragoza (687,000 inhabitants in 2024). From whichever direction the wind blows, the central part of the Ebro basin is always in the rain shadow of mountains. Therefore, it is a dry and hot area, in some places reminiscent of the great deserts of North America. Spectacular and thinly populated (apart from Zaragoza and its environs), this area supports some well-known bird sites, such as the steppes of Los Monegros and south of it Belchite. On page 108 we provide a detailed account of this area as an introduction to the routes.

Sierras Exteriores

The second region is a belt of mountains collectively called the *Sierras Exteriores* or *Prepireneos* (although we won't be using the latter term in this book). Routes 7 to 11 cover this area. The central, largest and highest part of this mountain range is the Natural Park Sierra de Guara, but other fairly famous areas, such as Riglos and Loarre, are part of this chain too.
The *Sierras Exteriores* are, with peaks around 2000 metres, not as high as the central Pyrenees, but nevertheless form a respectable mountain chain. The mountains rise steeply up from the *Somontano* and are virtually deserted. The few villages that exist are at the southern base of the mountains (Riglos, Alquézar) and along the few valleys that connect the lowlands with the high Pyrenees.
The *Sierras Exteriores* form a considerable geographical barrier. Traffic through the chain is concentrated to a few valleys. The main traffic route (at the time of writing being converted into a motorway) is the

The four main landscapes of the Pyrenees: the steppes of the Ebro basin, the green *Somontano*, the Mediterranean *Sierras Exteriores* and the Alpine landscape of the high Pyrenees.

A23 which connects Huesca with Sabiñánigo. Towards the west there is only the road that connects Ayerbe with Jaca (via, with a small diversion, the village of Riglos). East of Huesca the next option to cross the *Sierras Exteriores* is near Alquézar at the far eastern end of the Sierra de Guara. East of Barbastro, the *Sierras Exteriores* disintegrate into a series of smallermountain ranges, pierced by larger rivers that run down from the Pyrenees, like the Cinca, Esera, Isábena and Ribagorzana. Beside these rivers, north-south traffic is much easier.

On page 140 we provide a detailed account of this area as an introduction to the routes.

Depresión and High Pyrenees

The third region lies north of the *Sierras Exteriores* and stretches out to the French border. Routes 12 to 21 cover this region. It is a large area with hills and smaller mountains, intersected with broad valleys separating the main Pyrenean chain and the *Sierras Exteriores*. This is known as *Las Depresiones*. Most of the Pyrenean towns, such as Jaca, Sabiñánigo, Fiscal, Aínsa and Campo, are here.

Broad shallow rivers, small areas of agriculture and vast areas of rocky hillsides covered in scrub and Portuguese Oak woodlands dominate the landscape. Only locally are there larger mountains of which the isolated twin mountains of San Juan de la Peña and Oroel (route 12) are the most noteworthy.

The High Pyrenees themselves rise up north of a line drawn between Jaca, Aínsa and Campo. Alternating valleys and mountains, orientated north-south, connect with the central Pyrenean 'spine' that runs all along the border with France. This is the highest part of the Pyrenees (see page 16).

Due to this topography, a visit to the High Pyrenees always takes one of these north-south valleys. Each has its special character and they are, therefore, separately described in this book. In general the western valleys (Ansó, Hecho, Canfranc) are the most 'Atlantic' (meaning that they are relatively green and moist). The eastern valleys (Plan, Benasque and Barrabés) are more 'Mediterranean', thus drier and sunnier (although not necessarily warmer). In the centre lie the great massifs of the National Park Ordesa and Monte Perdido, both of which, being limestone, have a more dramatic character of massive gorges and impressive cliffs.

On page 162 we provide a further account of the Depresión and High Pyrenees as an introduction to the routes in this area.

Opposite page: Overview of the area covered by this guide book.

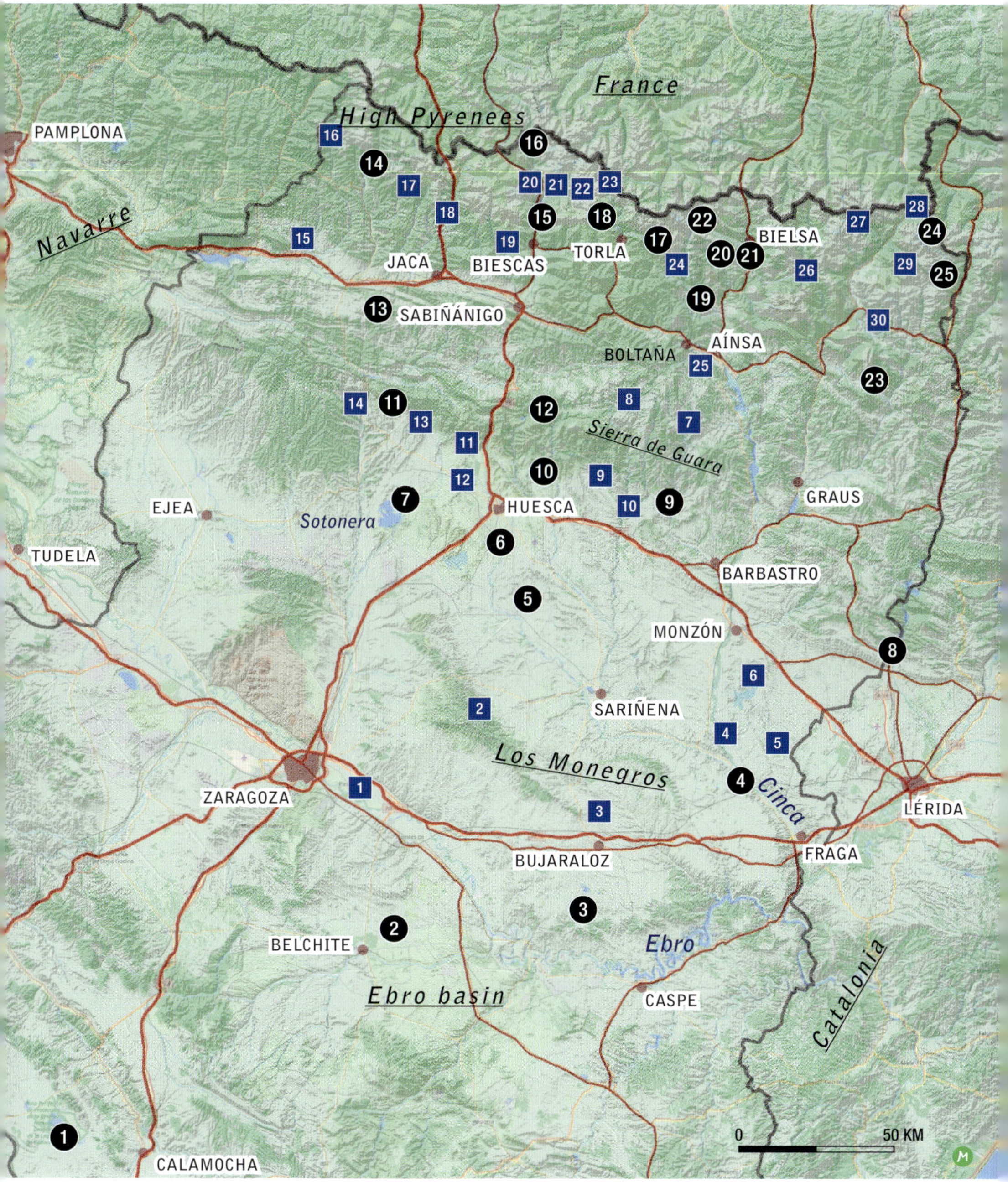
France
High Pyrenees
PAMPLONA
Navarre
JACA
BIESCAS
TORLA
BIELSA
SABIÑÁNIGO
BOLTAÑA
AÍNSA
Sierra de Guara
EJEA
Sotonera
HUESCA
GRAUS
TUDELA
BARBASTRO
MONZÓN
SARIÑENA
Los Monegros
ZARAGOZA
Cinca
LÉRIDA
FRAGA
BUJARALOZ
BELCHITE
Ebro
Ebro basin
CASPE
Catalonia
CALAMOCHA
0
50 KM

Geology

The complex geology of the Pyrenees makes it one of the most interesting places in Europe for geologists, amateur and professional alike. In fact, anyone with the slightest interest in landscape will be spell-bound by the spectacular geological phenomena. The geological features are not confined to the Pyrenees and *Sierras Exteriores* – but extend to the 'Wild West' landscape of gypsum and sandstone sculptures in the Ebro basin.

The region is composed of a range of high mountains along the French border (the high Pyrenees), followed by a broad zone of lower mountains with broad valleys in between (the *Depresión*). Further south the land rises again to form the *Sierras Exteriores,* before dropping down again to the lowlands of the Ebro valley. Within this region a wide range of rock types occur – limestone, slate, granite, sandstone, gypsum and younger sediments.

The first range

Four main events shaped this complex landscape. In the Paleozoicum (some 500 million years ago) there were no mountains in this area at all. On the contrary, a shallow sea covered what is now northern Spain with a ridge roughly where the Ebro flows today. During the earliest period of mountain building, the Hercynean (300 million years ago), the pressure from colliding tectonic plates steadily pushed up a range of mountains, along the line of the present Pyrenees. The central Pyrenees (or Axial Pyrenees, as geologists say) were formed. The old bedrock still surfaces on some of the highest ranges and contain both volcanic or *igneous* (e.g. granite) and metamorphic rocks (rocks that changed in composition due to extreme tectonic pressure, like marble, slate and

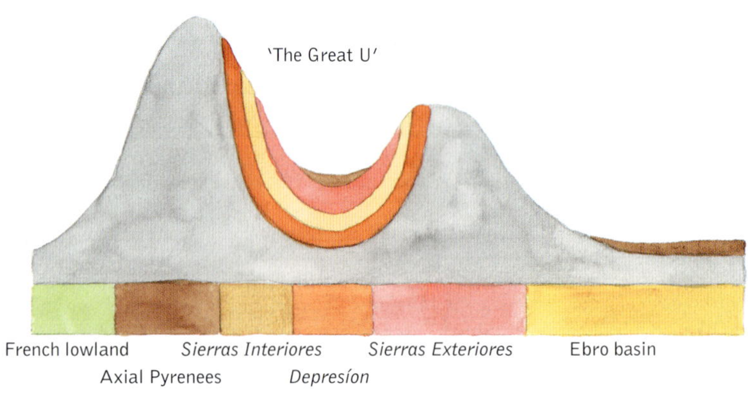

Geological cross-section of the Pyrenees and Ebro lowlands.

quartzite). Most of this bedrock is acidic and not easily penetrated by water. As a result, water runs off over the surface and creates a green, Alpine landscape. You'll find these landscapes near Benasque (Maladeta massif), Pineta, and areas of Hecho and Canfranc.

The great U

The second geological event occurred during the period of Alpine mountain building (some 55 million years ago). Prior to this, parts of the region had been covered by a shallow sea. When the Iberian plate pushed towards the neighbouring Eurasian plate, the land rose and the sea drained, exposing the underlying marine sediments. These are the limestones, sandstones and conglomerate rocks we find today.

During the collision, the gigantic pressure folded the bedrock such that, in cross-section, it formed a giant U shape (an anti-clinal in geological terms; see facing page). The northern peak of the U is known as the *Sierras Interiores*. They merge with the Axial Pyrenees to the north and together form the High Pyrenees.

The southern peak of the U emerges some 50 km further south and corresponds with the aforementioned *Sierras Exteriores* – the belt of high mountains of which the Sierra de Riglos and Sierra de Guara are a part. The trough of the U is the *Depresión* – the broad area with lower mountains and broad valleys that separate the two Pyrenean ranges.

This U-shape is unique to the Spanish Pyrenees and most visible in the western half of the province of Huesca. On the French side there is not a double row of mountains. This is because the Iberian plate is much lighter and more easily deformed than the larger European plate of the French Pyrenees. The Spanish Pyrenees are like a small car that crashed into a truck: its crumple zone at the front is completely folded and deformed, but the truck barely has a scratch.

This bedrock formation consists of multiple layers of rock. Limestone has created giant massifs in the *Sierras Interiores* (e.g. Ordesa – route 15, Turbón – route 20) and dominates the *Sierras Exteriores*. Because limestone easily dissolves in water, rivers were able to cut out impressive canyons and caves. The Gorge of Añisclo (route 17) and the many canyons in the Sierra de Guara are all the result of rivers (sometimes surprisingly small ones) that ate their way into the brittle bedrock.

Limestone layers are sandwiched between deposits of sandstones and slates. These dusty-yellow sandstones dominate the hillsides in the *Depresión* and *Somontano* today.

A very peculiar rock type is that of the conglomerates. It is a mixture of large rounded stones in a matrix of hard, petrified sand and clay. Conglomerate rock is very resistant to erosion so where it occurs it rises out of the surrounding limestone like giant pillars. The conglomerate *Mallos* of Riglos (route 10) are the most famous and spectacular example,

but other impressive conglomerate rocks are present at Roldán, Vadiello (route 9) and San Juan de la Peña (route 12).
This geological picture is further complicated by at least two glacial phases, which created icecaps on the axial Pyrenees and the *Sierras Interiores*. Glaciers ran down through the Pyrenean valleys and created impressive 'cirques' in some higher areas, most notably the Ordesa (route 15) and Pineta valleys (route 17). The length of the glaciers varied from 10 to over 40 km in the valley of the Gállego River.

Younger sediments

The geological formations in the Ebro valley are much younger than the Pyrenees. They find their origin in the sediments that ran off from the Pyrenean mountains and – to lesser extent – the Spanish Meseta.
This sea was filled up with sediments from the edges towards the centre of the Ebro basin. The hardest conglomerates and sandstones are found along the edges of the basin (in the *Somontano*) and towards the edge of the Iberian plateau. The centre is filled with younger marine sediments: sandstones, clays and gypsum soils.
Severe drought has hardened these sediments to a very erosive type of rock. The spectacular forms of erosion of these young and brittle sediments are found in the form of table mountains and isolated rock pillars or *torrellones* (routes 2, 4 and 5). These sediments are rich in salt and alkaline minerals. Evaporation draws up ground water, and with it these minerals, to the surface. As the water evaporates, they are left behind creating the special, desert-like vegetation of the Monegros heartland (route 2, 3).
In the *Depresión* a similar type of semi-petrified sediment occurs, brought down from the Pyrenean rivers. Here the bluish, softly rolling hills, devoid of vegetation, are not unlike hardened cement (page 173). These sediments are in the Jaca valley and south of Turbón (route 13 and 20).

There are many odd geological formations throughout Huesca, such as the old man (*El Abuelo*; left) and the Dolphin (*El Delfin*; opposite page). *El Abuelo* consists of sandstone, while *El Delfin* is a hole in a limestone cliff (next page).

New soils

The rivers that run down from the Pyrenees add the final touch to the landscape. They bring down sediments – clay, sand, pebbles – from the bedrock through which they flow. Where the current is sluggish, such as on the plains of Jaca and the river floodplains in the lowlands, these sediments sank down and formed fertile soils. Permanently moist and loaded with nutrients, these are the soils that traditionally supported the most verdant vegetation. They are also the most suited to agriculture. However, in the last century, irrigation made it possible to farm much further from the river whilst, in places, hydro-electric dams made farming along the streams impossible. Where the land is fertile and permanently moist, such as near the Cinca and along the Flúmen, riverine forests still thrive.

Climate

There are few – if any – places in Europe with such climatic differences as Huesca. This is the obvious result of strong altitudinal differences and the fact that the Spanish side of the Pyrenees lies in a rain shadow. Average annual precipitation decreases very rapidly when descending from the Pyrenean mountain tops to the Ebro lowlands. Less pronounced, but still noticeable, is the higher precipitation in the Atlantic west in comparison with the more Mediterranean east. Hence the southeast is the driest (and sunniest) part of the province. Fraga, the main city in the south-east, has and annual rainfall of only 347 mm. To put this into perspective, an annual precipitation of under 250 mm qualifies as a desert climate. In Spain, only the far south-east (Murcia, south-east Andalusia) sees less rain.

At the other extreme Candanchú, a ski resort on the French border in the high Pyrenees, has 1,957 mm., close to 6 times more rain than Fraga. It is also 3 times as much as London and twice as much as Amsterdam.

The climate in the Ebro valley is a Mediterranean one although with a distinct continental slant. Winters, which reign supreme until the end of March, are much colder than at the coast. The strong winds over the open plains make it even colder. The cold *cierzo* blows from the northwest and the warmer *bochorno* from the east, and both can build up speeds of nearly 100 km per hour. Fog is another typical feature of the lowlands in winter. Some valleys see fog regularly and there it is an important source of water for the vegetation.
But sun and clear skies are the usual conditions in the lowlands. Over much of the year, the sun relentlessly desiccates the land. The summers are extremely dry and hot. Two months without a single drop of rain is standard.

Fog is frequent in winter, but, like most weather types, local. Usually the lowlands experience fog (such as here the *Depresión*) and the mountains are clear.

In contrast in the Pyrenees a mountain climate predominates, with precipitation possible throughout the year. Between December and March I it mostly falls in the form of snow in the valleys. On the peaks however, the snowy period extends well into spring. The dominant wind direction, north-westerly, brings moist air to the western Pyrenees (Basque and Navarra) and the northern, French slopes. In Huesca, the mountains are relatively dry. Most rain and snow falls close to the border. It is frequently the case that if one travels over the Pyrenees, it pours on the French side, rains on the border, becomes dry a few kilometres further on with the sun coming out as one enters the valley. We have never experienced differences this stark elsewhere in Europe.
In summer, clouds often build up during the day over the Pyrenees, bringing rain and sometimes thunderstorms in the late afternoon. Such rains usually don't last long, but can be dangerous for hikers at high altitudes, particularly as the deluges are accompanied by lightning.

Habitats

Given the extreme climatic differences, it is not a surprise that there is a large range of habitats in the Spanish Pyrenees. Some habitat types reappear, in different forms, throughout the area. A heat and drought adapted forest (consisting of Spanish Juniper, Aleppo Pine and Holm Oak) occurs in the Ebro lowlands. A very different forest type, adapted to cool, moist conditions, consists of dense stands of Beech and Silver Fir, and occurs in the mountains. Cliffs and wetlands too, have their specific forms in each of the regions of the province.

Other habitats are restricted to a specific part of the province, like the steppes and semi-deserts in the Ebro basin and the Alpine meadows of the High Pyrenees.

We distinguish five general habitat types, which are described in detail in the following chapters. These are steppe and farmland (page 22), wetlands (page 26), cliffs and canyons (page 31), forests and scrublands (page 33) and high mountain habitats (page 39). These are further divided into the specific habitat types that occur at different altitudes. The illustration below gives an overview of these different habitats and their position in the landscape.

Each habitat has its own ecology, landscape, atmosphere and unique inhabitants – in other words, its own specific charm. Therefore, we have selected the routes and sites (described from page 111 onwards) to cover each of these habitats. At the beginning of each description we refer to the routes and sites that best showcase each specific habitat.

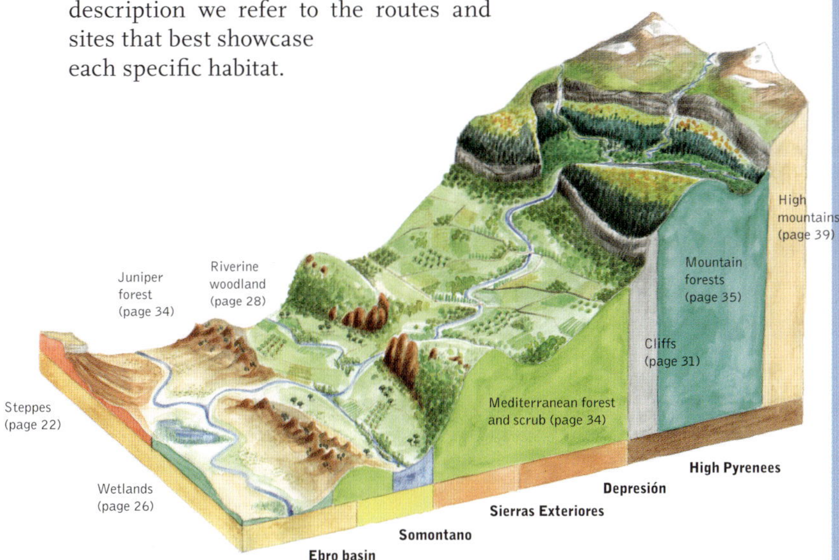

Cross-section of Huesca with its typical habitats.

Steppe and dry farmland

Routes 1-5 lead through steppe and dry farmland.

What is missing in this 'western' landscape is the poor lonesome cowboy. Otherwise, the steppes of the Monegros and the plains of the Ebro, with their badlands, table mountains and sandstone cliffs, appear like the Spanish version of the Wild West. This 'Wild Huesca' extends from the drylands of Lérida (Lleida) in Catalonia over Aragón to the Bardales Reales in Navarra (see map on page 15). It collectively forms one of the most important arid environments in Europe.

Dryland farming – using drought-resistant cereal crops – and sheep herding are the dominant forms of land use. The scenery appears terraced: flat-topped mountains are separated from flat lowlands to create a landscape in which plain and slope continuously alternate. Both slopes and plains have their own attractions.

Most of the flat or gently sloping areas, both in the valleys and on top of the table mountains, are ploughed and planted with cereals. The fields are not in production every year thus in a given area, you'll encounter

The salt steppes of el Planerón ornithological reserve at Belchite (route 2).

The table land steppe of the Ebro basin, with on the left the natural situation with Gypsum steppe on the top and salt steppe on the bottom of the hill. This is the situation at Belchite (route 2). On the right, the flat areas on the top and in the valley are farmed, as is the case in much of the Monegros.

a mix of cereals, fallow and ploughed land. Some of the flat areas have been abandoned, or have escaped cultivation altogether, because of their high salt or alkaline (gypsum) content which makes them unsuitable for agriculture.

On saline soils, endorheic lagoons – shallow water bodies present only after periods of heavy rain – add to the natural diversity. This extreme environment is the realm of many rare specialist plant species and some insects and crustaceans that are unique in the world (see route 3).

The natural vegetation on gypsum soils is a scatter of low bushes and grasses over barren ground. This fragile environment is home to another group of specialist plant species (see page 74) and a wealth of birds, of which the highly endangered Dupont's Lark is the most noteworthy.

The flat areas are the most attractive for steppe birds, with large numbers of larks, Stone Curlews, Pin-tailed and Black-bellied Sandgrouse. All of these do best on the natural steppes or on fallow land. Little and Great Bustards occur as well, albeit in much lower numbers. They prefer the cereal plots and areas with tall grass.

The hillsides and cliffs are left unused and are covered with a mix of Mediterranean and semi-desert scrub. This pristine vegetation supports a wealth of wildflowers and butterflies, with many species that are restricted to regions of extreme aridity. The reptile and amphibian fauna is diverse and consists almost solely of southern species. Typical dryland species are Ladder Snake and Spanish Psammodromus, which

If you look carefully, you'll find that the steppes are home to a wide variety of plants and animals, such as this Wood Fairy* (top), Spiny-footed Lizard (centre) and Spanish Aizoon (bottom).

are common alongside the more widely occurring Large Psammodromus, Moorish Gecko and Montpellier Snake. The birdlife consists of Thekla Larks, Black-eared Wheatear, Dartford and Spectacled Warblers.

The sometimes spectacular cliffs and isolated rock pillars greatly add to the drama of the arid landscape. Cliffs and crags also support large numbers of breeding birds and cave-dwelling bats. Eagle Owls, Egyptian Vultures and Golden Eagles are frequent – the latter even breeds in higher densities here than in the Pyrenees. A very typical bird of dry rocky slopes is one of the target species of many birdwatchers: the Black Wheatear. This bird, restricted to the Iberian Peninsula and northwest Africa, is typically seen flying from rock to rock along the sand-coloured cliffs.

The lark indicator

There are several types of arid landscapes in the Ebro plain, and each have their own natural treasures. One very good indicator for the type of arid land you are dealing with, is the species of lark you find there (or vice versa, recognising the habitat type is a good way to finding the lark species). Although there is a degree of overlap, each of the six species of lark favours its own habitat type:

Calandra Larks are common in steppe and cereal fields.

Crested Lark: Open disturbed land, road and field edges, car parks, wastelands near villages. Locally common.
Thekla Lark: Steppes with bushes – both small and large. Common.
Calandra Lark: Flat, grassy steppes or ploughed fields, but highest densities in cereal plantations. Common.
Short-toed Lark: Short-grass steppes (natural and man made), abandoned fields, dry farmland. Common.
Lesser Short-toed Lark: exclusive to saline areas and natural gypsum steppes. Very Local.
Dupont's Lark: exclusive to natural steppes, mostly gypsum, with patches of tall herbs and Esparto over barren ground. Very local.

We would have liked to end our description of this prinstine arid landscape here, but than we would leave you with an unrealistic account of the Ebro plains. For many years, the dryland farming existed as a nature-friendly way of land use in which birds and other animals could exist and thrive alongside the agricultural practice. During the Franco years, large scale irrigation projects changed the face of the Ebro basin (see maps on page 54). The Pyrenean rivers bring down plenty of water and much of the land in the Ebro basin is quite fertile, so all ingredients were there for large-scale integration. After the Franco era, the number of irrigated fields increased rapidly, thanks to EU subsidies. Since most of the land had no protected status whatsoever, the unique dryland habitat dwindled and became fragmented with severe consequences for, above all, the birdlife. At present, the area of irrigated fields is still slowly increasing, while wind farms and solar panels also occupy increasingly large sections of land. A visit to the Monegros or Belchite, though still of interest for the birdlife, is no longer a trip to the 'Wild West'. The lonesome cowboy is now just a distant memory.

Wetlands – rivers, marshes and temporary lagoons

Routes 1, 2, 3 (best) and 4 visit saline lagoons. Explore freshwater habitat on route 3, 5 and 6 and riverine forest on route 5 and sites B and D on page 137-138. Mid-altitude rivers are present on routes 11 and 20. Mountain streams are present on route 13, 15, 16, 17, 18, 29. Glacial lakes (Ibóns) are present on route 14, 21 and sites E and F on page 182 and site D on page 203.

Water is one of the defining factors of the landscape in Huesca – either through its presence or, equally striking, its absence. Huesca's basic hydro-logy is simple. Several major rivers (e.g. Aragón, Gállego and Cinca) flow from the high Pyrenees. Numerous much smaller rivers (e.g. Flumen, Alcanadre, Vero) run down from the *Sierras Exteriores*. All of them meet the mighty river Ebro in the south.

Waters from the mountains flow south into an area with progressively less precipitation, creating a lush ribbon of vegetation that snakes through a vast area of contrastingly thirsty steppe.

All in all, this produces a large variety of wetlands in the region, which can be roughly grouped into four major types: high altitude rivers and glacial lakes, mid-altitude rivers, slow-flowing lowland rivers and freshwater lakes, and saline lagoons.

Mountain streams and *Ibóns*

Melting snow trickles down wet slopes and collects in gullies. Joined by springs that gush from rocky cracks, the water soon collects in small streams which, engorged by meltwater and powered by gravity, thunder on down the valley.

Mountain streams are cold, oxygen-rich and nutrient-poor. Water levels vary greatly throughout the seasons. In winter, prolonged periods of subzero temperatures lock the water in an icy grip. In spring, the combination of growing warmth and an abundance of melting snow, transforms the murmuring streams into raging torrents. These drastic changes require special adaptations of the inhabitants of mountain streams. Brown Trout, Pyrenean Frog (see box on page 95) caddisflies and various dragonflies (e.g. Common and Sombre Goldenring) have all adapted to cope with these conditions. The most emblematic bird of these rivers is perhaps the Dipper: a member of a small family of songbird that can, uniquely, plunge into cold water to swim (using its wings) or walk on the riverbed in search of its favourite food, the larvae of caddisflies.

Unique to the Pyrenees and Cantabrian mountains is the mole-like Pyrenean Desman: a rare, nocturnal and highly secretive mammal of rapid mountain rivers.

The high mountain lakes or *Ibóns*, as they are called locally, offer a home to a number of rare animal species.

The source area of mountain rivers forms a very different habitat. Water seeping out of bedrock or meltwater dripping into a small depression creates permanently wet surfaces. There is a set of particular plants that occur only in these small boggy wetlands. It is the realm of the butterworts – a group of insectiverous plants of which four species occur in the Pyrenees. Lower down, Black Bog-rush, Robust Marsh-orchid and Marsh Helleborine are typical of such sites.

Where water collects in depresions in the mountains, peatlands and mountain lakes are formed (locally called *Ibóns*). These beautiful, high altitude habitats are poor in nutrients, which, together with the extreme winter cold, create a landscape reminiscent of the Scottish and Scandinavian lakes and peatlands. Not much of the northern flora and fauna has survived this far south, but the waving cottongrasses and Bogbeans starkly remind one of the north. There are also a number of northern dragonflies, such as Moorland Hawker and Small Whiteface, which reach their southern limit here in the Pyrenees. Thus, from a Spanish perspective, the *Ibóns* are very special.

Mid-altitude rivers

Once in the valleys, the mountain streams merge and flow over flat ground. In some valleys, the streams have created floodbeds tens of metres wide, through which multiple streams snake around islands and pebble banks in a continuously changing web of intricate channels. A gallery forest – where willows and poplars arch over the water – flanks the waterways.

The riverine habitat here (called *Soto* in Spanish) is often overlooked by visitors who are distracted by the splendour of the high mountain landscapes. The Spanish do remarkably little with their rivers. Angling,

The rivers in the lower valleys and in the *Somontano* have a distinct Mediterranean touch. The gallery woodland lining the streams support a rich birdlife.

canoeing, riverside picnics and swimming are virtually unknown here. Hence these riverine threads remain largely untouched. Unfortunately, they are also difficult to access. Yet where possible it is worth exploring the shorelines a little (such as on routes 11, 20 and site A on page 181). The riverine woodland is the realm of a particular subset of birds, with Golden Oriole, both kites, Iberian Green Woodpecker and Wryneck among the key species. Little Ringed Plovers, Grey and White Wagtails and Grey Herons are frequent on the pebble banks. Bee-eaters breed in the sandy cliffs of the river.

Lowland rivers and freshwater lakes

In the lower sections of the Ebro, Cinca and Gállego, the waters have slowed to a sluggish pace. What is true for the middle sections of the river, applies to the lowland rivers even more: the thick gallery forests are a refuge for many birds in this dry region. One might expect in this hot, dry and populated area, that people would also congregate along the riversides, but again there are almost no leisure activities here. Granted, the quality of the river water hasn't been very good. Run-off from the irrigated fields is dumped in the river. But, in the course of the last decade, the waste water has been better treated and the river water quality is gradually improving. Some species sensitive to pollution, like Otter, are frequent in some river sections (particularly in the Cinca River).

The lowland rivers are, in comparison to the mid-section ones, richer in nutrients and have soft, deep soils. Consequently, the vegetation is dominated by a few vigorous species of plants (e.g. willows, poplars, reeds) that push out all other plants. The lack of a varied vegetation takes its toll on the insect diversity, but these 'flaws' are easily forgotten when the birdlife is considered. In the generally arid and hilly Aragón, the bulk of the marshland birds breed along the river. And given the small size of the riverine wetlands, they do so in exceptional numbers. In particular, Purple Heron is surprisingly common along the Ebro river. Other riverine bird species that occur only, or predominantly, along the larger rivers are Night Heron, Little Egret, Kingfisher, Sand Martin and Penduline Tit.

The few freshwater lakes in the area essentially support the same species as the riverine habitat, but are more accesible, and therefore popular, amongst birdwatchers. The freshwater lakes, such as Sariñena (route 5),

Sotonera (route 6) and Candasnos (route 3) were created by man to produce a reservoir of freshwater for agriculture. Nonetheless, their reedy shores are an oasis for birdlife. Not all human-created wetlands are successful havens for nature. The large reservoirs with their steep sides and deep bottoms are biologically close to dead. The same goes for the recently created rice paddies. But in this case it is not the topography but the heavy use of pesticides that makes them uninteresting for most birds.

Temporary, saline lagoons

If you look at a map of the Monegros you find quite a large number of lagoons dotted throughout the steppes. These temporary lagoons (endorheic lakes in jargon) are the natural wetlands of the arid Ebro basin. They are saline in nature due to the very high evaporation that draws up water with soluble salts from the ground. At the surface, the water evaporates and the salt remains.

These lagoons are fed by rain but since the evaporation rate much exceeds that of the precipitation, the 'lagoons' are usually dry, leaving nothing but a salt crust surrounded by a ring of 'halophytes' (salt adapted plants). Some dry lagoon beds lack the white salt crust and in their habitually dry state they are hard to distinguish from the surrounding steppe vegetation. Being nothing more than a brownish disc of scruffy

The freshwater lakes in the Monegros are small in number and size, but still harbour large numbers of ducks, herons, Marsh Harriers, and other wetland birds (left). Night Herons occur along the Ebro River (top).

This is La Playa, a dried out saline lagoon in the Monegros (route 3). Such salt steppe vegetations are home to rare steppe birds, such as Short-toed and Lesser Short-toed Larks, Stone Curlews and sandgrouse.

plants under the brutish Spanish sun, they could not be more different from the optimistically bright blue patch on the map.

In spite of their unspectacular appearance, the temporary saline lagoons can be very attractive places for naturalists. The salt flora, though not very rich in species, is special. This far inland, with conditions that are different from those at the coast, the flora contains typical steppe species, some of which are unique to the arid regions of inland Spain. One peculiar type of glasswort occurs only in the Monegros, Southeast Spain and ... Central Turkey. This Relict Glasswort* (*Microcnemum coralloides*) is evidence for the theory that in the past the Mediterranean once nearly dried out and formed a giant area of salt steppes (an event called the *Messinean Salinity Crisis*). After the Mediterranean refilled, the formerly widespread Relict Glasswort* only survived in the two far corners of its original range: Turkey and Spain.

The prolonged drought makes it impossible for fish to survive in the saline lagoons. This offers opportunities for other animals to prosper that are otherwise eaten by, or are in competition with, these fish. Natterjack Toad and Western Spadefoot thrive here because of the lack of predatory fish. Several species of single celled organisms in the lakes of the *La Playa* complex (route 3) are unique to this area.

Birdwatchers do well at the temporary lagoons too. The larger lagoons which usually carry at least a little water, have breeding birds like Black-winged Stilt, Kentish Plover and, at Gallocanta (route 1), Gull-billed Tern. The surrounding zone with glassworts and other salt adapted plants is at least as interesting, with Lesser Short-toed Lark a typical breeding bird. Stone Curlew and Pin-tailed Sandgrouse do well here too.

Cliffs and canyons

Cliffs are a prominent feature on routes 8, 9, 10, 13, 15, 16 and 17. Sandstone escarpments in the Ebro basin feature on routes 3, 4 and 5.

Cliffs are everywhere. Even in the Monegros, sandstone rock walls and table mountains dominate the landscape. These grand escarpments make the Spanish Pyrenees one of the most dramatic landscapes of Europe.

Cliffs are flora and fauna hotspots, characterised by a high concentration of endemics – species that occur only in a very small area. In the Pyrenees and *Sierras Exteriores*, this is perhaps even more the case than elsewhere. No less than 5 of the 8 highly attractive plants we highlight on pages 62-63, are cliff dwellers. Many of the birdwatcher's most wanted – Lammergeier, Wallcreeper, Black Wheatear – breed in this mountainous landscape.

In an ecological sense, cliffs are special because they are places where competition and disturbance are naturally low. Chance is a big factor in determining whether seeds find the isolated spots where plant growth is possible. And, since chance doesn't favour specific species, all cliff dwellers are able to spread and grow on cliffs. The steep terrain is difficult or downright impossible for herbivores to access, so once a seed has germinated there is little danger.

The mighty rock faces of the Pyrenees and the Guara, such as here at Ordesa (route 15) support large colonies of cliff-breeding birds. The Griffon Vulture (next page) is undoubtedly the most numerous of them.

The Griffon Vulture is the most numerous of the three vultures of Huesca.

The inaccessibility also favours birds. Mammalian egg thieves (including humans) can't reach birds' nests. Soaring birds like raptors take advantage of the rising air. Cliff ledges are the vulture's equivalent of an apartment with elevator: the air warms on the vertical surface and rises. The bird only needs to spread its wings to be effortlessly wafted upwards.

This is also a reason why south-facing cliffs, quickly warmed by the sun, are more in demand than north-facing ones. Wallcreepers too prefer south-facing cliffs where their favourite prey, insects, are more abundant. Butterflies and reptiles which need the warmth of the sun to become active, are often found on south slopes too.

Plant life is also sensitive to exposure to the sun's rays, but this time, many species prefer the shadier, moister north face, where the microclimate is generally less extreme. Ramonda or Bear's-ear (page 63) is an obvious shade-lover, as are many ferns, like Maidenhair Fern, Maidenhair Spleenwort, Hart's-tongue and Smooth Spleenwort. On the sunny side of the rock, drought-resistant Snapdragon, Long-leaved (page 63) and Live-long Saxifrages and Sarcocapnos are typical (page 70).

The lowland rock slopes have their own distinctive set of species. Among the birds, Blue Rock Thrush and Black Wheatear are typical of lowland cliffs. The steep slopes of the table mountains are a refuge for steppe flora, because the flatter surfaces are mostly converted to agricultural use.

Forests and scrubland

Mediterranean oak woodlands are a prominent feature on routes 6, 9, 11, 12, 20 and sites A, C and F on pages 161-163. The special dry Aleppo pine and Spanish Juniper woodlands are part of route 5 and site A on page 137. Well-established mountain pine forests are to be found on routes 11, 12, 14, 16, 20 and site D on page 203. Beech and beech-fir forests of the moist areas of the Pyrenees feature on routes 13, 15 and 18 and site E on page 182, whereas subalpine open pine heathlands are present on routes 14, 15, 19 and site D on page 203. Route 17 is all about canyon forests.

Before the arrival of humans, the larger part of Huesca was forested. Only the saline and gypsum soils, areas where rocks surface, and the regions above the treeline are naturally forest-free.

In comparison to many other regions in Spain, Huesca has retained a fair chunk of its forests. With the exodus of people from the mountains (see history section), forest cover has increased over vast areas. Woodland occurs in inaccessible places and often isn't managed nor serves any particular purpose. In fact, apart from the odd hunter or rambler, no one sets foot in many of these areas. Large parts of the forest have developed into a natural state.

The large range of climates in the region gives rise to many different forest types, ranging from subalpine, open pine forests, mountain woodlands of Beech and Fir, Scots and Austrian pine forests, Mediterranean oak forests and drought-resistant stands of Aleppo Pine and Spanish Juniper.

Different types of scrubland and forest are found at different altitudes. Spanish Juniper forest covers the driest soils (see site A on page 137). Oak woodlands cover much of the *Somontano* and *Depresión* (e.g. routes 9 and 12). Scots Pine forests dominate the sunny areas of the mountains (e.g. routes 11 and 12), while Pyrenean Pine is found on the high slopes (e.g. route 15). In shady areas, mixed Beech-Fir forests are frequent (e.g. routes 13 and 15).

Forest or scrubland?

The lowland forests are strikingly different from those of the mountains and those of temperate and northern Europe. Trees are not as tall, are more widely spaced and much more scrubby than what most would consider a typical forest.

There is debate among ecologists about how dense the original forest canopy was in the Mediterranean range. The general consensus is that, although there is now much more scrub, scrubby areas have always existed in ancient woodlands.

Scrub appears after forest fires and when grazing is less intense or stops. In the Mediterranean climate, particularly on poor and rocky soils, tree growth is very slow, so scrubland persists for many years before gradually giving over to forest. Higher up in the mountains, the combination of winter cold and poor soils has the same effect. Since forest fire is a natural phenomenon, scrubland has always been a component of Mediterranean woodland. This also is evidenced by its flora and fauna. Scrublands have evolved their own specialised set of inhabitants.

Oaks, Pines and Junipers – Mediterranean forests

The rocky sandstone hills in the *Depresión*, the lower reaches of the Guara and the isolated sierras in the upper Ebro basin are covered in scrubby oak woodland, locally known as *carrascal*. The carrascal once covered the larger part of the Aragonese lowlands before the arrival of agriculture and, in the Aragonese Province of Huesca, it still does.

In the *Depresión* and *Somontano*, Portuguese and Holm Oak dominate the woodlands, but it is locally mixed with or replaced by (planted) Austrian and Scots Pine. The woodland's canopy can range from very open to completely closed. In the open patches a thick scrub of Kermes Oak, Rosemary, Box and other shrubs dominates.

The Blue Aphyllanthes is a conspicuous flower of Mediterranean scrublands and woodlands in May and June.

The trees and shrubs are adapted to withstand drought, heat and poor soils. Unlike the forest in central Europe and the woodlands higher up in the Pyrenees, trees keep their leaves in winter (and are thus evergreen). The trees are fairly short with small, leathery leaves, both adaptations to the environment. Because the winters here are not very cold, there is no need to shed the leaves. This is a great advantage because no valuable nutrients are wasted. Thick wax layers protect the leaves from water loss in the summer and give these woods a more dusty appearance than the name 'evergreen forest' might suggest.

The *Carrascales* are excellent sites to search for wildflowers in spring. There are many different species to be found, including a large variety of orchids. The exact species composition depends on the local climate and soil type. Blue Aphyllanthes (facing page) is often a common species on limestone soils. It is an inconspicuous and grass-like member of the lily family when not in bloom, but very showy when it opens its bright blue flowers.

The scrublands and evergreen forests are home to a fauna that is very different from that of northern and montane forests. Mediterranean species dominate, such as Bonelli's Warbler, Cirl Bunting, Hoopoe, Short-toed Eagle and Scops Owl. The open scrublands are also frequented by Mediterranean warblers, such as Sardinian, Dartford, Subalpine and Orphean.

Deeper down into the dry lowlands, the oaks disappear and make way for a similarly scrub-rich open woodland. Ecologically it functions roughly the same, but plants are even better adapted to drought. Coniferous plants now take a lead role, with dusty Aleppo Pine woods and bushes of Phoenician and Spanish Junipers. The largest areas with this habitat type are found in the Sierra de Alcubierre in the south of the province (site A on page 137).

Holm Oaks dominate the Mediterranean forest, but in between you'll discover a high diversity of shrubs and small trees in this woodland type.

Pine, Fir and Beech – the forests of the mountains

Higher up the slopes, winters are too cold and moist for evergreen trees and a mixed forest of coniferous and deciduous (leaf-shedding) trees becomes the dominant vegetation. On the dry south-facing slopes, Scots and Austrian Pines are the most frequent trees, whilst the cooler north slopes are covered in dense forests of Beech and Silver Fir.

These beech-fir forests are enchanting places: green, cool and mossy, with massive trees and dotted with big boulders carpeted with saxifrages and Ramonda, a pretty, endemic species (page 63). From a Spanish perspective, where 'hot-and-dry' is the norm, the cool mountain forests are something special. For northern Europeans familiar with the extensive beech-fir forest of the central European hills and mountains, this zone in the Pyrenees may, at first, appear less exotic. But many of the

Beech and Fir forests cover the cooler slopes of the Pyrenees. These forests are proper to the central European mountains and reach their southern limit in the mountains of northern Spain.

Pyrenean forests are much older than the average stands elsewhere (e.g. the Selva de Oza on route 13 and Ordesa of route 15). Massive woodland giants tower over moss-covered decaying snags. This is the mountain jungle par excellence.

The flora and fauna of the Pyrenean mountain forests are reminiscent of that of the central European forests. As a consequence of the heavy shade, the undergowth is generally poor in species: Box (a shrub that seems to thrive just about anywhere), Martagon Lily, Green Wintergreen and Bird's-nest Orchid are among the few wildflowers. As for the birdlife, Nuthatch, Song Thrush and Black Woodpecker emphasize the central/northern-European character of the beech-fir forests.

Pines dominate the more exposed and warm forests on south slopes of the Pyrenees. On acidic soils the forest floor is rather mossy with a little Heather, Bilberry and Round-leaved Bedstraw. Pinewoods over limestone soils often have a richer mixture of wildflowers including several wintergreens and, locally, Creeping Lady's-tresses (a small, white orchid). These forests support a typical birdlife, with Firecrest, Bonelli's Warbler, Crested and Coal Tits and Bullfinch.

Avalanches and streams – veins of diversity

Gravity is a major factor in shaping the mountain forests. Avalanches of snow and rocks, and meltwater streams open up the mountain forest. Landslides, aided by lightning strikes, have created a 'gapped' forest where, in older stands, giant Silver Firs and Beech trees alternate with open patches.

The alternation of dense forest with sunny, open areas accounts for the high biodiversity and attractive wilderness feel of the mountain forests. Open patches allow more light-demanding plants and insects to prosper. These generally belong to widespread (mountain) species such as Peach-leaved Bellflower, Common Columbine and Common Spotted-orchid (for the plants) and Spanish Heath, Purple-shot Copper and Heath Fritillary (for the butterflies). Along moraines there is often a surprising flora, with plants normally more common at higher altitudes. We have seen Edelweiss and Alpine Toadflax for example at only 1,000 metres on the edge of a rocky scree. The avalanche which brought down the rocks also carried plant seeds from much higher altitudes. And so frequent rock and snow slides not only create an open terrain, but also 'weed out' the previous flora, creating gaps for new plants to germinate.

Where rivers have dug out canyons, the alternation between sunny and shady environments (on rocks or avalanche slopes and in gorges respectively) is particularly swift. In the deep rifts, which enjoy a generally moist, nutrient-rich and protected environment, a special type of forest thrives. This canyon forest has a high diversity of trees, including Fir, Beech, Maple, Linden, Elm, Box, Hazel, Alder and various oaks. The high nutrient levels, shade on the canyon floors and shelter from wind gives rise to superbly tall trees. Nowhere in the entire region do trees grow as tall as in the canyon forests.

The humid and shady gorges are covered in a dense, moist and moss-covered vegetation, in which Box takes a prominent place.

The Pyrenean Pine forests form the highest woodland zone in the mountains (top). The Citril Finch is one of the typical birds of this forest type (bottom).

Subalpine forests

At higher altitudes, the forest gradually disintegrates into a parkland with scattered trees. This is not, as often thought, necessarily associated with the climatic limit of trees. In the Pyrenees, many upland areas were cleared to accommodate grazing cattle. Hence the existing forest line is a much lower, man-made level than would be the case were it left untouched.

In the gap between natural and artificial forest line, the subalpine 'forest' comes into being. Scattered coniferous trees, rose bushes, Alpenrose heathland and flowery grasslands characterise this zone. The Pyrenean Pine – a tree-sized relative of the Dwarf Pine of the Alps – is the tree that reaches the highest altitudes. But there is a shrub that climbs even further, the Green Alder. It is common along high mountain streams. In winter it becomes completely snow-covered, sparing the buds the freeze-dry treatment that wreaks havoc on the exposed pine tree buds. The subalpine parkland forest is a hotspot for wildflowers, butterflies and birds. Mountain specialists like Citril Finch, Ring Ouzel, Crossbill, Red-backed Shrike, Yellowhammer and Ortolan Bunting primarily inhabit this zone. The first three occur mostly in open pine stands, whereas the latter three prefer deciduous bushes.

The high mountains

Alpine meadows feature on routes 13, 14, 15, 16, 18, 19 and 21. The latter route incorporates the rocky terrain of the highest reaches. The Ordesa bus route (site B on page 202) is another excellent way to get above the tree level. Hedgehog Broom vegetation is present on routes 11, 12, 21 and the Ordesa bus route.

At an altitude of roughly 2,000 metres, the coniferous forest gives way to an open Alpine landscape. This is a wonderful world for naturalists. It is as if, within an ascent of a few hundred metres, you arrive on another planet, inhabited by entirely different life forms. The lowland plant species have been replaced by a new flora – one that is highly diverse and packed with impressive and colourful species. Clouds of butterflies and a few birds (largely high altitude specialists) make the landscape metamorphosis complete: above the treeline there is a new world to discover.

A severe climate and a short growing season set the ecological conditions in the high mountains. The higher up, the shorter the growing season and the thinner the vegetation until, eventually, around the summits of the highest peaks, plant life disappears altogether.

Not only the cold inhibits plant growth. In depressions in the landscape and in the shadow cast by rocks, snow lingers well into the summer and thus shortens the growing season. But snow is also a blessing. In winter, when wind chill and clear, icy night skies make life tougher than ever, the snow protects the vegetation from severe temperature drops. Any bud that ventures through the snowy blanket is destroyed by the frost. This is also the main reason why tree growth, with the exception of dwarf trees protected in snow bound gullies, is impossible at high altitudes.

What the growing season lacks in length, it compensates for in intensity. Extreme solar radiation and the occurance of many lush, wind-sheltered patches behind rocks or in gullies create golden opportunities for bees, butterflies and other insects. Within a short time, the Alpine meadows are alive with pollinating insects, and consequently with wildflowers begging for their attention.

Alpine meadows at Otal (route 16), home to both choughs, Quail, Grey Partridge, Citril Finch and a wealth of butterflies.

These environmental conditions require exactly the opposite adaptations found in the wildflowers of lower altitudes. Alpine plants cannot survive in areas where tall herbs, grasses and trees might shade them out. However, these species cannot cope with the short growing season and damaging UV-radiation. This is why the vegetation changes so drastically higher up in the mountains. And with this new vegetation comes a new insect world, often adapted to specific high mountain plant species.

The high mountain habitat is to its inhabitants a refuge amidst a deadly environment. Isolated from other similar areas in the Alps and Cantabrian Mountains, the high peaks became what biologists refer to as hotspots of endemism: areas with a high number of species that occur nowhere else in the world. The Alpine realm is, indeed, a unique world.

Superdiversity

As a rule of thumb, small 'islands' in an ecological sense (meaning, isolated from similar terrain), support few species because populations are – due to limited space – inevitably small and thus vulnerable to extinction. 'Islands' with an extreme climate are even poorer in terms of diversity, because only few species can adapt to such conditions. The Alpine habitat has both these 'red flags' for biodiversity, so it is all the more astonishing to encounter a tremendous variety of species at high altitudes.

One explanation for the high diversity of plants and butterflies is the mix of many different habitats. Rock-littered meadows, patches of heathland, peaty depressions, scree fields, mountain lakes, streams and snow patches all occur within the small area of a single high mountain valley. In the rough terrain of the Alpine meadows, average snow depths vary strongly from place to place. This determines the species composition in the summer months. Hollows where snow lingers have a distinct flora with Pyrenean Dragon's-mouth, Yellow Mountain Violet and Alpine Snowbell.

Glandon Blue and its host plant Woolly Rock-jasmine are both confined to the meadows at and above the treeline.

Another factor that explains the rich flora is the variation in soil depth. In the meadows bordering the river, a deep and peaty soil supports a very different flora than the shallow cracks in rocks. Exposed thin soils dry out easily, requiring a vegetation able to cope with drought. At the opposite extreme the plants of stream borders, which are permanently wet, suffer a different set of constraints.

The caterpillars of butterflies are picky eaters and occur only on specific groups of plants in a particular vegetation. Since both plant species and vegetation types are very diverse in the Alpine meadows, the butterfly diversity is equally high.
Another explanation for the remarkable biodiversity of the Alpine meadows is that the whole idea of the Alpine habitat as a 'small island' doesn't apply to plants and butterflies. These are species that generally need only a small area and do not roam very far, so the Alpine habitat is quite large from their perspective. In contrast, the diversity of species that require a larger territory, like birds and mammals, is, as expected, much smaller. Nevertheless, there are a number of species confined to the higher mountains (e.g. Chamois, Marmot, Alpine Chough, Snowfinch).

Alpine Marmots are very frequent in the Alpine meadows. They are not native, but were introduced from the Alps for the hunt.

Alpine haymeadows

Cows and sheep do well on Alpine meadows, much better than in the woodlands further below. Therefore, farmers have 'extended' the Alpine meadows further down into the valley, by cutting forest and creating hay meadows.
These hay meadows are superficially similar to the Alpine meadows and the two are not always easy to tell apart. Further down still, where the growing season is longer and there are more nutrients (thanks to cow dung and deeper soils), tall grasses and herbs dominate the meadows. Only the big, competitive herbs of high altitudes, like Globeflower, Monk's-hood and Leafy Lousewort invade these meadows.
Intensively grazed hay meadows are easily recognisable by the presence of tall toxic herbs which cattle do not eat and have, therefore, spread unchecked. Among them are some very beautiful plants, like Pyrenean Iris (p. 62), White Asphodel and Great Yellow Gentian.
Scenic as these meadows may be, the abundance of these species means that you are not likely to find many other wildflowers, and by extension, butterflies.
Rosebushes and other shrubs are also largely left alone by cattle and they provide the type of vegetation structure that is favoured by a large number of interesting bird species. Bushy hay meadows are excellent sites for Garden Warbler, Red-backed Shrike, Yellowhammer and Ortolan Bunting. Close to coniferous forest, Ring Ouzel and Citril Finch are also often present.

Below the climatic treeline farmers created meadows to accommodate their cattle. Red-backed Shrikes prefer these bush-dotted meadows.

The realm of the Hedgehog Broom

'When the big herds of thousand heads or more still roamed the mountains, the slopes were beautiful and clean.' – the words of one of the older inhabitants of the village of Torla, near Ordesa. His reference is to the spread of the 'dreadful' *Erizón* or *Alison*, alias Hedgehog Broom. The beautiful cushions, which appear so soft but are so spiny, now entirely dominate some of the subalpine slopes around the forest line (1,000 – 2,000 m.).

The Yellow Hedgehog Broom (p. 47) spreads rapidly and massively when grazing stops. In the age of the big herds, the unpalatable Hedgehog Broom had to be controlled, usually by frequent burning. Now that farmers have retreated from the mountains, the Hedgehog Broom spreads unchecked. Its massive flowering forms a yellow belt on the mountain slopes in early July that is visible from kilometres away.

Where Hedgehog Broom has pushed out most of the other flora, there is little to interest the naturalist. But where it occurs in lower densities, there is much to discover. Here, the spiny broom protects other wildflowers from herbivores. Where the Hedgehog Broom is scattered amongst coniferous trees at altitude, an interesting bird community is often present with Rock Thrush, Citril Finch, Rock Bunting and Wheatear all playing their part.

History

It is not easy to provide a historic account of the province of Huesca, for the simple reason it didn't exist as an entity over much of history. For long, it was part of the much larger Kingdom of Aragón. Moreover, the Pyrenees, an isolated and inhospitable place, has experienced a very different history from the fertile, well-populated plains and the large cities of Huesca and Zaragoza.

The Pyrenees formed a mighty barrier for travel and trade. Hence, the infrastructure of Huesca has always been directed towards the Mediterranean coast.

Dawn of history

Rock paintings and excavations confirm that the human story in this part of the world goes back to the Neolithic, some 22,000 years ago. The Sierra de Guara and the valley of the Río Vero area (near Barbastro) in particular has a very rich collection of dolmens and cave paintings for which there is an interpretation centre set up in Colungo (between Barbastro and Aínsa). At this time, the glaciers of the last ice age retreated and the Pyrenees became forested.

The picture of the primeval Huesca is largely speculative, but it is likely that the general vegetation layers we find in the mountains today, were present before the arrival of humans or at least before humans were able to change the vegetation on a noticeable scale. The Ebro lowlands were probably covered in open Holm Oak forests of the type that you still find widely, though patchily, throughout the *Somontano* (see page 33 and site F on page 163). The vast areas of grain and irrigated fields of today's Monegros once sported extensive evergreen oak forest. The area of natural steppe was restricted to those sites with high salt and gypsum concentrations and to unstable ground (e.g. slopes of the table mountains).

The Romans and the Moors – early history

Sedentary life began in the Bronze Age, but it was with the arrival of the Romans that the Pyrenees and the Huescan lowlands became firmly placed on the map. The Roman emperor Augustus founded a city, *Caesaraugusta*, along the Ebro river. This city, later known as Zaragoza, ruled over the Ebro Basin. The Roman bridge over the river Ebro, the *Puente de Piedra*, is still in use. Ruins of Roman houses are everywhere beneath the city.

Apart from Zaragoza, the Romans also founded the cities of Huesca, Lérida / Lleida, Barcelona and Pamplona, all of which became, as they remain, important cities. By doing so, the Romans laid down the blueprint for the human topography that is largely intact today: important towns lie along an east-west line and the 'in between lands' of the Monegros were little more than a throughfare between cities. Towards the north, the Pyrenees formed a barrier that inhibited trade between the French and the Spanish parts of the Roman empire.

During the 4th century AD the Christian faith became the major religion in the region, but this status quo was threatened when the Moors arrived and introduced the Islam. In 714 the Moors reached Zaragoza

The Moorish Citadel of Alquézar village (route 8).

and soon thereafter penetrated the mountains, as far up as Aínsa, but their hold on this mountainous area was brief and tenuous.
The province of Huesca has a special place in Spain's rich history because it was here that the gradual re-conquest (or *reconquista)* started – the long period of battles in which Christian lords gradually took Spain from the Muslims. As early as 780, Jaca became the first town to be re-conquered. It also became the capital of the newly founded Kingdom of Aragón. In the 10th century, Christian kings conquered the important parts of the Pyrenees near Jaca and further east, in Sobrarbe and Ribagorza.

The Kingdom of Aragón

The *Sierras Exteriores* were conquered shortly afterwards and the Christians, under the leadership of García I, set up a line of defence on the southern rim of the sierra. The famous castles near Loarre and Huesca (the town), plus a series of defence towers still stand as evidence of the reconquista. The beautifully restored village of Alquézar (*Al-Qasr*; route 8) was once an important fort of the Moors, built to protect their northernmost important city in the area: Barbastro. Zaragoza fell in the hands of the Aragonese in 1118 and then became the capital of the Kingdom of Aragón.
As the Christian frontier pushed south, immigrants crossed the Pyrenees and settled in the mountains and the plains. Not all Moors were expelled though, and many continued to live in Christian Aragón. They were called *Mudéjar* and became famous builders. Mudéjar style buildings of the 12th to 16th century form an important cultural heritage in the Ebro valley. The most important is the Seo in Zaragoza which was consecrated as a cathedral in 1119.
During the 15th century, Aragón, with Zaragoza as its capital, had become one of the dominant kingdoms of Europe. It acquired, through marriage or arms, Catalonia, Sardinia, Corsica, Sicily and even a part of Greece.
The marriage of Queen Isabella I of Castile and King Ferdinand II of Aragón in 1469 – together called the Catholic Monarchs (*los Reyes Católicos*), created the mighty kingdom of Spain and finally sealed the fate of the remaining Moors. The *Reyes Católicos* did not accomplish this without bloodshed. Breaking solemn promises to the contrary, they pushed both the Moors and the Jewish population out of the rest of the Peninsula and financed the discovery of America. So celebrated are the *Reyes Católicos* that few communities in Spain lack some edifice or road named in their honour.
The next centuries, thanks to economic growth, human population increased steadily. Within our region, especially the Ebro valley prospered. More and more land was cultivated and, along the rivers,

irrigation schemes were increasingly developed, often using techniques learnt from the Moors. This relative wealth of the valley towns and cities lured people from the impoverished Pyrenees which thereby became even more of a backwater.

The feudal system of Medieval Catholic Spain, as elsewhere, created a society in which the riches were channelled to a very small, select group of noblemen, leaving the bulk of people in serfdom and intense poverty. In a thinly populated and wild region where travellers journeyed from city to city over long and lonely roads, robbery was rife. Mountainous areas like the Sierra de Alcubierre were particularly dangerous. *Bandoleros* could strike easily and quickly vanish into the wilderness. These bandits have shaped folkloric history of the many backwaters of the region. In popular imagination, the culprits are frequently seen as champions who stood up for the poor in a deeply unequal and unfair society.

The mass vegetation of Yellow Hedgehog Broom* is not natural, but indicate abandoned grazing grounds. The Pyrenees and *Sierras Exteriores* have suffered from depopulation, and large areas of former meadows are now overgrown with Yellow Hedgehog Broom*.

Agricultural reform and depopulation – onto the modern age

Spain's powers were already declining in comparison to the other great European powers, when the War of the Spanish Succession broke out. The Spanish allied with the French against the British and the Dutch, but this alliance was broken, leaving Spain a much more modest role at the table of the world powers. This position further deteriorated and eventually lead to Peninsular War, in which Spain and Portugal were occupied by Napoleon. With the aid of the British, the French were thrown out of the Iberian Peninsula in 1814, but for the common man, this was hardly an improvement. The Spanish King established an absolute monarchy in which repression and economic malaise went hand in hand.

In the 19th century the province saw a major rural exodus to Zaragoza and other major Spanish cities. And not without reason. The development of rural areas, with the exception of the irrigated areas along the main rivers, had been close to zero. Basic utilities (clean water, sewers, roads etc.) were non-existent. People in the Monegros were far away from modern services and for those in the Guara and Pyrenees, the isolation was almost complete. In the Pyrenees, it was easier to travel to the villages over the border in France (on foot of course) than it was to get to Huesca or Zaragoza. This poverty and isolation pushed many people to seek a better life elsewhere.

A 30-year-old slide of times gone by: sheep grazing on the Alpine pastures of Ordesa. Sheep husbandry has nearly disappeared. The result is that the pastures become overgrown with shrubs.

The Civil War and the Franco era

The Spanish Civil War (1936-1939) left deep wounds in this part of Spain. The political left and right took extreme positions. Neighbours, friends and even family members ended up fighting each other. The frontline ran from the border with France, through the valley of Tena (Formigal) to Huesca, past the Sierra de Alcubierre in the Monegos and on to Teruel further south (see box 'Orwell' opposite). Large parts of Aragón and the Pyrenees further to the west sided with the Republicans of the left. However, under General Franco, the rightwing Nationalists were victorious and by the end of the struggle, many areas had suffered heavy losses. One tragic but very moving testimony to this time is the village of Belchite – which was completely razed. The new Belchite was built next to the old village, which' ruins now stand as a mute, yet tragic, monument to the catastrophic violence of the Civil War (route 2).

In the decades after the war, the new regime improved the roads in the Pyrenees and built new bridges. A series of hydro-electrical dams, which flooded some of the Pyrenean valleys, were also constructed.

Orwell and the Ebro front

The British author George Orwell (famous for his books *Animal Farm* and *1984*) fought for the Republicans in the outskirts of Huesca and in the Alcubierre mountains. In 1937 he was wounded near Huesca and was transported to Barcelona to recover. Here he found out that the Communists (who were then in control) had declared the POUM, for whom Orwell had fought, to be an illegal Trotskyist organisation and, therefore, his life was in danger. Only after a perilous and difficult journey did he manage to return to England. Fresh from the front he wrote *Homage to Catalunya* (1938) which remains a vivid key source for an understanding of the conflict. Had he not succeeded, neither *1984* nor *Animal Farm*, hugely influential books in part forged by his experiences here, would not have been published.

When the Ebro front broke just south of Sabiñánigo, the Republican army withdrew to Catalonia. Some villages in the isolated mountains north of Aínsa resisted the furious attacks of the Francoist army for several months without any outside help. When the resistance was finally broken, the last Republicans had to flee over the snowy peaks to France. Their stronghold – Bielsa village – was burned to the ground, but today various books and the Bielsa Museum proudly tell their story.

With the improvement of agriculture in the lowlands, it became virtually impossible to make a living by farming the poorer lands of the Pyrenees and *Sierras Exteriores*. This led to the second, even greater wave of emigration. Vast areas were now completely abandoned and the number of cattle and sheep was decimated. One (beautiful) route that connects several of these *pueblos abandonados* (deserted villages) is route 11.

The Nationalist government also planted huge areas of (Aleppo) pines in the lowland hills where many of them still stand – a hot and dusty testimony to another grand but failed economic project. Some

From the Franco years right up to the present day, one reservoir after another is created to quench the nation's insatiable thirst for water and the need for electricity. The water has swallowed many beautiful villages and valuable natural areas.

The old town of Belchite (route 2) was almost completely razed in the civil war. The village was rebuilt, but the original, ruined village centre remains as a monument to that black period in history.

completely new villages were built and the inhabitants used irrigation to convert more steppes into agriculture.

The birth of tourism

The beauty of the Pyrenees, the Ordesa valley and the canyons of Guara were discovered in the early days of modern tourism. French mountaineers and nature lovers such as Lucien Briet published photos and books about the Pyrenees at the beginning of the 20th century. Their landscape images, now over a century old, are an invaluable source of information of how the landscape changed. One of the most striking differences, compared to today's landscape, is the far higher percentage of scrub and pasture – a clear sign that sheep and cattle were much more numerous a century ago.

With these books, the scenic and natural value of the mountains became evident to a larger public. Walking, hunting, mountaineering and skiing gradually became an economic development that needed to be taken seriously.

Spanish tourism started under Franco, but the tourism in the Pyrenees really took off with the development of ski pistes in the 1970s. Aided by the death of Franco in 1975 (and soon after the collapse of his regime), the number of foreign tourists grew rapidly. This trend was boosted when Spain joined the European Union in 1986. In recent decades, people have returned to the previously abandoned villages to set up small tourism ventures and attractions. Again route 11 is helpful in this respect: the tiny villages of Bara and Nocito were all abandoned, but now a modest green tourism development brings life back to these places.

When agriculture improved in the fertile lowlands, villages in the remote parts of the Sierra de Guara were abandoned. With the increase of tourism, people are gradually returning to set up small-scale ecotourism businesses.

After Franco – Modern Spain

The Pyrenees and the lowlands developed in very different directions after Franco's death. Whereas the ecological and touristic value of the mountains was recognised at an early stage, the unique steppes and dry agricultural land of the Monegros still await the recognition they deserve. The agricultural reforms initiated in the 1960s were accelerated after Spain joined the EU in 1986. The irrigation schemes (*regadíos*) in particular changed the face of the Monegros (see page 53).

Today, the Pyrenees and the Ebro valley are still amongst the most sparsely populated parts of Europe, but the per capita income of the inhabitants is now at European level. Agriculture, with its subsidies from Brussels, is still an important source of income, but new industries, including the General Motors factory near Zaragoza, are gaining in importance. A recent and major success is the growth of viniculture, especially in the *Somontano* region of Barbastro.

In the mountains, tourism is still growing and reviving more of the semi-abandoned mountain villages. However, most of the original mountain people are now living out their retirement. It seems only a matter of time before the last herdsmen return from the pastures for good.

Nature conservation

With the protection of Ordesa as a National Park in 1918 (the second Spanish National Park, after Picos de Europa), one is tempted to believe that in this region the need to preserve nature was recognised early. But this early act of preservation lacked any thorough awareness of the concept of nature conservation. The Ordesa valley was protected to preserve its beautiful and unique landscape and thereby, to attract tourism. The canyon, with its awe-inspiring scenery, was simply regarded as too beautiful to be destroyed by logging, hunting or electric plants. Any concept of its ecological importance was still rudimentary at best.

A painful testimony to this lack of insight is the sad tale of the Pyrenean Ibex. The National Park status protected it in the valley, but not on its feeding grounds on the plateau above the gorge. The plateaux were were at that time not part of the National Park and the Ibex were awaited with blazing guns. The animal was brought to extinction right on the edge of the National Park (see also box on page 81).

A more modern approach to nature conservation did not surface, and then only gradually, until the late 1960s. Raptors in Spain were not protected until 1968 and bear hunting wasn't banned until 1973. The change came around the time the country entered the EU in 1986. Within 30 years, the country's attitude towards nature conservation flipped round 180 degrees. Nature conservation became an important topic, not just on the political agenda but also in the hearts of the people. But at the same time, modern developments, partially accelerated by EU subsidies, posed severe threats to many ecosystems, some of which are still hardly recognised as important parts of Spain's natural heritage.

Tourism

In the late 1970s, the Pyrenees became popular tourist destination and with tourism came an elaborate infrastructure: large roads, hotels, car parks, camp sites, shops and ski resorts appeared in previously uninhabited valleys. The winter sports industry puts great strain on the landscape. Valley sides were bulldozed for hotels and car parks and hillsides smoothed for the pistes (the most recently at Formigal in 2009). Especially in the valleys of Canfranc, Formigal and Benasque, ski tourism is a damaging phenomenon.

The problem with skiing, apart from the obvious scars on the landscape, is that skiers

Tourism has taken off in the last few decades. Nevertheless, there are only a few areas truly busy, such as here, in Ordesa.

The two main conservation problems in one image.
First, the immense increase in irrigation, which uses vast amounts of riverwater and sprasys it over the fields, even when it is windy, sunny and 40 degrees celcius.
Second, the rise of (usually unmanned) pigfarms that are being built everywhere in the remote part of the lowlands.

disturb wildlife in their most vulnerable time of the year: winter. High mountain specialists, like Ptarmigan and Capercaillie, are most at risk. And these species are special because the Pyrenees are right at the edge of their range. Their populations are small and, this far south, threatened by climate change. Ski tourism puts an additional strain on them which may, in time, prove to be too much. And yet the regional governments want to build more pistes...
On the bright side, local governments increasingly value nature-friendly tourism too. Villages close to natural parks and reserves have grown both economically and in population thanks to this new brand of tourism. In fact, economic opportunity is now the most important incentive to create natural parks and reserves.

The water problem

Spain is not only an arid country, it also lies in a region where precipitation is highly irregular: years with abundance of water alternate with years in which hardly a drop falls. The Pyrenees are one of the country's few exceptions where precipitation is much more reliable. Hence, everyone wants a share of the abundant waters of the Pyrenees. Even the southern regions of Valencia and Murcia claim the Pyrenean waters to irrigate their lands and to water their golf courses. Rivers are dammed in various places to retain water for the irrigation of the fields in the nearby Ebro valley.

From an agricultural angle this makes sense, but ecologically it is nothing short of disastrous. In a nutshell, unspoilt river valleys are destroyed in order to ruin superb steppes. Reservoirs are constructed to collect water for irrigation (*regadíos*), which transforms steppe and dry fields (both good for steppe birds) into biologically dead agricultural monocultures. Vast areas of the Monegros have fallen prey to this process already. Fortunately, the remaining steppe land seems to have been spared, at least temporarily, the same fate. But this was not because politicians wanted to protect the remaining area, but because under EU pressure subsidies for irrigation have ceased. The remaining steppes are under a weak form of protection as ZEPA (*Zona Especial para la Protección de Aves*; Spanish for IBA – important bird area) or LIC (*Lugar de Interés Comunal* – area of communal interest). This is unlikely to stop further developments.

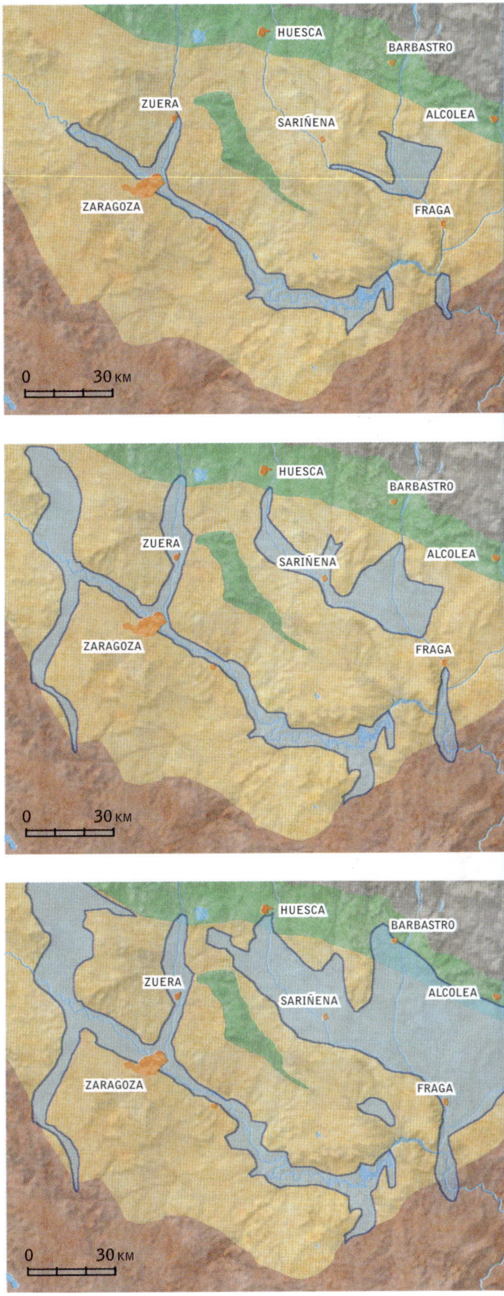

The fast expansion of irrigation in the Monegros: 1926 (top) 1975 (centre) and the current situation (bottom).

FLORA AND FAUNA

The ecological rule of thumb dictates that a topographically varied region houses a diverse flora and fauna. A mere glance on the map shows that Huesca promises a rich biodiversity. And it more than delivers on that promise!

One can experience both arctic conditions and semi-desert landscapes, and everything in between, in just one, modestly sized, province. Soil conditions vary from rocky to sandy, acidic to basic. Ground water ranges from saline to fresh, each with its own set of plants and animals.

The Pyrenees as a whole act as a mountain barrier between the Mediterranean and temperate worlds. Like any borderland, it is an area where differing biological realms merge. The Alpine meadows, rocky slopes and snow fields of the high mountains are a spectacular backdrop for species of northern environments. A few of them, such as the Ptarmigan, Bog Bilberry, and Small Whiteface even reach northernmost Scandinavia. These isolated, relict populations of the Pyrenees are a legacy of the ice ages when they were widespread throughout Europe.

Many plants, butterflies and birds are exclusively found in the mountains. Among them is the most enigmatic bird of the region: the Lammergeier or Bearded Vulture. Other examples of mountain species include Wallcreeper, Snowfinch and Alpine Chough. The flora and butterfly fauna of the mountains are particularly striking. The Pyrenees share a large number of bellflowers, rock-jasmines and orchids with other European mountains. Among them is the most well-known Alpine flower – the Edelweiss, which can occur quite commonly on limestone soils in the Alpine regions. Of the butterflies, there are many fritillaries, blues and ringlets that are exclusively found in the high mountains of Europe. Some of them are unique (endemic) to the Pyrenean mountains (such as the impressive Long-leaved Saxifrage and the Pyrenean Iris – pages 62-63), or shared only with nearby mountains in Cantabria and Central Iberia (e.g. Ramonda) or the Massif Central in France (e.g. Pyrenean Fritillary).

The Bearded Vulture or Lammergeier is one of the key species of the Pyrenees and *Sierras Exteriores.* Huesca has the highest densities of this magnificent raptor in Europe, perhaps the world.

The secluded mountain valleys are covered in dense forests, where one encounters a flora and fauna that resembles that of central Europe (e.g. Black Woodpecker, Beech, Birch and Bird's-nest Orchid). For some of these species, the Pyrenees forms the southernmost outpost (e.g. Viviparous Lizard and Small Whiteface).

Descending deeper into the valleys one encounters an increasing number of Mediterranean species. This is already demonstrated by the evergreen oak woodlands of the valleys of the *Depresión* (the lowlands between the high Pyrenees and the *Sierras Exteriores*; see page 14), where there's a mix of temperate and Mediterranean species. Once the exterior mountains are crossed, on the south-facing slopes of the Sierra de Guara, the flora and fauna consists mostly of Mediterranean species. Mediterranean birds are frequent (e.g. warblers of the *Sylvia* genus, Bee-eaters, Bonelli's Eagles, Blue Rock Thrushes). Even more radical is the change in the reptilian world. With the exception of the water loving European Pond Terrapin and Viperine Snake, there is almost no overlap between the reptilian species north of the Pyrenees and the Mediterranean species to the south.

Further south in the lowlands of the Ebro valley, the flora and fauna changes yet again, with a different set of Mediterranean species adapted to dry, open country, such as Lesser Kestrel, Lesser Mouse-eared Bat and the small East Iberian Painted Frog. Interesting here is the occurence of many Ibero-African species – which are unique to the very arid parts of the Mediterranean and North Africa. It is this group that brings many birdwatchers to this area. Dupont's Lark, Thekla Lark, Spotless Starling, Black Wheatear, Pin-tailed and Black-bellied Sandgrouse and Spectacled Warbler are representatives of the birdlife of arid Iberia and North-Africa. The plant and insect life of these driest parts of the Ebro basin are unique as well. The gypsum and saline soils, the result of prolonged periods of desiccation, support specialists of desert-like environments (see flora section).

Some striking Pyrenees endemics

Mammals Isard or Pyrenean Chamois, Pyrenean Desman (shared with other Iberian mountains)

Reptiles and amphibians Pyrenean Frog, Pyrenean Brook Newt, Pyrenean Rock Lizard

Butterflies Gavarnie Blue, Lefebvre's Ringlet (both with Cantabrian Mnts.), Forster's Furry Blue, False Dewy Ringlet, Gavarnie Ringlet, Pyrenees Brassy Ringlet

Wildflowers Ramonda, Long-leaved Saxifrage, Pyrenean Valerian, Pyrenean Bellflower (with Cevennes), Pyrenean Lily, Pyrenean Iris, Pyrenean Pheasant's-eye, Pyrenean Yam

Ibero-African region
Black Wheatear
(Oenanthe leucura)
Dry rocky area

Central European region
Lady's-slipper
(Cypripedium calceolus)
Beech forest

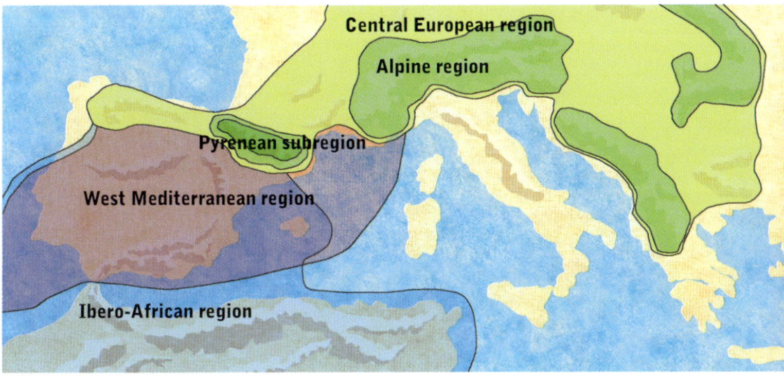

Pyrenean subregion
Ramonda
(Ramonda myconi)
Damp rocks

Alpine region
Shepherd's Fritillary
(Boloria pales)
Haymeadows, alpine meadows

West Mediterranean region
Ladder snake
(Rhinechis scalaris)
Scrub and steppe

Flora

For flora of alpine meadows and scree, try routes 13, 14, 15, 19 and 21, and sites sites C, E, F and G on pages 181-183, site B on page 202, and B and D on page 215. Subalpine heathlands are present on routes 14, 15 and 19 and for wildflowers of the hedgehog broom zone, visit routes 9, 11, 12 and 20 and site B on page 202. The botanically richer beech and mixed mountain forests are along routes 13 and 15, while the flora of the Scots pine forest is interesting on routes 12, 14, 16, 20 and sites D on page 203 and D on page 215. Open oak woodland and Mediterranean scrubland flora can be found almost throughout the province, but we found some excellent wildflowers along routes 7, 9, 11 and 20. The steppe flora of the Ebro basin is exquisite, albeit not particularly showy, along routes 2, 3 and 5 and site A on page 137.
A list of the orchid sites and routes in the Huesca region can be downloaded from **crossbillguides.org**.

It is impossible to do justice to the flora of Huesca Province in the limited space this book allows. Between the summits of the Pyrenees and the arid plains of the Monegros, there is a plant diversity that is so high that it has placed this small region amongst the botanical hotspots of Europe, alongside the mountains of southern Spain and Italy, the southern slopes of the Alps, Crete, the Peloponesos and Caucasus. In Huesca alone, 2,656 species of vascular plants have been recorded, which is close to twice the number of wildflowers in the Netherlands and almost as great as the entire flora of the British Isles. To put this into perspective, Huesca is only a fifth the size of Scotland. On page 221 we provide a list of wildflower identification books and sites that will help you towards naming these species. In the following chapter, we will limit ourselves to locating and describing the best sites and habitats and the most typical wildflowers found here.

General remarks on the flora

The botanical diversity of this region is a direct reflection of the variety of climates and soil types. Each rock or soil (limestone, sandstone, quartzite, gypsum, saline clay and peat) supports its own type of vegetation. The orientation of the slope towards the sun (i.e. north, east, west or south) create different (sub)climates as does, of course, the altitude. In the province of Huesca, the climatic variety is further enhanced by the extreme differences in precipitation and sun hours between the high Pyrenees and the lowlands (see climate and geology – page 16). Less pronounced, but sufficiently so to create clear local differences, is the influence of the progressively cooler and moister Atlantic regime to the west and the drier and warmer Mediterranean areas to the east. This is even noticeable at the highest altitudes, where the species of Rock-Jasmine

Huesca is a mecca for wildflowers, both in diversity and in number.

and Saxifrage on the western tops differ from those on the eastern peaks. Not only the variety makes the flora of Huesca so exciting, but also its exclusivity. Both the Pyrenees and the plains rejoice in many endemics: species that have only a very small distribution range and do not occur elsewhere. These rarities are present mostly in isolated 'islands' where conditions differ from the surrounding regions. These conditions require special adaptations which only few plants can meet. In isolation of other sites with similar conditions, these plants evolve into separate species.

The Pyrenees as a whole can be seen as such an 'island', separated from the Picos, the Central Iberian Mountains and the Alps. On a smaller scale the extreme environments like the mountain tops and the hottest parts of the plains are climatic islands. Therefore, these sites boast the highest numbers of rarities.

High mountain flora

The short growing season on the highest slopes of the Pyrenees is between mid June and late August. During this period, the scree, cliffs and Alpine meadows boast a fascinating range of wildflowers. On exposed sites, where the cold is extreme, the solar radiation high and soils poor, many plants with numerous small stems form a 'cushion' (or an umbel) to minimise frost and UV damage. The most conspicuous 'cushion plant' is the Yellow Hedgehog Broom* (*Echinospartum horridum*), which occurs at altitudes up to 2,000 m. Higher up, Moss-campion, rock-jasmines and saxifrages grow in a cushion-like form. The latter group, especially, is diverse at high altitudes. Moss Saxifrage, Rock-jasmine Saxifrage* (*Saxifraga androsacea*), White Musky Saxifrage, Purple Saxifrage, Livelong Saxifrage, Neglected Saxifrage and Irati's Saxifrage* (*Saxifraga irati*), are all recorded at altitudes exceeding 3,000m. On high altitude stream banks, Starry Saxifrage, Yellow Saxifrage and the Pyrenean endemic Water Saxifrage are found. Unfortunately, the highest parts are difficult to reach without serious effort, often involving multiple day trips. The easiest places are near Aneto (see routes 19 and 21).

Pyrenean Honeysuckle (top) and Water Saxifrage (bottom) underline how special the Pyrenean flora is: both are beautiful species that are endemics of the Pyrenees.

The Alpine meadows – the vegetation zone between 1800 and 2500 metres – are easier to access (routes 13, 14, 15, 16 and 19). In places where trees have disappeared due to ski tourism or cattle grazing a semi-natural type of Alpine meadow occurs where many wildflowers are present (see page 41).

Alpine meadows are an absolute delight. Various species of bellflowers, gentians and, on limestone soils, Edelweiss and Vanilla Orchids, are easy finds. The Pyrenean Iris forms large drifts of beautiful deep purple flowers. Locally, this is also the terrain of the Pyrenean Fritillary (p. 62) and Pyrenean Pheasant's-eye, two beautiful, endemic wildflowers. The Parnassus-leaved Buttercup is one of several white-flowered buttercups, easily recognisable by its leaves that resemble those of the Grass-of-Parnassus (which also occurs on limestone soils in the high Pyrenees). Ashy Crane's-bill and Pyrenean Stork's-bill* (*Eroduim glandulosum*) are fairly frequent and have conspicuous markings on their flowers.

Little hollows and rocky cracks where the snow lingers in spring

High altitude flora (roughly over 2,200 metres)

Highest crests and rock slopes Pyrenean Columbine (*Aquilegia pyrenaica*[△]), Alpine Pasqueflower (*Pulsatilla alpina*), Aragon Scurvy-grass (*Cochlearia aragonensis*[△]), Moss Campion (*Silene acaulis*), Tufted Soapwort (*Saponaria caespitosa*), Pink Sandwort (*Arenaria purpurascens*), Mountain Avens (*Dryas octopetala*[△]), Snowy Cinquefoil* (*Potentilla nivalis*), Irati's Saxifrage* (*Saxifraga pubescens iratiana*[△]), Neglected Saxifrage (*Saxifraga praetermissa*[△]), Purple Saxifrage (*Saxifraga oppositifolia*), Hariot's Saxifrage* (*Saxifraga hariotii*[△]), Mossy Saxifrage (*Saxifraga bryoides*), White Musky Saxifrage (*Saxifraga exarata moschata*), Blue Saxifrage (*Saxifraga caesia*), Yellow Mountain Saxifrage (*Saxifraga aretioides*[△]), Pyrenean Rock-jasmine (*Androsace pyrenaica*[△]), Vitaliana (*Androsace vitaliana*), Lagger's Rock-jasmine (*Androsace laggeri*[△]), Woolly Rock-jasmine (*Androsace villosa*), Pygmy Hawk's-beard (*Crepis pygmaea*)

Hollows where snow lingers Pyrenean Willow (*Salix pyrenaica*[△]), Glacier Crowfoot (*Ranunculus glacialis*), Bird's-eye Primrose (*Primula farinosa*), Entire-leaved Primrose (*Primula integrifolia*), Alpine Snowbell (*Soldanella alpina*), Sibbaldia (*Sibbaldia procumbens*), Samnitic Milkvetch (*Oxytropis neglecta*[△]), Yellow Mountain Violet (*Viola biflora*), Pyrenean Dragon's-mouth (*Horminum pyrenaicum*), Pyrenean Lousewort (*Pedicularis pyrenaica*[△])

Streamsides and streamside meadows Aconite-leaved Buttercup (*Ranunculus aconitifolius*), Globeflower (*Trollius europaeus*), Common Butterwort (*Pinguicula vulgaris*), Alpine Butterwort (*Pinguicula alpina*), Water Saxifrage (*Saxifraga aquatica*[△]), Yellow Saxifrage (*Saxifraga aizoides*), Starry Saxifrage (*Saxifraga stellaris*), Purple-beaked Lousewort* (*Pedicularis mixta*[△]), Heath Spotted-orchid (*Dactylorhiza maculata*), Broad-leaved Marsh-orchid (*Dactylorhiza majalis*)

Alpine meadows Moonwort (*Botrychium lunaria*), Pyrenean Buttercup (*Ranunculus pyrenaeus*), Alpine Pasqueflower (*Pulsatilla alpina*), Pyrenean Pheasant's-eye (*Adonis pyrenaica*[△]), Pyrenean Eryngo* (*Eryngium bourgati*), Alpine Clover (*Trifolium alpinum*), Pink Rock-jasmine (*Androsace carnea*), Ashy Crane's-bill (*Geranium cinereum*), Pyrenean Stork's-bill* (*Erodium glandulosum*[△]), Yellow Betony (*Stachys alopecuros*), Alpine Bartsia (*Bartsia alpina*), Leafy Lousewort (*Pedicularis foliosa*), Snow Gentian (*Gentiana nivalis*), Burser's Gentian (*Gentiana burseri*), Great Yellow Gentian (*Gentiana lutea*), Spring Gentian (*Gentiana verna*), Alpine Gentian (*Gentiana alpina*), Trumpet Gentian (*Gentiana acaulis*), Scheuchzer's Bellflower (*Campanula scheuchzeri*), Clustered Bellflower (*Campanula glomerata*), Pyrenean Rampion (*Phyteuma pyrenaicum*[△]), Round-headed Rampion (*Phyteuma orbiculare*), Graceful Globularia* (*Globularia gracilis*[△]), Arnica (*Arnica montana*), Alpine Aster (*Aster alpinus*), Pheasant's-eye-leaved Ragwort* (*Senecio adonidifolius*[△]), Goldenrod (*Solidago virgaurea*), Edelweiss (*Leontopodium alpinum*), False Helleborine (*Veratrum album*), Pyrenean Iris (*Iris latifolia*[△]), Pyrenean Fritillary (*Fritillaria pyrenaica*[△]), Frog Orchid (*Dactylorhiza viride*), the vanilla orchids *Gymnadenia austriaca* and *Gymnadenia gabasiana*

[△]=endemic to the Pyrenees and nearby mountains

Pyrenean Stork's-bill* (top) and Ashy Crane's-bill (bottom) are two conspicuous members of the Geranium family that are frequent in the Alpine meadows.

are rewarding wildflower spots. Being more sheltered, they support a different and more luxurious flora than the exposed areas, with Alpine Snowbell, Yellow Mountain Violet, and the attractive Dragonmouth (p. 176). The latter is numerous in the upper valleys of Hecho and Tena (route 13 and 14).

Many species occur either in the western or the eastern Pyrenees, giving each mountain chain its own peculiarities. If you want to see as many species as possible, you'd best visit various mountains in the west, central and eastern part of the Huescan Pyrenees. This is more rewarding than combing every nook and cranny of a single peak.

Flora of subalpine heaths and coniferous forests

A little lower than the Alpine meadows – roughly between 1,700 and 2,000 m – shrubs dominate the slopes and patches of Pyrenean Pine enter the scene. The flora here is an attractive mixture of woodland and Alpine meadow plants. In this zone, there is a strong difference between shady and acidic soils on the one extreme, and sunny, calcareous parts on the other. The cooler and moister (acidic) parts support grassland and 'heathland' with Alpenrose, Bilberry and various ferns – not unlike the subalpine zone in the Alps.

Limestone retains moisture very poorly, and sun-exposed limestone slopes are strikingly different from acidic northern slopes at the same altitude. The vegetation on limestone is adapted to drought and high solar radiation – with species reminiscent of Mediterranean mountains. This is the realm of the Yellow Hedgehog Broom* (*Echinospartum horridum*), which forms splendid dense 'cushions' of sharp spines and flowers in June. The Hedgehog Broom zone appears at exposed sites as low as 1,000 metres, and is accompanied with different flowers at each altitude. On the slopes of Ordesa, there are Alpine plants like Pyrenean Stork's-bill* (*Erodium glandulosum*) and Bearberry, whereas further down, Mediterranean species like Rush-leaved Jonquil, Spanish Fritillary, Wild Tulip, Woodcock and Dull Bee Orchids can be found (e.g. Roldán – route 9).

Flora of subalpine heaths (1,700-2,200 m)

Subalpine heathland (mostly on cool, acidic slopes) Alpine Pasqueflower (*Pulsatilla alpina*), Narcissus-flowered Anemone (*Anemone narcissiflora*), Alpenrose (*Rhododendron ferrugineum*), Bilberry (*Vaccinium myrtillus*), Burser's St. John's-wort (*Hypericum richeri burseri*$^{\Delta}$), Lesser Masterwort (*Astrantia minor*), Great Masterwort (*Astrantia major*), Pyrenean Saxifrage (*Saxifraga umbrosa*$^{\Delta}$), Burser's Gentian (*Gentiana burseri*), Beech Fern (*Phegopteris connectilis*) Wild Daffodil (*Narcissus pseudonarcissus*), Pyrenean Iris (*Iris latifolia*$^{\Delta}$), Alpine Leek (*Allium victorialis*)

Hedgehog Broom vegetation Mountain Milkvetch (*Astragalus sempervirens*), Pyrenean Vetch (*Vicia pyrenaica*$^{\Delta}$), Yellow Hedgehog Broom* (*Echinospartum horridum*), Bearberry (*Arctostaphylos uva-ursi*), Hyssop-leaved Ironwort (*Sideritis hyssopifolia*), Common Lavender (*Lavandula angustifolia*), Pyrenean Germander (*Teucrium pyrenaicum*$^{\Delta}$), Tuberous Valerian (*Valeriana tuberosa*), Celandine Bellflower* (*Campanula ficarioides*$^{\Delta}$), Pyrenean Hyacinth (*Brimeura amethystina*), Wild Tulip (*Tulipa australis*)

High nutrient depressions (Megaforbias) Monk's-hood (*Aconitum napellus*), Wolfsbane (*Aconitum vulparia*), Cambrian Poppy (*Meconopsis cambrica*), Pyrenean Valerian (*Valeriana pyrenaica*$^{\Delta}$), Hairless Blue-sowthistle (*Cicerbita plumieri*), Adenostyles (*Adenostyles alliariae*), Giant Saw-wort* (*Rhaponticum centauroides*$^{\Delta}$), Streptopus (*Streptopus amplexifolius*)

$^{\Delta}$=endemic to the Pyrenees and nearby mountains

Yellow Hedgehog Broom* grows between 1,000 and 2,000 m and can turn entire hillsides yellow.

In little hollows where snow lingers, by river banks or where water is present throughout summer, the soil is better and contain more nutrients. This gives rise to a vegetation that the Spanish aptly call *Megaforbias* – giant weeds. Here you will find robust plants like Wolfsbane, Adenostyles and Pyrenean Valerian.

Martagon Lily and Pyrenean Squill (opposite page) are wildflowers of the Beech forests. The first flowers in spring, the second in summer.

Mountain forests and clearings

In contrast to the previous zones, the forest flora of the mixed beech forests of the montane zone (1,000-1,600 m) is rather poor in species. Interestingly on limestone soils, the orchids are among the most frequent plants in these forests. Red Helle-borine and Bird's-nest Orchid are a frequent sight in late spring, while in summer Dark-red, Broad and Small-leaved Helleborines can be quite abundant. Again, the angle of the slope towards the sun greatly determines the flora in the montane zone. The previous description pertains to north facing slopes. Those looking to the south are dominated by pine forests, and support wildflowers like Liverleaf, various wintergreens and Round-leaved Bedstraw.

Flora of mountain forests and clearings (altitude 1,000-1,600 m)

Mixed and Beech Woodlands Soft Shield-fern (*Polystichum setiferum*), Yellow Anemone (*Anemone ranunculoides*), Pinnate Coralroot (*Cardamine pentaphyllos*), Pyrenean Saxifrage (*Saxifraga umbrosa*$^{\Delta}$), Alpine Figwort (*Scrophularia alpestris*$^{\Delta}$), Irish Spurge (*Euphorbia hyberna*), Wood Speedwell (*Veronica montana*), Purple Lettuce (*Prenanthes purpurea*), Martagon Lily (*Lilium martagon*), Lily-of-the-Valley (*Convallaria majalis*), Pyrenean Squill (*Scilla lilio-hyacinthus*), Bird's-nest Orchid (*Neottia nidus-avis*), Broad-leaved Helleborine (*Epipactis helleborine*), Narrow-leaved Helleborine (*Cephalanthera longifolia*)

Mixed and Pine forests Liverleaf (*Hepatica nobilis*), Round-leaved Bedstraw (*Galium rotundifolium*), Red-berried Elder (*Sambucus racemosa*), Slender St. John's-wort (*Hypericum pulchrum*), Common Wintergreen (*Pyrola minor*), Green Wintergreen (*Pyrola chlorantha*), One-flowered Wintergreen (*Moneses uniflora*), Serrated Wintergreen (*Orthilia secunda*), Yellow Bird's-nest (*Monotropa hypopitys*), Yellow Foxglove (*Digitalis lutea*), Bubani's Goldendrop (*Onosma bubanii*$^{\Delta}$), Bastard Balm (*Melittis melissophyllum*), Dark-red Helleborine (*Epipactis atrorubens*), White Helleborine (*Cephalathera damasonium*), Red Helleborine (*Cephalanthera rubra*), Creeping Lady's-tresses (*Goodyera repens*)

$^{\Delta}$=endemic to the Pyrenees and nearby mountains

Pyrenean Squill

A different flora is present in forest edges and along the sides of streams. The flora here has a distinctly central European touch, with species present that are frequent throughout the mountains and temperate lowlands of Europe. Moist spots in the beech forests have Herb-paris, Adenostyles, Baneberry, Sanicle and Wolf's-bane.

On rocky patches, there is a variety of bellflowers, Wild Marjoram, Bloody Crane's-bill and Yellow and Fairy Foxgloves and Grass-leaved Buttercup. In scree fields – areas with loose rock where the ground is constantly disturbed – there are often unexpected finds of plants from higher up, which' seeds were brought down in the avalanche.

Flora of cliffs and gorges

The cliffs, rocks and canyons support perhaps the most interesting flora, containing several spectacular species, many of which are endemic or highly localised. Best are limestone cliffs, such as those in the Sierra de Guara (routes 8 and 9) and in and around Ordesa (routes 15 and 17). Many cliff species are not confined to a specific altitude. The plants just flower at different times of the year. At the base of the mountains (e.g. routes 8 and 9) the flora starts to bloom at the end of April, whereas at higher altitudes (for example route 15), it reaches its peak in early July.

One emblematic group of rock hugging plants is that of the Petrocoptises, a genus of the Pink family exclusive to the Pyrenees. (see boxed text).

Another Pyrenean beauty is the Ramonda (see page 63) – a relict of an ancient flora from before the ice ages. Ramonda always grows on sheltered, damp rocks. Where water trickles down the limestone cliffs, the endemic Long-leaved Butterwort is very common (p. 63). The long,

pale leaves of this insectivorous plant hang down like flypaper, trapping any insects that dares to land on it. Be careful not to confuse this species with the Large-flowered Butterwort, which is also common on moist rocks. Another emblematic plant of the Pyrenees is the Long-leaved Saxifrage (p. 63 and 165). It has a large, radially arranged rosette of stiff leaves. After several years of vegetative life, it produces a spike up to 60 cm tall with up to 500 individual flowers – a very conspicuous sight on cliffs. A closer inspection will reveal many more Saxifrages (see box on previous page). On scree and loose gravel at higher altitudes, look for Pyrenean Yam* (*Borderea pyrenaica*; p. 63), a member of the predominantly tropical Yam family. This is a very special plant because there are only two Borderea species in the world and both are endemic to the Pyrenees. The second, very similar species is *Borderea chouardii*, which is only found in the Ribagorzana and Noguera valleys in the east of Huesca!

Sarcocapnos is endemic to the Iberian Peninsula. It frequents exposed limestone cliffs at the base of the mountain, including old walls such as here, on the citadel of Alquézar (route 8).

Petrocoptis – an ultralocal delight

The Pyrenees abound in highly localised species of plants, but the group of the Petrocoptises are in this respect something special. This genus of showy relatives of the Pink family counts nine species world wide. With the exception of two, they all occur in the province of Huesca, and no less than five are exclusively found in Huesca. Most species occur only in one or a few valleys, where they can be quite common. For example, *Petrocoptis guarensis* is unique to the eastern Guara (e.g. route 8), while *Petrocoptis pseudoviscosa* is only found along a few kilometre stretch of gorge along the road between Campo and Castejon de Sos.

Petrocoptis guarensis

^Δ^=endemic to Pyrenees and nearby mountains.

Flora of cliffs and crags

Shaded rocks, water sources Maidenhair Fern (*Adiantum capillus-veneris*), Maidenhair Spleenwort (*Asplenium trichomanes*), Brittle Bladder-fern (*Cystopteris fragilis*), Black Spleenwort (*Asplenium adiantum-nigrum*), Smooth Spleenwort (*Asplenium fontanum*), Ramonda (*Ramonda myconi*^Δ^), Long-leaved Butterwort (*Pinguicula longifolia*^Δ^), Large-flowered Butterwort (*Pinguicula grandiflora*), Globularia-leaved Valerian* (*Valeriana apula*^Δ^), Marsh Helleborine (*Epipactis palustris*), Robust Marsh-orchid (*Dactylorhiza elata*)

Dry limestone cliffs (mostly over 1000 meters) Green Spleenwort (*Asplenium viride*), Pyrenean Columbine (*Aquilegia pyrenaica*^Δ^), Pyrenean Whitlowgrass (*Petrocallis pyrenaica*), Charmeli's Rampion* (*Phyteuma charmelii*), Heart-leaved Globularia* (*Globularia cordifolia*), Leafless-stemmed Globularia (*Globularia nudicaulis*), Creeping Globularia (*Globularia repens*), Heart-leaved Globularia (*Globularia cordifolia*), Snapdragon (*Antirrhinum majus*), Evergreen Snapdragon (*Antirrhinum sempervirens*^Δ^), Sarcocapnos (*Sarcocapnos enneaphylla*^Δ^), Lax Cinquefoil (*Potentilla caulescens*), Pyrenean Honeysuckle (*Lonicera pyrenaica*^Δ^), Lady's-mantle-leaved Cinquefoil (*Potentilla alchemilloides*^Δ^), Livelong Saxifrage (*Saxifraga paniculata*), Long-leaved Saxifrage (*Saxifraga longifolia*^Δ^), Mountain Alison (*Alyssum montanum*), Saxifrage Catchfly* (*Silene saxifraga*), Fragile Saxifrage* (*Saxifraga fragilis*), Malling Toadflax (*Chaenorhinum origanifolium*)

Dry limestone and sandstone cliffs (mostly under 1000 meters) Long-flowered Valerian* (*Valeriana longiflora*^Δ^), Petrocoptis (*Petrocoptis sp.*), Pyrenean Figwort (*Scrophularia pyrenaica*^Δ^), Thick-leaved Stonecrop (*Sedum dasyphyllum*), Snapdragon (*Antirrhinum majus*), Woolly Snapdragon (*Antirrhinum molle*), Sea Mallow (*Lavatera maritima*), Rock Tea (*Jasonia glutinosa*), Malling Toadflax (*Chaenorhinum origanifolium*)

Rocky clearings, moraines, scree Limestone Fern (*Gymnocarpium robertianum*), Sticky Columbine* (*Aquilegia viscosa*^Δ^), Thore's Buttercup (*Ranunculus thora*), Grass-leaved Buttercup (*Ranunculus gramineus*), Parnassus-leaved Buttercup (*Ranunculus parnassifolius*), Pyrenean Germander (*Teucrium pyrenaicum*^Δ^), Pona's Speedwell* (*Veronica ponae*), Fairy Foxglove (*Erinus alpinus*), Alpine Toadflax (*Linaria alpina*), Prostrate Toadflax (*Linaria supina*), Spreading Bellflower (*Campanula patula*), Pyrenean Bellflower (*Campanula speciosa*), Whorled Solomons-seal (*Polygonatum verticillatum*)

Flora of the Mediterranean scrubs and woodlands

Vast areas of the *Depresión*, the lower *Sierras Exteriores* and the *Somontano* are clad in an open, scrubby woodland of Portuguese and Holm Oaks. The plant life here differs, depending on the soil and geographic location. The binding factor is the dominance of Mediterranean type shrubs. These are evergreen, small-leaved, sturdy bushes with a tolerance for heat and grazing. Most of them are heavily scented, often poisonous, frequently spiny, with leathery or hairy leaves and with resilient woody

Bellflower Flax* (*Linum campanulatum*) – one of several colourful flax species that is common in scrublands.

stems. Widespread shrubs are Kermes Oak, Rosemary, Scorpion Broom, Sage-leaved Cistus and Shrubby Globularia.

In spring, the scrub and open woodlands are remarkably rich in wild-flowers. This is the realm of the small, usually colourful orchids, such as Fly, Woodcock, Early Spider and Dull Bee Orchids. Close to Rosemary bushes, you often find the stout, parasitic Rosemary Broomrape (p. 144). In spring the bright blue tussocks of Blue Aphyllanthes are very common (p. 34). This plant resembles a rush, but is actually a member of the lily family.

The common blue flower in summer is the Blue Catananche. There are not many other wildflowers around in the summer months, but White Cephalaria is a frequent and conspicuous flower of the hottest months.

Exploring the scrublands and open woodlands is easy: park anywhere along the road and stroll in. There is bound to be something of interest. Yet finding specific scrubland species is another matter. There appears to be a large degree of randomness as to exactly where species occur, and you can do little more than explore similarly random sites in this widely spread habitat. Hence, there is a certain amount of luck involved in finding that one particular orchid or ironwort, although perseverance

Flora of Mediterranean scrub and woodland

Trees and shrubs Phoenician Juniper (*Juniperus phoenicea*), Portuguese Oak (*Quercus faginea*), Holm Oak (*Quercus ilex*), Kermes Oak (*Quercus coccifera*), Strawberry Tree (*Arbutus unedo*), Laurustinus (*Viburnum tinus*), Etruscan Honeysuckle (*Lonicera etrusca*), Box (*Buxus sempervirens*), Rosemary (*Rosmarinus oficinalis*), Laurel-leaved Cistus (*Cistus laurifolius*), Sage-leaved Cistus (*Cistus salvifolius*), Shrubby Globularia (*Globularia alypum*), Wayfaring Tree (*Viburnum lantana*)

Widespread flora of the woodlands and scrub Silver-lined Broom* (*Argyrolobium zanonii*), False Vetch (*Astragalus monspessulanus*), Bearberry (*Arctostaphylos uva-ursi*), Pygmy Bindweed (*Convolvulus lineatus*), Southern Bindweed (*Convolvulus cantabrica*), Shrubby Gromwell (*Lithodora fruticosa*), Rosemary Broomrape (*Orobanche latisquama*^Δ^), Hairy Ironwort (*Sideritis hirsuta*), Lavender-leaved Sage (*Salvia lavandulifolia*), Iberian Jerusalem-sage (*Phlomis lychnitis*), Iranian Jerusalem-sage (*Phlomis herba-venti*), Coris (*Coris monspeliensis*), White Rockrose (*Helianthemum apenninum*), White Cephalaria (*Cephalaria leucantha*), Leuzea (*Leuzea conifera*), White Flax (*Linum suffruticosum*), Sticky Flax (*Linum viscosum*), Bellflower Flax* (*Linum campanulatum*), Beautiful Flax (*Linum narbonense*), Rush-leaved Jonquil (*Narcissus assoanus*), Round-headed Leek (*Allium sphaerocephalon*), Blue Aphyllanthes (*Aphyllanthes monspeliensis*), Pyramidal Orchid (*Anacamptis pyramidalis*), Lady Orchid (*Orchis purpurea*), Dull Bee Orchid (*Ophrys fusca*), Woodcock Orchid (*Ophrys scolopax*), Fragrant Orchid (*Gymnadenia conopsea*), Early Spider Orchid (*Ophrys aranifera*)

Flora of Depresión and Somontano Grass-leaved Buttercup (*Ranunculus gramineus*), Common Lavender (*Lavandula angustifolia*), Common Globularia (*Globularia vulgaris*), Blue Catananche (*Catananche caerulea*), Rosy Garlic (*Allium roseum*), Spanish Fritillary (*Fritillaria lusitanica*), Fly Orchid (*Ophrys insectifera*)

Flora of Ebro basin scrubland Large Joint-pine* (*Ephedra major*), Sad Stock (*Matthiola fruticulosa*), Boleum (*Boleum asperum*^Δ^), Large Moricandia* (*Moricandia moricandioides*), Pamirian Winterfat (*Krascheninnikovia ceratoides*^Δ^), Dwarf Scorpion-vetch (*Coronilla minima*), Foxtail Milk-vetch* (*Astragalus alopecuroides*), Grey Milk-vetch (*Astragalus incanus*), Woolly Bindweed (*Convolvulus lanuginosus*), Purgative Thymelea* (*Thymelaea tinctoria*), Rosemary-leaved Cistus* (*Cistus clusii*^Δ^), Wall Germander (*Teucrium chamaedrys*), Cudweed Germander* (*Teucrium gnaphalodes*^Δ^), Ruthenian Globe Thistle (*Echinops ritro*), Brown Bluebell (*Dipcadi serotinum*), Slender Sternbergia (*Sternbergia colchiciflora*),Violet Bird's-nest (*Limodorum abortivum*), Dull Bee Orchid (*Ophrys fusca*), Mirror Orchid (*Ophrys speculum*)

^Δ^=endemic to arid regions of Spain

Opposite page: The Mediterranean scrublands boast a high variety of orchids. In April and May, the Early Spider Orchid (left), Dull Bee Orchid (centre) and Woodcock Orchid (right) are frequent.

obviously improves your chances. The best approach is to visit scrublands in a variety of areas. This habitat holds different species in the comparatively moist *Depresión* and *Somontano*, than it does in the arid

Ebro and Sierra de Alcubierre. For maximum diversity, spend time in the hills around Fraga and near the reservoir of Santa Ana (route 7), where species with a more Mediterranean distribution occur.

Flora of the steppes

The steppe flora is appreciated by the connoisseur. Many species are rare, localised and adapted to extreme soil and climatic conditions. The admirer though, needs to be somewhat of a specialist to appreciate the often tiny flowers and scruffy, dust-covered plants.

In the lowlands of the Ebro depression, the botanical hotspots are found in the natural steppe vegetation. Agricultural land is only of interest when it is abandoned or in the small zones between the plots to which the original steppe vegetation has retreated.

The modest peak of the flowering season lies between late April and early June, but those brave enough to explore the steppes in the baking summer season are treated to the delicate flowers of no less than nine species of Sea Lavender that occur in the Ebro depression.

When exploring the flora of the steppes, you should focus on three different vegetation types. The first is the native scrubland of Spanish Juniper and Rosemary. These areas of scrub are easily recognised and can be explored on routes 1, 3, 5 and the Alcubierre mountains (site A on page 137). The second botanical vegetation type is the gypsum steppe, which occurs on hillsides and table mountains in the hottest parts of the steppes (routes 2 and 3). This steppe land is patchy with scattered bushes over bare soil. Typical and frequent plant species here are the robust Spanish Gypsophila* (*Gypsophila struthium hispanica*), the purple-flowered

The sweet-vetch *Hedysarum boveanum* grows at La Lomaza reserve (route 2). This is one of the more colourful steppe specialists. It can be found both on saline and gypsum soils.

Three-toothed Restharrow* (*Ononis tridentata*), Pale-leaved Rockrose* (*Helianthemum squamatum*), Golden Dwarf Gromwell* (*Neatostema apulum*) and the oddly fine-leaved *Herniaria fruticosa*. On more grassy patches, there is Brown Bluebell, Upright Yellow Flax and the orange-flowered Toothed Pheasant's-eye* (*Adonis dentata*). The grasses are very beautiful, particularly against a low, setting or rising sun. Various of the oddly-shaped needle-grasses (*Stipa ssp.*) and the Esparto Grass are typical plants of the steppes.

The sturdy False Esparto Grass can be dominant in certain types of steppe. It is a beautiful species (particularly in the setting sun) but the seeds can be a real nuisance when they bore themselves into your clothing when you walk through the grassland.

Third is the flora of the saline steppes (routes 2 and 3) which consists of a few species uniquely able to survive such hostile environments. White Frankenia* (*Frankenia pulverulenta*), Shrubby Seablite (*Sueada vera*) and various glassworts and sea lavenders.

Finally, fallow and wasteland areas are worth exploring too. They vary strongly in botanical interest, and it is not always easy to predict which might be the good sites. However, a little searching around Belchite and the interior Monegros should produce Peganum and Spanish Aizoon (page 24), two very typical wildflowers of the lowlands, as well as various spurges and species of the borage family.

Flora of the Ebro basin

Gypsum steppe species Small-seeded Pheasant's-eye* (*Adonis microcarpa*), Toothed Pheasant's-eye (*Adonis dentata*), Narrow-leaved Rue (*Ruta angustifolia*), Spanish Gypsophila (*Gypsophila struthium hispanica*), Gypsum Pepperwort* (*Lepidium subulatum*), Upright Yellow Flax (*Linum strictum*), Pale-leaved Rockrose* (*Helianthemum squamatum*$^{\Delta}$), Thyme-leaved Frankenia* (*Frankenia thymifolia*), Three-toothed Restharrow* (*Ononis tridentata*$^{\Delta}$), Sand Broomrape (*Orobanche arenaria*), Starry Scabious* (*Scabiosa stellata*), Gypsum Hawkweed* (*Launaea pumila*$^{\Delta\Delta}$), Lagasca's Needlegrass (*Stipa lagascae*), Small-flowered Needlegrass* (*Stipa parviflora*), Esparto (*Lygeum spartum*)

Saline steppes Shrubby Orache (*Atriplex halimus*), Mediterranean Saltwort (*Salsola vermiculata*), Shrubby Seablite (*Suaeda vera*), Halopeplis (*Halopeplis amplexicaulis*), Relict Glasswort* (*Microcnenum coralloides* – endemic to East Spain and Turkey), Aizoon (*Aizoon hispanicum*), African Tamarisk (*Tamariscus africanus*), Cressa (*Cressa cretica*), the sea-lavenders *Limonium echioides, Limonium costae, Limonium latebracteatum, Limonium stenophyllum, Limonium tournefortii, Limonium catalaunicum*

Fallow land Wild Camphor* (*Camphorosma monspeliaca*), Hypecoum (*Hypecoum imberbe*), Peganum (*Peganum harmala*), Platycapnos (*Platycapnos spicatus*), Serrate Spurge (*Euphorbia serrata*), White Wormwood* (*Artemisia herba-alba*), Hollow-stemmed Asphodel (*Asphodelus fistulosus*)

$^{\Delta}$=endemic to Spain and North-Africa
$^{\Delta\Delta}$=endemic to arid Spain

Pyrenean Iris *Iris latifolia*
A stunning deep purple iris that forms large drifts.
Range: endemic to the Pyrenees and Cantabrian mountains
Flowering time: July
Habitat: fresh mountain meadows
Frequency: fairly widespread and abundant
Routes: 14, 15, 16, 18, 19

Pyrenean Germander
Teucrium pyrenaicum
Prostrate germander with typical cream and purple flowers.
Range: mountains of northern Spain and southern France
Flowering time: June-August
Habitat: rocks, cliffs, roadsides
Frequency: fairly common
Routes: 12, 13, 14, 15, 17, 18, 20, 21

Pyrenean Lily
Liliumpyrenaicum
Large lily of the Martagon Lily group but with yellow flowers.
Range: northern Spain and Massif Central (where very rare)
Flowering time: June-July
Habitat: open woods, roadsides
Frequency: local and rare
Routes: 18, site A on page 202

Pyrenean Fritillary
Fritillaria pyrenaica
Pretty small fritillary of species-rich grasslands.
Range: Pyrenees and Cévennes
Flowering time: late May-June
Habitat: alpine meadows
Frequency: local but abundant where present
Route: 14

Pyrenean Yam *Borderea pyrenaica*
Member of the tropical Dioscorea family.
Range: Pyrenees
Flowering time: January-April
Habitat: rocky forests, old walls
Frequency: very local and rare
Routes: 15, site B on page 202

Long-leaved Butterwort
Pinguicula longifolia
Pale-flowered Butterwort with long,
yellowish leaves.
Range: Iberian mountains
Flowering time: April-July
Habitat: wet limestone rock faces
Frequency: local but abundant where present
Routes: 15, 16, 17

Ramonda *Ramonda myconi*
Relict species from the Tertiary period, isolated member of the tropical Gesneria family.
Range: Pyrenees and Catalonian mountains
Flowering time: May-August
Habitat: sheltered, moist, shady rocks
Frequency: widespread and common
Routes: 8, 9, 12, 13, 14, 15, 16, 17, 18, 19, 20

Long-leaved Saxifrage *Saxifraga longifolia*
Superb saxifrage with stiff rosette and large inflorescence with hundreds of flowers.
Range: mountains of northern Spain
Flowering time: May-early August
Habitat: exposed rocks, cliffs
Frequency: widespread and common
Routes: 8, 9, 10, 11, 12, 13, 14, 15, 17, 20

Mammals

To find Chamois and Marmots, try routes 13, 15, 16, 18 and 20. Very good routes for bats are 3, 5, 6, 7, 9 and 13. The best way to find carnivores and Wild Boar is by driving minor roads at dusk or dawn. Route 3, 5 and 11 can be rewarding.

The mammalian fauna of the region is a blend of temperate, Mediterranean and mountain species. The majority of them is difficult to find, or require specialist equipment such as bat detector or live traps. However, if you pay close attention, you should be able to find some of the larger animals, such as Red Fox, Roe Deer, Chamois and Alpine Marmot.

The Chamois of the Pyrenees are darker than those of the Alps. The Pyrenean species is sometimes called *Isard*.

Herbivores

The high mountains were once the realm of the Pyrenean Ibex, but it sadly became extinct in January 2000 (see box on page 81). Two other mountain specialists inhabit the steep slopes and windy plateaux: the Alpine Marmot and the Pyrenean Chamois (or *Isard*). The latter closely resembles the Chamois of the Alps and is not too difficult to find. It grazes the upland pastures (often close to woodland cover) and in summer gathers around the last patches of snow, which they visit to cool down.

The second high altitude species is the Alpine Marmot, a species that is easily heard (a loud high pitched whistle) but requires careful scanning to find. Marmots are big, badger-sized herbivores that live in groups in Alpine meadows, where they build an extensive system of burrows. They are a favoured prey for Golden Eagles, and are therefore shy and alert. Although well adapted to the habitat, Marmots are not native to the Pyrenees. They were introduced from the Alps by French hunters in the 1960s, and quickly spread all over the high altitude meadows.

Another hunting-related introduction concerns the Iberian Ibex. Several animals escaped from a private hunting area in the Sierra de Guara and are colonising this mountain range. In 2014, a successful introduction program started in the French Pyrenees. Animals crossed the border to the Bujaruelo valley (route 16) and are roaming widely in the Monte Perdido and Aneto massifs. Feral goats are widespread and easy to observe in the Guara. Once, goat herding was a living that could sustain a farmer, but with the exodus from the mountains (see history section), herds were left unattended and today fend for themselves on the dry slopes of the southern Guara.

Red Deer occupy the mountain forests and oak woodlands of the valleys. They are most abundant in the western part of the Pyrenees near Jaca, where they were introduced. In the southeast part of Huesca, on both sides of the river Ebro, a small population of the original Iberian subspecies survives. They are smaller in size and sport a black line along their spine. Roe Deer and Wild Boar are much more widespread, occurring throughout the mountains. In Spain, Roe Deer used to be an animal of the mountains. Over the last few decades, it has gradually colonised much of the Ebro lowlands. They occur all along the Ebro and its tributaries and during one of our preparatory trips, we even found one at La Lomaza, the driest of steppe reserves near Belchite (route 2).

Wild Cats roam the mountain forests throughout the province.

Carnivores

Red Fox is the most common carnivore. It is equally at home on the snow-covered Alpine meadows as it is in the hot lowland steppe, and everywhere in between. In wooded lowlands, it shares its habitat with the Genet, which is related to the cats. The Genet is generally nocturnal, spends nearly all its life in trees and is, as a consequence, very hard to see. However, its presence can be detected by its latrines, containing long, dark grey droppings.

Beech Marten are abundant in woody areas and in shrubby terrain throughout the mountains, and occur locally in the Ebro basin as well. Although shy, Beech Marten often live close to human habitation. The closely related Pine Marten, in contrast, occurs far away from villages and farms, deep in the thick mountain forests. This is also the realm of Wild Cat and Badger. The characteristic foot prints and dropping of the Otter can be found along many rivers below 1,000 m. Look for them along the banks of the rivers Cinca and Ara.

As in many places in Europe, large mammals were heavily hunted in the Pyrenees. Wolf and Lynx disappeared in the 20th century. The biggest and most famous carnivore however, the Brown Bear, survived in the remote valleys of Ansó and Hecho. Although, 'survive' is, perhaps,

The Desman is exclusively found in mountain streams in northern Spain. This odd-looking creature has only one relative: a type of Desman that lives in Russia.

too optimistic, because heavy persecution reduced the original population to only one old male which was then officially declared dead in November 2010. However, thanks to reintroductions on the French side from 1993 onwards, a new population of Brown Bear is now present in the mountains. They seem to be doing well since there are currently (2025) around individuals roaming the mountains. They are mostly on the French and Catalan side, but in autumn and spring some animals cross the border at the western Ansó and Hecho valleys as well as near Benasque and Campo in the east.

Bats

An area with as many caves, cracks and old trees as the Spanish Pyrenees has to be a paradise for bats. And indeed, no less than 27 species have been recorded, many in high numbers.
Lesser and Greater Horseshoe Bats are common in caves and (abandoned) buildings. The regular 'streetlight' bats are Common Pipistrelle in the mountains and Soprano's and Kuhl's Pipistrelles in the Ebro basin.
Most bats can only readily be identified by the sound they produce. Unfortunately, this is only audible to humans via a 'bat detector'. The only exception is the relatively low (but still very high) ultrasonic calls of the European Free-tailed Bat. This big bat makes feeding flights of several kilometres and can be heard almost everywhere. A rather rare species is the Greater Noctule, which lives in the extensive old forests of Ansó and Hecho. The odd and difficult to find Barbastelle probably

occurs throughout the mountains. Finally, the Alpine Long-eared Bat occurs in Ordesa.

Other mammals

There is a large number of small animals (voles, shrews, etc.) present in the region, none of which are likely to be seen by the casual visitor. A few species deserve mention though, starting with what is probably the oddest and rarest of all the Pyrenean mammals, the Pyrenean Desman. This is an insect-eating animal of about 12 cm with a long, flexible, trunk-like snout. It is strongly tied to rivers and streams in the mountains up to an altitude of about 1,500 metres. This odd animal is restricted to the Pyrenees and Cantabrian mountains. It is a strong swimmer and catches aquatic insects, larvae and shrimp by using its sensitive nose. Desmans live in pairs, marking their territory with their scent and defending it against intruding Desmans – to the death if necessary. The species used to be quite common in the wetter parts of the mountains. At present (2025) however, this species is listed as Endangered by the IUCN. The population is falling as a result of habitat fragmentation and a decrease in precipitation associated with climate change. There are probably more factors at play that are currently not well understood.
Not nearly as radical looking, but much easier to spot, is the Iberian Hare. It is smaller and more reddish coloured than the European Hare, but is most easily identified by having white backs to the legs. The Ebro river roughly divides the ranges of European and Iberian Hares. Towards the south of Huesca, the Iberian Hare is the more frequent whereas to the north most are European Hares.

The large numbers of caves and many old trees mean that the Pyrenees support huge numbers of bats. These are Schreibers' Bats in a cave in Vadiello (route 9).

The sad story of the Pyrenean Ibex

The Spanish Pyrenees has the dubious honour of producing the first global extinction of the 21st century. The century was only six days old when the last Pyrenean Ibex was found dead in Ordesa.

The *Bucardo*, as it was called in Aragonese, was endemic to the Pyrenees and lived on both sides of the border. It was distinct from both the Alpine and Iberian Ibexes. The males had bigger, broader horns and the females were heavier with bigger heads. Genetically, the *Bucardo* was midway between the Alpine and Iberian species.

Due to its impressive horns and, not least, the wild and challenging habitat in which it lived, the Bucardo was an esteemed trophy. By 1880, hunting had reduced the population to one small area in and around the Ordesa valley. In 1918 it finally received some protection with the establishment of the Ordesa National Park where it could not be hunted. But this was not enough. The upland plateaux, which provided its main summer pastures, wasn't part of the National Park (not until 1984). From the Civil War onwards and into the 1950s, poaching in the Park took a heavy toll on the population.

This skull is the only remains of the Pyrenean Ibex on public display. You can admire it at the reception of the Parador de Bielsa in the Pineta valley; route 18.

Paradoxically, the establishment of the National Park itself turned out be another nail in the coffin. The valley with its harsh winter climate never was a favourable place for the Ibex. It became even less suited as new Park regulations banned tree felling and grazing, causing the valley to become overgrown with bushes, not leaving enough food for the Ibex. Sadly, the *Bucardo* was being preserved in the one place it couldn't survive. Some 80 years after the establishment of the National Park, there were only ten to twenty animals left.

Shortly after Spain joined the European Union, an active *Bucardo* conservation plan was launched. By the start in 1993, there were three females left, but no males (the last male died in 1991). The plan was to crossbreed the Pyrenean females with males from the Iberian Ibex, as a last attempt to save the species, but to no avail. One female died after nine months in captivity, another female just disappeared and the last was found dead under a tree on the 6th of January 2000. More information: **bucardo.es**.

Birds

The best routes for high mountain birds are routes 13, 15, 16 and 21. Vultures and other cliff breeding raptors are very visible on routes 7, 9, 10, 12 and 15, plus sites A, C and D on pages 161-162 and sites B and C on pages 202-203. Mediterranean birds are more scattered, and are often found alongside the road (sites A on pages 137 and 161). Rewarding routes are 3, 5, 6, 8, 9, 10 and 11. The best sites for steppe birds are on routes 1, 2, 3 and 4. Wetlands birds are present on routes 1, 3, 5 and 6. A detailed per species site description is given on page 226.

The Spanish Pyrenees became, together with places like the French Camargue, one of the first popular birdwatching destinations abroad. Before travel by airplane became something for the masses, the Pyrenees was one of those magical places where a large number of 'new' species (to the predominantely 'northern' observers) could be seen in an area that could still be reached conveniently within an average holiday period. The quantity and variety of birds plus the spectacular, undisturbed landscape was legendary. Today, cheap fly-drive package deals create more competition with other areas, but the Spanish Pyrenees, together with the nearby steppes, remain as they were: an exceptionally rich birdwatching destination. Moreover, the presence of many good hotels and camp sites and increased accessibility, now make travel a lot more comfortable.

There is a high diversity of birds, which can be broadly grouped into five 'domains'. First, there are the mountain specialists, most of which occur at altitude (e.g. Rock Thrush, Snowfinch). Then there is the rich birdlife of Mediterranean scrub, agricultural land and open woodlands (e.g. Bee-eater, Woodchat Shrike). And third, there are the arid landscapes of the Ebro basin with its bustards and sandgrouse.

Raptors in general and vultures in particular make the Pyrenees a spectacular place for birdwatching.

The three vultures of the Pyrenees: the Bearded (top), the Griffon (previous page) and the Egyptian Vulture (bottom). A fourth species, Black Vulture, extinct here for over 100 years, is now the subject of a re-introduction project.

These, the first three of our five domains, provide the greatest attraction to visiting birdwatchers. The two others, although arguably less exciting, greatly add to the overall diversity. The fourth domain encompasses the extensive forests and fresh meadows of the Pyrenees, which support a large variety of temperate European species. Familiar they may be, but here in Spain some of them reach their southern limit (e.g. Song Thrush, Marsh Tit). Finally we come to the wetlands (with species such as Red-crested Pochard and Little Bittern). Huesca being land-locked, arid and mountainous, wetland is not the first habitat that comes to mind. And indeed, the wetlands are limited in extent, but the number of birds is unexpectedly high. In this chapter we describe these five bird 'domains' in further detail.

Birds of the high mountains

The open woodland, bushes and Alpine meadows around the tree limit (between 1,600 and 2,100 metres) support many mountain species. The subalpine zone, with its scattered trees and heath and alpenrose bushes, is the haunt of Ring Ouzel and Citril Finch with a fine supporting cast of Tree Pipit, Rock Bunting, Dunnock, Yellowhammer, Linnet and Red-backed Shrike. In flat areas with tall herbs, both below and above the treeline, you may encounter two unexpected birds. This is the natural habitat of Quail and Grey Partridge. Quail is frequently heard if rarely seen. The Grey Partridge is particularly interesting as they

Cliff breeding species

	High Pyrenees	*Sierras Exteriores*	*Lowland cliffs*
Lammergeier	common	common	
Griffon Vulture	very common	abundant	local
Egyptian Vulture	frequent	common	local
Golden Eagle	frequent	frequent	fairly common
Bonelli's Eagle	extinct	rare	
Peregrine	frequent	frequent	rare
Kestrel	fairly common	fairly common	fairly common
Crag Martin	very common	very common	local
House Martin	very common	very common	very common
Alpine Swift	frequent	frequent	local
Eagle Owl	rare	fairly common	common
Rock Dove	rare	fairly common	
Wallcreeper	frequent		
Rock Thrush	frequent	frequent	
Blue Rock Thrush	rare	frequent	rare
Black Wheatear		local	frequent
Alpine Chough	fairly common		
Red-billed Chough	very common	very common	fairly common
Raven	frequent	frequent	frequent
Rock Bunting	fairly common	common	local

are of a relict population and a distinct subspecies. Other than in the Cantabrian mountains (where this subspecies is also found), there are no Grey Partridges elsewhere in Spain nor are they found in the nearby lowlands to the north. So the isolated population of the Pyrenees has evolved into a distinct subspecies.

Rocky Alpine meadows above the treeline support in addition to the aforementioned species, also Water Pipit, Northern Wheatear, Rock Thrush, Alpine Accentor, Alpine Chough and Black Redstart (with the latter in particular in high densities). Where rocky slopes turn into a solid rockface, the birdlife changes yet again. Warmer, insect rich south-facing cliffs have a very rich community of breeding birds. This is the realm of the Wallcreeper which, like Crag and House Martins and Alpine Swift, breeds in cracks in the escarpments. The often abundant Red-billed Chough breeds on small ledges and in larger cracks in the rock. At 1,900 m and above, the Alpine Chough takes over from its red-billed cousin. Both species often feed on Alpine meadows.

Other cliff breeders include Egyptian and Griffon Vultures, Lammergeier, Golden Eagle and Raven. Particularly common is the Griffon Vulture, a colonial breeder. There are colonies all over the Pyrenees, *Sierras Exteriores* and on cliffs deeper in the lowlands. It can be seen cruising the skies almost anywhere.

Cliffs are clearly a feature of mountains, but not necessarily of high altitudes (see box above). For example, all three vulture species occur in large numbers in the High Pyrenees, but the densities in the lower *Sierras Exteriores* are even higher. The spectacular conglomerate walls of Agüero, Riglos (route 10), Roldán and Vadiello (route 9) and Mascún hold spectacular colonies of Griffon Vultures. Egyptian Vulture, Lammergeier, Peregrine and Golden Eagle are present as well, but more widely dispersed and never in colonies. The warmer, more Mediterranean cliffs typically support Rock Dove, Blue Rock Thrush and Black Wheatear, although the latter is declining in the region.

Finally, the highest slopes of the Pyrenees – well over 2,000 metres – are the realm of Ptarmigan and Snowfinch. Although, these two species share their summer habitat with birds like Alpine Accentor and Black Redstart, they themselves are true cold-loving birds that descend only a little in winter. Since climbing up to altitudes in excess of 2,000 metres requires a considerable effort, these two species are easiest to find in winter.

The Spanish Pyrenees are right on the meeting point of of the temperate European and Mediterranean worlds. The Woodchat Shrike (top) is a Mediterranean bird, frequent in the *Somontano* and Ebro Depression. The Red-backed Shrike (bottom) of temperate Europe is common in the small scale agricultural land in the Pyrenees.

Mediterranean birdlife

A special attraction of the Spanish Pyrenees – and a striking difference with the French side – is the swift succession of Alpine birdlife to a Mediterranean avifauna at lower levels. Mediterranean scrublands, evergreen forests, small scale plots and arid mountains are found as far north as the *Depresión* (near Jaca for example), but the most extensive areas cover the south-facing slopes of the Guara and *Somontano* plus the Sierra de Alcubierre in the Ebro valley.

The Mediterranean birdlife is famously rich and this is no exception in Huesca, where large areas of Mediterranean-type woodlands are in an unscathed state. Some delightful species, like Hoopoe, Woodchat Shrike, Bee-eater and Rock Sparrow, are widespread and common. Most impressive are the high numbers of kites. Black Kites are simply everywhere in the lowlands, circling low over the fields, taking carrion from the road or resting on electricity poles. Red Kite is widespread as well, with high densities in the west and in the *Depresión*. Here it outnumbers Black Kite.

The evergreen wood and scrub is home to a large variety of small passerines. Rock Bunting is locally abundant in semi-open rocky country while Cirl Bunting, which prefers open woodland, is widespread. Corn Bunting is very common in areas with cereals and open steppes, where it occurs with the much rarer Tawny Pipit and Montagu's Harrier. In the complex of Mediterranean wood and scrub, Melodious, Dartford, Sardinian, Subalpine, Spectacled, Orphean and Bonelli's Warblers are all present. These birds present a daunting task to inexperienced birdwatchers. Careful observation reveals that these species tend to seek out

Vulture fashion

Vultures do not have a very good name, often being described in terms such as disgusting, cruel, unsanitary, glutinous and brutish. Granted, with a wingspan of up to 2.80 metres (in case of the Griffon) they are appreciated as spectacular birds, but most frequently in a beastly kind of way. It is time, though, to break down this unfairly negative image of the vulture and reveal its other side.

When Joni Mitchell famously sang that *'you don't know what you've got until it's gone'*, she could have had vultures in mind. In India vulture populations have suffered a massive decline due to accidental poisoning by the use of veterinary drugs that proved to be highly toxic to these resilient birds. Subsequent research revealed unexpectedly huge economic and social health cost as a direct result of their disappearance. Without vultures, carrion-eating dogs spread rapidly through India, causing a huge increase in rabies. Instead of spreading disease, as commonly supposed, vultures are vital in maintaining a hygienic environment.

Neither do vultures deserve their reputation as savage animals. Did you know that vultures are highly romantic (to put it anthropomorphically) and loyal birds? Pairs really do stay together 'until death do us part'. Only if one dies, does the other look for a new partner. The pair raises the chick together, and when mature, teaches it how to raise chicks of their own.

Another little known oddity of some vultures is that they henna their feathers. This was first discovered when Lammergeiers were brought up in captivity and it turned out that their paler colouring was naturally white. The 'typical' rusty-orange was not the 'natural' colour of the feathers, but one that was obtained, it transpired, by bathing in water rich in iron oxide. Egyptian Vultures are no natural blondes either. They too, dye their feathers.

This vulture fashion is part of a highly sophisticated form of courtship, that bonds together a pair for life. So don't let a negative predisposition towards carrion eating birds trick you into thinking these animals are unfeelingly savage. Vultures are social and hygienic birds. Well almost. Egyptian Vultures also colour their feathers with cow and horse dung, so something of an unsavoury streak remains... but then you have to admire their robust constitution that enables them to emerge unharmed from such filthy habits!

distinct habitats. Melodious prefers large, isolated bushes and trees, often in moister terrain. Subalpine Warbler inhabits large bushes as well, with a special liking for Holm Oaks. Dartford Warbler seeks out scantier terrain of low bushes (roughly up to a metre), whereas Spectacled appears only when scrub has reduced to the size of bushy steppe. Orphean and Bonelli's Warblers occupy the other end of the range and breed in open woodland.

Other widespread birds in Mediterranean habitat are Turtle Dove, Nightjar, Black-eared Wheatear, Short-toed and Booted Eagles and Iberian Grey Shrike (although the latter seems to be declining in numbers). Woodlark can be found in many places, but tends to have a preference for almond groves.

For some Mediterranean species Huesca is, so it seems, too distant from the coast. They are more widespread in Catalonia, but occur only locally in Huesca, mostly in the lowlands near the Catalonian border. The Roller is a good example. It occurs only in the eastern part of Huesca, close to the Cinca river. Red-necked Nightjar is another Mediterranean species that occurs in the region, but only in low (though largely unknown) numbers. The same applies to Great Spotted Cuckoo: it occurs but is not frequent. This being said, there are vast areas in the lowlands which hardly a soul ever visits, let alone a binocular wielding birder. Some of these species may be much more common than is currently known. If you want to make some new discoveries, you have come to the right place.

The Hoopoe is a frequent bird of the *Somontano.*

Birds of steppe and dryland farming

The third major bird region is the steppe zone in the Ebro basin. This habitat, and with it its birds, is the most threatened of the province.

The characteristic steppe birds are a challenge to find. Camouflage is an important survival mechanism in open terrain where predators have unimpeded view. Low activity during the hot hours of the day is another necessary requirement here. This combination makes birdwatching difficult, yet very enjoyable for those who like a challenge.

The Ebro basin is one of Spain's top areas for steppe birds. Unlike the steppes of the upland mesetas and Extremadura, the steppes of

Huesca and Zaragoza are not a gently rolling landscape, but consist of various plateaux, each separated by cliffs and steep rocky slopes. Indeed they are as much 'stepped' as steppe! The vegetation is also more patchy, with scattered dwarf bushes and mostly small plots of grassland and cereals. It is in this respect more reminiscent of the steppes and semi-deserts of southeast Spain.

This shows in the birdlife which has important populations of Pin-tailed and Black-bellied Sandgrouse, Stone Curlew, Black Wheatear, Short-toed, Lesser Short-toed and Dupont's Lark – all species of very scanty steppes of southern Europe, North Africa and the Middle East.

Within the region, the richest areas for steppe birds are the flat areas with primary (original) steppe vegetation. This habitat is now very rare. The best remaining parts are near Belchite (route 2). This is the haunt of the rare and essentially North-African Dupont's Lark. Short-toed and (near saline areas) Lesser Short-toed Lark do well here too, as do the sandgrouse and Stone Curlew.

Most other flats are cultivated. When such areas are left fallow or are planted with cereals, they attract sandgrouse and Stone Curlew, in addition to Short-toed and Calandra Larks.

The larger, more rolling areas of cereals are the prime habitat for Calandra Lark, and, in the east, for Roller. The grain fields also offer home to the region's modest population of Great Bustard which numbers about 60 birds. Little Bustards are widespread, but generally uncommon, in the more varied types of steppe.

The bushy and rocky slopes give the Ebro basin its exotic 'Wild West' look, but for steppe birds they are of lesser value. You will find Thekla Lark here (found throughout the steppe), Black-eared Wheatear and Dartford Warbler – species that also occur in areas with scanty Mediterranean scrubland. Perhaps the most interesting species is the Spectacled Warbler, the most heat-and-drought-loving of the warblers of the *Sylvia* group. It is not restricted to slopes, but to areas of low, steppe-like scrub which cover these slopes. Its tolerance of saline habitats gives it an odd distribution: bone dry shrubby steppe and coastal salt marsh.

The mountains support an attractive birdlife. Rock Thrush (top) is frequent in rocky terrain throughout the *Sierras Exteriores* and Pyrenees. The Alpine Accentor (bottom) is an altitudinal migrant: inhabiting rocky terrain above 1,800 metres in summer, and descending to the lower parts in winter.

Rocky slopes are the preferred domain of Black Wheatear – a species that is restricted to North-west Africa and the dry regions of Spain and Portugal.

Birds of deciduous woodlands

Perhaps the largest group of birds is what we loosely call the species of temperate Europe: the thrushes, tits, robins, finches, pigeons and others, which are a familiar sight to most European birders. Many of these species occur widely in Europe, such as Great Tit, Wren, Chaffinch, and Great Spotted Woodpecker. They are found widely in Huesca as well, although their numbers thin out on the steppes.

Black Woodpeckers breed in old beech-fir forests in the High Pyrenees.

Other birds that are so common further north, stick to Huesca's higher regions. Song Thrush, Nuthatch, Goldcrest, Chiffchaff and Marsh Tit for example, find refuge in the cool mountain forests. The fresh beech-fir forests here form a southern outpost of their ranges and from a Spanish perspective, this is a special group of birds.

There are several birds of the deciduous and coniferous mountain forests that are absent from the UK. Black Woodpecker, for example, is a frequent bird of the old mountain forests of Huesca. Eurasian Treecreepers occur, but so does Short-toed. The first is generally found in high coniferous forests, and the latter at lower elevations. Unless you venture into Scotland, Crested Tit is another species for which British birders have to cross the Channel. Both the tit and Short-toed Treecreeper are common in coniferous forest. The deciduous forests, especially those along the mountain rivers, are also home to the Iberian Green Woodpecker. This bird used to occur in riparian forest throughout the lowlands as well, but strongly declined here.

Surprisingly, the old pine woods of the high Pyrenees also support some birds that are more often thought of as native to the vast taiga forests of Scandinavia and Russia. They are a relict of the ice ages, when these species occurred much further south. When the climate warmed, a part of the original population sought refuge in the cold coniferous mountain forests. Two examples are Tengmalm's Owl and Capercaillie. Both species are highly threatened and very difficult to find in the Pyrenees.

Evening flight of Cranes at the Sotonera reservoir (route 6).

Birds of wetlands

It is almost unfair: wetland birds like Purple Heron and Great Reed Warbler, which demand large areas of undisturbed, high quality habitat in northern Europe, make do with the most unspectacular little wetlands in Huesca. And so, even in this dry province, there is a good number of wetland birds. Granted, they cannot compete with the large coastal areas of Catalonia (primarily the bird-filled Ebro Delta), but it is still possible to see a good share of wetland species, like Black-winged Stilt, Penduline Tit, Night Heron, Little Bittern and Red-crested Pochard.

The small freshwater lakes of Sariñena (route 5), Candasnos (route 3), El Pas (site C on page 138) and the northern rim of the Embalse de Sotonera (route 6) have sizable reedbeds, which support Marsh Harrier, Water Rail, Coot, Moorhen, Reed and Great Reed Warbler, Purple and Night Herons and Little and Great Bittern.

Surprisingly rich in birds are the difficult-to-access riverine woodlands where Little Egret, Night and Purple Herons sit alongside Kingfishers and Little Ringed Plovers. Sand Martins wheel overhead whilst Golden Oriole, Penduline Tit and Wryneck call from the high trees. Cetti's Warbler and Nightingale are both very common in moist bushy areas while Zitting Cisticola is at home in riverine fields and grasslands.

Saline wetlands with permanent water are rare in the area. Gallocanta (route 1) is by far the best and biggest example. In fact it is the largest natural lake in Spain. Saline lagoons are less rich in wetland birds than the freshwater sites. The steppe birds are more typical here, but Shelduck, Kentish Plover and, at Gallocanta (route 1), Gull-billed Tern occur in small numbers.

Birds in the winter months

Winter is a an attractive period for birdwatching in Huesca. Large groups of birds flee the north's winter chill and come to feed in the fields of the lowlands. Likewise, the birds of high altitudes seek refuge at

Black-winged Stilts have increased in recent years with the estblishments of reservoirs.

lower altitudes making themselves more accessible to birdwatchers than in their remote breeding quarters. Add to this the large group of resident southern species and you come to a highly attractive mix.

In winter, the high mountains are strikingly devoid of birds. With the exception of some mixed groups of tits, some lone Ravens and a few other species, the high slopes and vast mountain forests are completely silent. The Snowfinches, Wallcreepers and Alpine Accentors find their food at much lower altitudes. Snowfinches frequent huts, barns and refuges on mountain passes and meadows. Alpine Accentor and Wallcreeper spend the winter at the base of mountains. The south-facing cliffs of the Guara (Roldán, Vadiello, Riglos, etc) are particularly rewarding spots for these birds in winter.

The cereal fields in the *Somontano* and Ebro basin are a magnet to song birds and pigeons of central and northern Europe. Large flocks of Wood Pigeons, Chaffinches, Cirl Buntings, Yellowhammers, Skylarks and various pipits spend the short days on the stubble fields. Red Kites, Marsh Harriers, Sparrowhawks and Buzzards are much more abundant during the winter months as well. The breeding population is augmented by thousands of birds from the north. White Storks, Grey Herons, Cattle Egrets and Lapwings feed on irrigated fields while Robins, Chiffchaffs and Blackcaps are common in all kinds of vegetation.

Many of the exotic breeding birds of the province are residents. Griffon Vultures and Lammergeiers, Golden Eagles, Great Bustards, etc. – all of them are as numerous in winter as they are in summer. Most steppe birds congregate in large flocks although many of the Sandgrouse and Little Bustards winter further south. Hundreds of Calandra Larks form huge flocks. Many steppe birds, instead of being widely spread, group together in discrete flocks making winter birdwatching here something of a famine-or-feast experience.

The most spectacular winter experience is undoubtedly the arrival of thousands of Cranes. Strictly speaking, most Cranes visit the region on passage. However, since the passage south begins as late as mid October and lingers on until early December and the passage north starts again in early February, good numbers are present for much of the winter. In recent years, an increasing number of birds do not move further south at all.

Cranes cross the Pyrenees and pass from lagoon to lagoon as they head south to congregate eventually at Gallocanta (route 1). At peak times, in November, over 50,000 birds are present at this lake – a spectacular sight!

Reptiles and amphibians

Routes 1 and 3 are good for finding the amphibians of temporary steppe lakes. Evening drives in warm, damp weather produces many amphibians on the road. Any quiet, local road in the lowlands can be productive, e.g. the *Somontano* road (site A on page 161). The Ibón of Plan (site D on page 203) and routes 14, 16 and 21 support Pyrenean Brook Newt. Rich areas for Mediterranean reptiles are in the Guara (routes 8, 9, 10 and in particular 11). Asp Viper is common in the alpine meadows of Hecho (route 13) and El Portalet (route 14).

With the Pyrenees as the great divide between the Mediterranean and the temperate regions, the province of Huesca is, for most species of reptiles and amphibians, a borderland – either representing the northern or the southern limit of ranges. But there is a third group, which is for experts the reason to visit the region. These are the highly localised Pyrenean endemics – species that occur only in the Pyrenees, and often even here only in a few spots.

Amphibians

Most, if not all, waters in the region have their collection of amphibians amongst which the Iberian Water Frog and Midwife Toad are the most constant factor (the latter is now considered to be a separate species, the Catalan Midwife Toad; *Alytes almogavarii*).

The Iberian Water Frog is, to the untrained eye, simply a Green Frog. Its Spanish name, *Rana Común*, is elucidating: you can find it in any type of water, pretty much everywhere and in large numbers too. In many shallow, standing pools, it is accompanied by the (Catalan) Midwife Toad. Its soft, melancholic *pjuup* calls are heard on warm evenings in many places.

The Spiny Toad is the third widespread species. It is known to wander and is often found far away from water, even in the arid south, where there are some huge specimens.

In the seasonal lakes and streams in the Ebro basin, the small Natterjack Toad, Western Spadefoot and Parsley Frog are the most typical species. All of them are fairly secretive, leading a largely hidden life, shielded from the desiccating sun. On wet, warm evenings, they suddenly emerge and are surprisingly abundant.

The Parsley Frog inhabits riverine habitats, ponds and pools in the warm lowlands, up to about 1,000 metres.

Cold blood in the high mountains

Owing to the isolation from other high altitude ranges, the Pyrenees support a few unique reptile and amphibian species, three of which occur in Huesca.

The **Pyrenean Frog** (*Rana pyrenaica*) was not recognised as a separate species until 1993, being previously mistaken for a dwarf version of Common Frog. Its more uniform skin pattern with slightly reddish colour and its modest length (5 cm at maximum) makes it quite different from the Common Frog. The Pyrenean Frog lives in and around cold mountain streams and torrents at an attitude of 800 to 2,100 m. It is confined to the southern slopes of the western central Pyrenees so that almost the entire world population lives in Huesca. The population is in strong decline, because its eggs are predated by trout. Moreover, the few rivers that still support this species are under threat because of forestry and infrastructure development.

Pyrenean Frog and Pyrenean Brook Newt, two endemic amphibians of the Pyrenees.

The story of the **Pyrenean Brook Newt** (*Calotriton asper*) is similar. This medium-sized newt is easily distinguishable by its uniform brown colour, yellowish line and coarse skin. It inhabits similar habitat as the Pyrenean Frog, in addition to cold mountain lakes and rivers. It is found from the foothills all the way up to an altitude of 3,000 m, an incredible range for a remarkably adaptive species. At high altitudes the newt hibernates from October to April, but, at low altitudes. its active period is reversed and the newt stays underground between June and September. The Pyrenean Brook Newt is much more common and widespread than the previous species, and is not too difficult to find when you search for it. Look underneath stones at lake edges (both under water and on the shore), or on the bottom of still lakes. The combination of broad head and small legs is characteristic.

The **Pyrenean Rock Lizard** (*Iberolacerta bonnali*) is the third species to occur only in the Pyrenees and also the only one to be found on the highest peaks. It resembles the Wall Lizard, with which it shares the alpine habitats around 2,000 m, but is distinguished by the pattern of scales on the head. The Pyrenean Rock Lizard occurs only in rocky terrain, avoiding closed vegetation. Recently, two very similar small lizard populations have been 'split' and are now considered different species – these two occur further east, on the border between Catalonia, Andorra and France.

In mountain lakes and streams, you may find Common or Grass Frog, here at the southern edge of its range. This is also the realm of the supeficially similar, and highly endangered, Pyrenean Frog (see box on page 95).
Another Pyrenean specialist is the Pyrenean Brook Newt, which occurs in Ibóns and fast-flowing mountain brooks. A further exploration of mountain lakes, particularly the better vegetated ones, may turn up Palmate Newt and, in the western lowlands, Marbled Newt.

Reptiles

Among the reptiles, the most encountered species are Wall Lizard, Iberian Wall Lizard and Large Psammodromus. The first two are difficult to tell apart and both occur on rocks, walls, houses and other stony places. The story is different with the Large Psammodromus. This large olive-brown lizard with its two light lines on each flank is easily distinguished. It is fairly common in leaf litter and scrub up to an altitude of about 1,600 m. Descending the Pyrenees from the north, this is the first representative of the distinct southern reptile fauna.

The Ladder Snake, the adult of which is recognisable by the two long dark lines on the back, is common in the dry Ebro Basin.

Further down into the warm lowlands of the *Somontano*, you enter the range of the Moorish Gecko – a splendid little dragon that rushes up and down rocks and walls in the evening (p. 98). It is known as an animal of good fortune and enters houses to catch insects.
In the gypsum steppes of Belchite and the Monegros, the reptile fauna consists almost entirely of species that are endemic to the Western Mediterranean or even restricted solely to the Iberian Peninsula. Here you may see the Spanish Psammodromus dashing from bush to bush

(page 24). It is rarely active in temperatures below 15 degrees and is, thereby, the most warmth-loving reptile of the area. The biggest lizard is the Ocellated Lizard (p. 138). It grows well over half a metre and is bulky, bright green and fast. It prefers dry, sunny and warm places, with rocks and scrub or light woodland. It is widespread, but numbers have decreased in recent decades.

Up in the mountains there are different species of lizards. Wall and Viviparous Lizards frequent the Alpine meadows with the rare and endemic Pyrenean Rock Lizard (see box on page 95) seeking the highest and most rocky parts of the mountain. In shady, damp places throughout the mountains, you may find Slow Worm. With its sensitive skin it

The Montpellier Snake has conspicuously large eyes. It is the most common snake of Huesca and occur in a variety of habitats from lowlands to the base of the Pyrenees.

avoids direct sunlight, and often hides in leaf litter, under stones or tree bark in the warmer part of the day.

The bigger rivers in the lowlands also support European Pond Terrapin. It occurs up to the Sotonera Reservoir (route 6).

Snakes are widespread but difficult to find. The most frequent species is the Montpellier Snake, which is also the largest, growing over 1.5 metres. It occurs in almost any dry bushy area, even fairly high up in the mountains. The Ladder Snake (p. 94) is also fairly common, but tends to stay in the lowlands.

Common does not mean easy to see. The easiest to find are the aquatic snakes. The two species of water snakes in the area are Viperine Snake (small, with a viper-like zigzag pattern on the back and large staring eyes), and the Iberian Grass Snake. The is quite different from the widespread, European Grass Snake, being much darker and lacking the yellow collar that is characteristic of this species elsewhere in Europe.

Amphibian and reptile list

Fire Salamander	mountain forest streams	HP	lc
Pyrenean Brook Newt	cold streams, Ibóns	P	fc
Marbled Newt	mountain pools	west P	lc
Palmate Newt	mountain pools	HP	lc
East Iberian Painted Frog	vegetated lowland pools	S, EB	fr
Midwife Toad	any pond	throughout	c
Western Spadefoot	temporary lowland pools	S, EB	fr
Parsley Frog	lowland scrub and pools	S, EB, SE	fc
Spiny Toad	throughout	throughout	c
Natterjack Toad	steppe, temporary pools	S, EB, SE	lc
Stripeless Tree Frog	vegetated waters	near Fraga	vl
Common Frog	mountain pools and rivers	HP, SE	c
Pyrenean Frog	cold streams	HP	vl
Iberian Water Frog	any water	throughout	c
Graf's Hybrid Frog	well-vegetated pools	EB	unknown
European Pond Terrapin	vegetated pools and rivers	EB	fr
Spanish Terrapin	lowland pools	EB	r
Moorish Gecko	walls, rocks, houses	EB, S, SE	fc
Turkish Gecko	walls, rocks, houses	EB	vl
Spanish Psammodromus	steppe, open scrub	EB, S	lc
Large Psammodromus	any terrain with scrub	EB, S, SE, D	c
Spiny-footed Lizard	steppe, open scrub	EB	vl
Ocellated Lizard	open wood, scrub, steppe	EB, S, SE, D	fc
Western Green Lizard	mountain and gorge forest	west P	l
Viviparous Lizard	alpine meadows	HP	lc
Pyrenean Rock Lizard	high altitude scree	HP	lc
Wall Lizard	scree, rocks, walls	mostly P	fc
Iberian Wall Lizard	scree, rocks, walls	mostly EB, S, SE	c
Western Three-toed Skink	Mediterranean scrub	EB, S	l
Bedriaga's Skink	scrub and steppe	EB	vr
Slow Worm	mountain heath and woods	P	c
Iberian Worm Lizard	loose or rocky soil	EB	l
Montpellier Snake	any scrub or steppe	throughout	c
Horseshoe Whip Snake	scrub and steppe	EB	vl
Western Whip Snake	mostly near wells	HP	vl
Aesculapian Snake	mountain forest near rivers	HP	l
Ladder Snake	dry lowland scrub, steppe	EB, S	fc
Grass Snake	vegetated waters	throughout	l
Viperine Snake	all kinds of waters	P, D, S, EB	c
Smooth Snake	alpine heath, open wood	P	fc
Southern Smooth Snake	rocky lowlands	EB	unknown
False Smooth Snake	scrub and steppe	EB	vl
Asp Viper	open habitat in mountain	HP	fc
Lataste's Viper	scrub and steppe	EB	vl

HP=High Pyrenees, SE=*Sierras Exteriores*, P=Pyrenees (HP+SE), D=*Depresión*, S=*Somontano*, EB=Ebro basin; c=common, fc=fairly common, lc=locally common, fr=fairly rare, l=local, vl=very local

Moorish Geckos are common in old walls and buildings in the lowlands.

Both Viperine and Iberian Grass Snakes are completely harmless. Viperine Snake is the more common of the two and prefers small rivers in the lower half of the mountains and foothills.

High up in the Pyrenees, the only widespread and potentially dangerous snake occurs: the small Asp Viper. Although it rarely exceeds 60 cm in length, this species is dangerous because of its potent venom. It is easily recognised by a combination of a clear zigzag pattern on the back, a short, thick body and the characteristic vertical cat's-eye pupils that gives it its vicious look. The Asp Viper lives in open, sunny and rocky places in the mountains up to 2,500 m. You won't find it easily though, since it frequently hides under rocks. It is most abundant in the western valleys (Hecho and Tena – routes 13 and 14) and rare in the *Sierras Exteriores.*

Perhaps the most beautiful of all the snakes is the large, slender green-and-yellow Western Whip Snake. This species, widespread in France, occurs only very locally in the region (see site C on page 215).

Rare or patchily distributed species

There is a number of reptiles and amphibians that, within the area, are rare or only occur in some specific locality. The majority of them are either typical of more northern areas and occur in a few isolated spots in the mountains, or, conversely, belong to the fauna of southern Spain and cling to a few outposts in the Ebro basin. Northern interlopers include Aesculapian Snake, Western Green Lizard and Western Three-Toed Skink. Southern species are Spiny-footed Lizard, Stripeless Tree Frog, Bedriaga's Skink, Turkish Gecko, Horseshoe Whip Snake, Lataste's Viper, Iberian Worm Lizard and Spanish Terrapin. These live on low densities or isolated spots in the Ebro valley. The relatively cold winters here prevent them from spreading further into the region.

Insects and other invertebrates

The better alpine meadows for butterfly watching are at Hecho (route 13), Portalet (route 14) La Sarra (site E on page 182), Ordesa (route 15 and site B on page 202), Otal (route 16), Pineta (18), Benasque (route 19 and site A on page 215) and Llauset (route 21). Route 11 and 12 are excellent butterfly routes, with species of Mediterranean scrub and dry, Mediterranean-influenced mountains.

Of the overwhelming diversity of invertebrates in the region, butterflies are especially eye-catching. The colourful clouds that accompany you on your walks through the Pyrenees, are an unforgettable sight.

Butterflies

The province of Huesca is one of Europe's top butterfly areas. Both in diversity and in quantity, the province stands out. Here in the Pyrenees, you may be forgiven for thinking you have accidentally entered a carefully designed butterfly garden.

Again it is the magnificently abrupt gradient from the high Pyrenees down to the lowland steppes that create a wealth of different habitats, each with its own butterflies. At least 191 species occur in this area. Thanks to the region's excellent accessibility, a good deal of these species can actually be found. We were able to find 130 different species in just two weeks in early July. If your main interest is butterflies, organise your trip to encompass not only different landscapes and altitudes, but also consider the soil (calcareous versus granite).

The butterfly fauna can be roughly divided in three different zones: First that of the higher Pyrenees, second the Mediterranean hills and mountains (*Depresión, Sierras Exteriores* and *Somontano*) and third the steppes of the Monegros.

The *Sierras Exteriores* and *Somontano* abound in southern delights. The beautiful Striped Grayling (top) and the Escher's Blue (bottom) fly in early July.

Butterflies of the high Pyrenees

Butterflies put up a magnificent show in the high Pyrenees in summer. Nearly every mountain habitat has its own specific species. The Alpine meadows are one of the highlights, supporting many species that you will only find at these altitudes. Usually, the richest meadows are those that are not too heavily grazed because they support the highest number of nectar plants and larval food plants.

The blues, skippers, fritillaries and ringlets are particularly well represented (see box on page 104). There are at least fifteen ringlet species in the Huesca province, some of which are unique, although often very local, to the Pyrenean mountains. The Pyrenees Brassy Ringlet, one of these localised species, is abundant in the Pineta valley (route 18). The Gavarnie Ringlet (another endemic) we found to be particularly frequent at the Alpine meadows above Baños de Panticosa (site G on page 182) and Benasque (route 19).

These Turquoise Blues sport, very appropriately, heart-shaped orange spots.

The most legendary Alpine butterfly meadows are found in the valley of La Sarra (site E on page 182). Purple Emperor, Silver-washed Fritillary, Lesser Marbled Fritillary, Pearly Heath, Pyrenees Brassy Ringlet, Pearl-bordered Fritillary and Safflower Skipper are just a quick taster of the many butterflies that visit the flowery grasslands here.

On tracks near rivers you will find mud-puddles with common species like Glandon, Turquoise, Chalk-hill, Argus and Escher's Blues, but also more rare species like Esper's Marbled White and Sage Skipper (see box on page 102).

Woodland edges, gorges and streams are other very productive butterfly habitats. This is the realm of some of the more enigmatic species, such as Southern White Admiral (common) and White Admiral (localised). The Añisclo gorge (route 17) is a good site for them. Look for the spectacular Purple Emperor around the canopies of the streamside willows and poplars and, since you are straining your neck anyway, look up to the oak and ash branches for Purple and Spanish Purple Hairstreaks respectively. In woodland clearings, Scarce Copper is anything but scarce, while in the shade of the open pinewoods, the elfishly delicate Wood White is a common sight.

Sunny, flowery meadows and glades in the lower mountain valleys support a different palette of species. Scarce Swallowtail, Black-veined White, Scarce, Sooty and Purple-shot Copper, Green-underside Blue, Meleager's Blue, Turquoise Blue, Mountain Argus, Alcon and Large Blue, Weaver's Fritillary, Lesser Marbled Fritillary, Heath and Spotted Fritillary, are all frequent and widespread 'valley butterflies'.

Butterflies of the Mediterranean hills and mountains

The warm and dry Mediterranean habitats of the *Depresión*, *Sierras Exteriores* and *Somontano* support a different set of butterflies, many of which are exclusive to the Mediterranean basin, the Spanish interior or mountains on the Peninsula.

The higher parts of the *Sierras Exteriores* and *Depresión* (e.g. San Juan de la Peña, route 12) are different from the High Pyrenees. They are less humid, hotter and sunnier, yet lack the heat and drought of the Mediterranean lowlands. These mountains support a mixture of mountain and Mediterranean species. The Apollo of the high Pyrenees flies here side by side with the essentially Mediterranean Great Sooty Satyr and Southern Grizzled Skipper.

Mountain species like Autumn, Piedmont and de Prunner's Ringlets live at altitudes in excess of 1,000 m in the *Sierras Exteriores* (routes 11 and 12 are good for them).

The open woodland, flowery scrub and grasslands at the foothills of the *Sierras Exteriores* and *Somontano* are another butterfly heaven. The quantity is perhaps not as great as in the high mountains, but the number of species is enormous. This zone, easily accessible (e.g. routes 7-11), is the realm of the *Satyridae* – the diverse group of graylings, browns, marbled whites, gatekeepers and other brown-with-eye-spots butterflies. Southern, Spanish and Common Gatekeepers are escorted by Striped Grayling, Dusky Meadow Brown and Dusky Heath.

The Forster's Furry Blue is one of those butterflies with a very small range: it is restricted to the *Sierras Exteriores*. These ones we found near Nocito (route 11).

In summer, the big Great Banded Graylings are a very common roadside (and car grill) species. Be aware of the similar Woodland and Rock Grayling, the latter being particularly frequent. In hot and dry areas, Tree and False Graylings are quite common. They rest on the ground where they are well camouflaged, often undetected until they fly off.
So far these were all *Satyridae*, but there are representatives of other butterfly groups too. Blue Spot and False Ilex Hairstreaks are common in areas with Holm and Kermes Oaks. Flowery grasslands are true butterfly gardens. Fritillaries like Cardinal, Queen-of-Spain and Knapweed Fritillary fly around. The nectar-rich Field Eryngos attract Adonis Blue, Black Satyr, Iberian Marbled White and Forster's Furry Blue.

Mud puddling

Is chasing butterflies an exhausting pastime? No way. On a warm day almost all species sit right on your trail, easy to observe and photograph. Skippers, blues and whites in particular gather in big groups amounting to over a hundred individuals of various species. They congregate around muddy, wet spots where they drink and collect minerals. As in your local traditional pub, the drinking parties consist largely of males, but here the chaps never forget to bring their lady friends a small token of their esteem! They collect the minerals to deliver to the females in return for which they get to copulate! This is no roguish seduction as the females require these minerals for the development of their eggs. To find the females, you still have to climb the mountains. Look for them near the caterpillar's host plants. You can find drinking groups particularly in the higher mountains and near small rivers at lower altitude. Species that frequent the mud puddles are Small White, Silver-studded Blue, Small Blue, Chalk-hill Blue, Marbled skipper and occasional Duke-of-Burgundy.

Wet tracks at high altitudes are the places where butterflies congregate to drink.

The Strawberry Trees near Agüero (close to Riglos) host, in addition to the rare Chapman's Green Hairstreak, Huesca's only population of Pasha. Another typical and eye-catching Mediterranean species is the Spanish Festoon, which is most frequent in the Mediterranean foothills to the east (route 7).

Butterflies of the steppes

The Mediterranean steppe with maquis vegetation is too hot and dry for most butterflies, but a select group of specialists, mostly of North-African origin, occur here.

True Spanish species like Southern Hermit, Provence Orange-tip and Sooty Orange-tip can survive typical semi-desert conditions and are present in Los Monegros. Another real steppe specialist is the African species Greenish Black-tip, found near Fraga and Valdecuernas (route 3) where it flies in early spring.

This being said, the vast Monegros is still very much terra incognita when it comes to butterflies. For many of the above-mentioned species, their status and location are not entirely clear. If you go and search for them, you might very well find new populations, or discover that they have disappeared from former sites.

The Hermit (top) is a well camouflaged butterfly of dry stony grasslands. The Spanish Festoon (bottom) flies in spring and is fairly rare. Look for it in the *Sierras Exteriores* (e.g. route 7).

△=endemic to the Pyrenees and nearby mountains

Conspicuous butterflies of Huesca

Widely occurring butterflies Swallowtail (*Papilio machaon*), Spanish Swallowtail (*Iphlicides feisthamelii*), Black-veined White (*Aporia crataegi*), Clouded Yellow (*Colias crocea*), Adonis Blue (*Polyommatus bellargus*), Red Admiral (*Vanessa atalanta*), Silver-washed Fritillary (*Argynnis paphia*), Provençal Fritillary (*Melitaea deione*), Marbled White (*Melanargia galathea*), Iberian Marbled White (*Melanargia lachesis*), Southern Grizzled Skipper (*Pygrus malvoides*)

Butterflies of Alpine meadows Apollo (*Parnassius apollo*), Clouded Apollo (*Parnassius mnemosyne*), Mountain Clouded Yellow (*Colias phicomone*), Purple-edged Copper (*Lycaena hippothoe*), Spanish Argus (*Aricia morronensis*), Gavarnie Blue (*Plebejus pyrenaicus*△), Glandon Blue (*Plebejus glandon*), Eros Blue (*Polyommatus eros*), Alcon Blue (*Maculinea alcon*), Pyrenees Brassy Ringlet (*Erebia rondui*△), Western Brassy Ringlet (*Erebia avernensis*), Mountain Ringlet (*Erebia epiphron*), Prunner's Ringlet (*Erebia triaria*), Lefebvre's Ringlet (*Erebia lefebvrei*△), Alpine Grizzled Skipper (*Pygrus andromedae*), Marbled Skipper (*Carcharodus lavatherae*)

Butterflies of Woodland clearings and gorges in the Pyrenees Cleopatra (*Gonepteryx cleopatra*), Spanish Purple Hairstreak (*Laeosopis roboris*), Turquoise Blue (*Polyommatus dorylas*), Purple Emperor (*Apatura iris*), White Admiral (*Limenitis camilla*), Southern White Admiral (*Limenitis reducta*), High Brown Fritillary (*Argynnis adippe*), Heath Fritillary (*Melitaea athalia*), Western Fritillary (*Melitaea parthenoides*), Marbled Fritillary (*Brenthis ino*), Glanville Fritillary (*Melitaea cinxia*), Knapweed Fritillary (*Melitaea phoebe*), Spanish Heath (*Coenonympha iphioides*)

Butterflies of dry Mediterranean mountains Apollo (*Parnassius apollo*), Niobe Fritillary (*Argynnis niobe*), Piedmont Ringlet (*Erebia meolans*), Prunners Ringlet (*Erebia triaria*), Common Grayling (*Hipparchia semele*), Sooty Satyr (*Satyrus ferula*), Silver Spotted Skipper (*Hesperia comma*)

Butterflies of scrub and open oak woodland False Ilex Hairstreak (*Satyrium esculi*), Forster's Furry Blue (*Polyommatus fulgens*△), Chalk-Hill Blue, (*Polyommatus coridon*), Rippart's Anomalous Blue (*Polyommatus ripartii*), Cardinal (*Argynnis pandora*), Great Banded Grayling (*Brintesia circe*), Striped Grayling (*Hipparchia fidia*), Black Satyr (*Satyrus actaea*), Dusky Meadow Brown (*Hyponephele lycaon*), Spanish Gatekeeper (*Pyronia bathseba*), Southern Gatekeeper (*Pyronia cecilia*), Dusky Heath (*Coenonympha dorus*), Lulworth Skipper (*Thymelicus action*), Cinquefoil Skipper (*Pyrgus cirsii*)

Butterflies of the steppes Berger's Clouded Yellow (*Colias alfacariensis*), Sooty Orange-tip (*Zegris eupheme*), Provence Orange-tip (*Anthocharis euphenoides*) Greenish Blacktip (*Euchloe charlonia*), Striped Grayling (*Hipparchia fidia*), Southern Hermit (*Chazara prieuri*)

More widespread dryland species are Clouded Yellow, Spanish Chalk-hill Blue, Western Marbled White, Provence Orange-tip, Hermit, Great Banded and Striped Graylings. Not surprisingly, spring is an important season for steppe butterflies – only the latter three fly in summer. They are mostly seen on thistles, one of the few nectar sources at that time. They also rest on rocks and soil, but here their cryptic colouration renders them near invisible.

Dragonflies and damselflies

Although Huesca prides itself in having a large variety of wetland types, the dragonfly and damselfly fauna, which depend on water, is not as diverse as might be expected. Many southern species do not range all the way up to Huesca, whereas various northern species do not make it all the way down to the Pyrenees. Nevertheless, there is much to discover in the region and, with fifty-seven species present, the diversity is still more than in the entire UK.

The dragonfly fauna can be roughly divided into those typical of the Mediterranean streams and wetlands of the Monegros and those found

The Ibóns form a good habitat for dragonflies of northern regions, such as this newly emerged Moorland Hawker at the Ibón de Piedrafita (route 14).

in mountain wetlands (including several species widespread in the cool European lowlands, but absent in lowland Iberia). Paradoxically, the hot and dry lowlands offer – at least for northern Europeans – the most interesting dragonflies. The warm lowland streams are home to several southern species, for instance Yellow-veined Skimmer (restricted to the Ebro River) and Small Red-eye. Faded Pincertail (a desert species) has only been found along rivers in the steppes of the far south whereas Desert Darter is reported more and more frequently in the drier areas of the Monegros. Here it reproduces in small ponds. Red-veined Darter remains the more common though. The spectacularly coloured Violet Dropwing deserves mentioning because it is expanding its distribution area rapidly to the north and inland. It occurs in the Catalan Ebro and, with new populations close to the Huescan border, it seems merely a matter of time before it can be added to the fauna of the province.

The rivers of the *Sierras Exteriores* and *Somontano* (top) harbour several attractive dragonflies, including the Western Spectre (centre) and the Western Demoiselle (bottom).

Conspicuous dragonflies of Huesca

Common Large Red Damselfly (*Pyrrhosoma nymphula*), Blue Hawker (*Aeshna cyanea*), Common Goldenring (*Cordulegaster boltonii*), Red-veined Darter (*Sympetrum fonscolombii*), Southern Skimmer (*Orthetrum brunneum*), Broad Scarlet (*Crocothemis erythraea*)

Ibóns Common Spreadwing (*Lestes sponsa*), Common Bluet (*Enallagma cyathigerum*), Moorland Hawker (*Aeshna juncea*), Four-spotted Chaser (*Libellula quadrimaculata*), Small Whiteface (*Leucorrhinia dubia – local*)

Streams Copper Demoiselle (*Calopteryx haemorrhoidalis*), Western Demoiselle (*Calopteryx xanthostoma*), Mercury Bluet (*Coenagrion mercuriale*), Mediterranean Bluet (*Coenagrion caerulescens*), Blue-eye (*Erythromma lindenii*), White featherleg (*Platycnemis latipes*), Western Spectre (*Boyeria irene*), Small Pincertail (*Onychogomphus forcipatus*), Large Pincertail (*Onychogomphus uncatus*), Yellow Clubtail (*Gomphus similimus*)

Rivers in the Ebro basin Small Red-eye (*Erythromma viridulum*), Faded Pincertail (*Onychogomphus costae*), Yellow-veined Skimmer (*Orthetrum nitidinerve*), Desert Darter (*Sympetrum sinaiticum*), Violet Dropwing (*Trithemis annulata*)

The slow-flowing rivers in the Ebro basin support a number of damselflies. White Featherleg is the most widespread and abundant species here. The Orange Featherleg is found only occasionally. In places where aquatic vegetation is well-developed, look for Mercury and Mediterranean Bluets and Blue-eye. The Bluetails in the lowlands nearly all belong to the Iberian species. Only further up in the mountains does the Common Bluetail gradually take over. In shady places, Western Spectre hunts over the water.

The latter also occurs in the streams in the *Depresión* and the lower Pyrenees. Though much more conspicuous here are the damselflies – Beautiful, Copper and Western Demoiselles. They are widespread and easily found. Along pebbly rivers, Small and Large Pincertails are frequent. Like many dragonflies, the males have divided the river into territories and defend the invisible borders with a vengeance. The rivers higher up in the Pyrenees only support Large Pincertail. It prefers faster flowing, more shaded and smaller streams than Small Pincertail.

Both Common and Sombre Goldenring occur along the smaller mountain streams, whilst Yellow Clubtail prefers larger rivers. It is fairly rare, but diligent searches in spring could reveal new populations. We found it along the road to Alastuey (site A on page 181).

The high mountain lakes (*Ibóns*) enjoy a special position with regard to Spanish dragonflies as they support some species that are rare in the country, such as Blue and Moorland Hawkers. Common Bluet, Common Spreadwing and Four-spotted Chaser are other typical *Ibón*-species. A rarity that occurs near Benasque (route 21) is the Small Whiteface. This is one of the few places in Spain where it is found. Since the Small Whiteface is also the nation's only representative of this group of dragonflies, this is a very special species for Spanish enthusiasts.

Widespread dragonfly species include Blue Hawker, Southern Skimmer, Broad Scarlet and Red-veined Darter. They can be found anywhere, but especially close to standing waters.

Other invertebrates

There are far too many invertebrate species to describe in detail in this guidebook. The vast majority of them are small and live their lives without coming to the attention of all but the most specialist traveller. But each of these 'other invertebrate groups' include some spectacular species that, when they cross your patch, you'd want to know what they are. These are the minibeast stars that are discussed here.

The Siberian Grasshopper, with its 'muscular' front legs, frequents the alpine meadows.

The best method to find the usually nocturnal moths is by checking lights, particularly those left on all night such as those at the sanitary facilities on your camp site. Beautifully coloured moths like Cream-spot Tiger and both Dark and Light Crimson Underwing can be encountered, especially in the Pyrenees. The largest of all is the Great Peacock Moth which is widespread in the Pyrenees and *Depresión*. The delicately beautiful Spanish Moon Moth (p. 171) is native to Spain and southern France. The caterpillar of this moth, which is difficult to find, primarily eats the needles of native pine trees.

Diurnal (day active) moths are much fewer in number, but obviously more visible. On large flowers in urban surroundings, but also in more natural habitats, the Broad-bordered Bee Hawk-moth and Hummingbird Hawk-moth are quite common.

Grasshoppers and crickets can be encountered everywhere and in large numbers. One conspicuous species of the higher mountains (e.g. around the Ordesa miradors – site B on page 202) is the Siberian Grasshopper. The curiously inflated front legs give this species the memorably descriptive nickname Popeye Grasshopper.

The warm valleys and hot lowlands are a hotspot for larger species. Here you may find, particularly in summer, Praying Mantis. The most remarkable light brown or greenish Long-nosed Grasshopper is found in grassy steppes. The elongated head resembles a twig. We found this species along the river at Buñales (point 1 of route 5), but we presume it is widespread. Other typical steppe and desert species are Steppe Cricket, which hides under stones, and the Iberian endemic *Ephippigerida pantingana*, a type of Saddle Bush-cricket.

The songs of grasshoppers and crickets is typical of the hot, sun-soaked lowland summer. This is also the season for the cicadas to produce their loud rasps. They usually 'sing' from a tree, hugging close to the bark and are difficult to spot. There are various species in the region.

Ascalaphids or Owlflies are another group of striking creatures. These colourful insects fly low over warm, flowery grasslands with the fast, straight flight of a dragonfly combined with the colourful wings of a butterfly. But it is neither, because it is a relative of the antlions. The Yellow-veined Ascalaphid* (*Libelloides longicornis*; p. 211) is the most frequent species.

The scrubby lowlands have more fascinating, multi-legged creatures. The poisonous Scolopendra or Megarian Banded Centipede hides under rocks and comes out at night to hunt. It is approximately ten centimetres long and has fifteen pairs of legs. There are various species of scorpions that share the same habitat as the Scolopendra. They too are nocturnal. Scorpions have a painful sting, as does the centipede, so be careful.

The bigger and more impressive beetles are found in the mountains although the Weaver Beetle, with a thick body of over 3 cm, is found in the Ebro basin. The beautiful black and blue Rosalia Longicorn occurs in old Ash trees along the rivers of the Pyrenees. This Europe-wide declining species lives on sun-exposed dead wood. The impressive Stag Beetle has a similar predisposition for dead wood, although the latter prefers oak.

The Long-nosed Grasshopper is an animal of the summer time. This curious creature inhabits grasslands and steppe in the Ebro basin.

ROUTES AND SITES

Scan the QR code to download GPX files of the routes. These can be used on GPS devices and GPS apps.

The natural beauty of Huesca needs no recommendation. A kaleidoscope of charming, picturesque villages, thundering rivers threading through dramatic canyons over which vultures drift, a profusion of wildflowers tumbling across the alpine meadows attended by clouds of nectar loving butterflies, all this, and much more, speaks for itself. But to find the endemic rock flora, the rare birdlife and the best spots for butterflies, you need a little help, and that is what this section provides. It also outlines the best routes to find steppe birds, the unique saline flora of the Monegros and the more dramatic wild-west landscapes of this unique, desert-like area.

The routes and sites that follow are grouped together in the three major landscapes of Huesca. The first six routes (pages 112 to 138) cover the lowlands of the Ebro Basin; route 7 to 11 (pages 139 to 163) explore the Mediterranean-tinged *Sierras Exteriores* and routes 12 to 21 in the high Pyrenees (page 164 to 215) constitute the third part of the route section. Each of the sections is, for the sake of completeness, closed by shorter descriptions of routes and activities for which space does not allow full coverage.

The geography of this part of the High Pyrenees lends itself to a further division into three distinct sections: the western valleys (page 167), the Ordesa and Monte Perdido massif (page 184), and the Benasque area (page 204). In each of these areas we have described several interesting routes, which cover all the habitats present and support the maximum variety of flora, birdlife and wildlife. As such they function as an introduction to that part of the Pyrenees. At the end of each of these sections, we have briefly outlined a number of other routes – some short, some long and strenuous – which permit exploration of that area in further detail. The location of each of these extra routes is given on the map in the introductory text of that part of the Pyrenees.

Each of our routes is accompanied with maps to help you find your way. However, for the hiking routes in particular, we advise to use a detailed hiking map as well (see 'maps' on page 221).

The options for naturalists to explore the mountains are endless. Here we are watching Lammergeier at Revilla, route 21).

The Ebro basin

The *Depresión del Ebro* is a large lowland basin south of the Pyrenees. Numerous rivers run down from the mountains to join the mighty river Ebro which snakes its way through Aragón.

The landscape and nature of the Ebro basin is unique and, in places, spectacular. Surrounded by mountains on every side, the depression lies always in the rain shadow, regardless of the direction of the wind. As a result, rain is scarce and the hours of sunshine are very high. With the exception of the southeastern corner of the country, the Ebro basin is the driest area of the Spain. The region is – apart from the cities around the Ebro itself – very thinly populated and there are vast areas that cannot be visited except by four wheel drive vehicles. It is an agricultural region, where grains are the dominant crop. In many places though, it is the natural steppe and the impressive, dry mountains that dominate the landscape. Although no more than 100 kms from the snow-capped Pyrenees, you find yourself in a completely different landscape.

The flora and fauna, of course, respond to the dry climate, with many species typical of Mediterranean and semi-desert areas. The region is

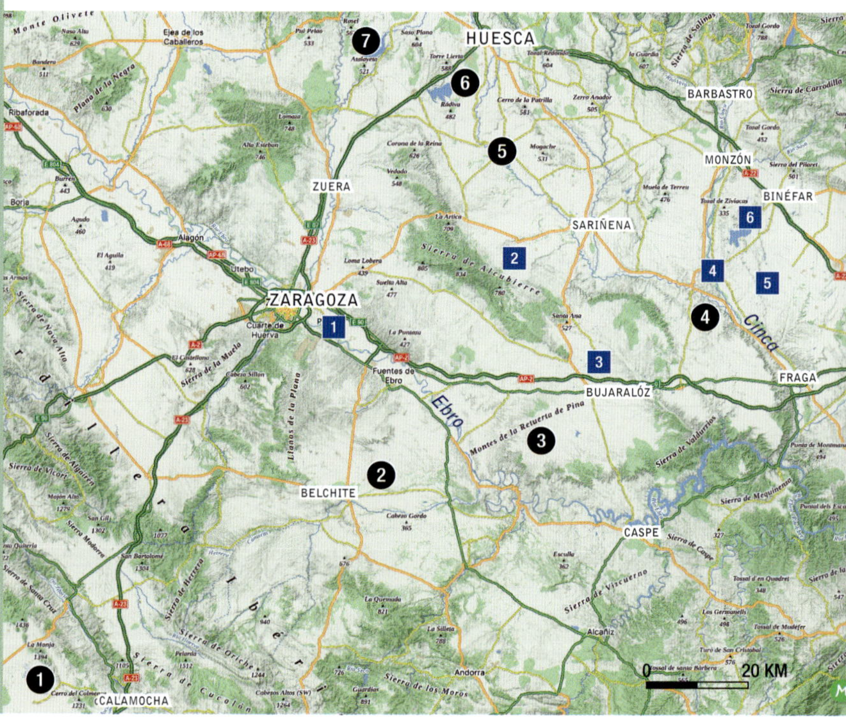

Overview of the Ebro basin.
In black are the locations of the routes described on the following pages; in blue are the sites described on pages 135-137.

best known for its birdlife, which consists of specialised species like Black and Black-eared Wheatears, Iberian Grey Shrike, Little Bustard, Stone Curlew, Pin-tailed and Black-bellied Sandgrouse and six species of larks, including the star, the Dupont's Lark. The flora is perhaps even more specialised, with many steppe and desert species. The reptilian and amphibian world too, has its share of warmth-loving species, with Ladder Snake, Ocellated Lizard, Spanish Psammodromus and Spiny-footed Lizard among the typical species.

The lands bordering the river Ebro are generally referred to as *Los Monegros* – a huge territory that stretches out from *Los Bardales Reales* in Navarre to the drylands of Lerida (Lleida) in Catalonia. The largest part lies in Aragón, on the border of Huesca and Zaragoza provinces.

The land around the Ebro may be modest in elevation, but it is far from flat. Low, rocky mountain ranges dominate the region. Heavy erosion of the soft strata give rise to a spectacular landscape of low tablelands. In places, this gives the impression of a desert rather than steppes, although technically the climate is not dry enough to qualify as such. Thousands of years of erosion by water and wind, combined with the effects of extreme evaporation and desiccation has sculpted a landscape that might well be nicknamed 'Little Arizona'. In the Monegros, gypsum steppes (route 2 and 4) and salt steppes (route 2 and 3) alternate with sandstone rocks (route 1 and 5), Mediterranean scrubland and open pine and juniper woodland (route 1 and 3, site A on page 137), saline lagoons or *saladas* (route 1, 2 and 3), rivers and (artificial) freshwater lakes (routes 1, 3 and 5). Each of these habitats has its own peculiarities. The soil – sediments from the Pyrenees – is generally quite fertile. Flat areas, either on the plateaux (*plataformas*) or in the gullies (*barrancos*) are planted with cereals, which are inhabited by sought-after birds (e.g. Great Bustard).

Desert-like landscape of the Ebro Basin, home to Black Wheatear (route 5).

The last few decades have brought many changes to the Monegros, which have greatly reduced the natural richness of the region. Vast irrigation networks of small canals and an elaborate network of sprinklers has given rise to an intensive form of farming which leaves little place for birds or other wildlife. Of the original total surface of 500,000 ha. of steppes and arid farmland,

The clay soils, here in the Alcubierre mountains, erode easily, leaving isolated table 'mountains' known as *torrellones*.

two thirds have disappeared under EU-financed irrigation schemes (see page 54). The remaining 180,000 ha is protected as Important Bird Areas (IBA) and Natura 2000 sites, and will not be irrigated.

This desolate landscape can best be explored by car, making stops to scan the area or take short walks in search of wildflowers, insects, steppe birds and other wildlife. All routes are good for birdwatching, but the best are perhaps route 2 (the famous steppes of Belchite) and route 3, which combines some very good cereal fields with *saladas*, and freshwater habitat. The most spectacular landscape and geological features are present on routes 2, 4 and 5. The butterfly fauna is best in rocky sierras (route 3 and 5) while the handful of Mediterranean dragonfly species are best found in the *saladas* and freshwater rivers (best route 3). The gypsum and saline vegetation is best in route 1, 2, and for the *saladas*, 3.

The rivers that run down from the Pyrenees form linear oases through the dry Monegros. In many places, riverine woodlands create a habitat for marshland birds. These forests are hard to visit, but route 5 and the Galacho de la Alfranca (page 137) offer an insight in this habitat.

South of the Ebro depression the land rises again to the Iberian upland plateau of the Meseta. No high peaks can be found on the plateau but most of the land lies above 1,000 m. Winters are very cold and spring arrives late.

The Iberian plateau is outside the scope of this book, but for one site, the natural steppe lake of Laguna de Gallocanta, we make an exception (route 1). This excellent bird area, famous for its autumn concentrations of Cranes, is situated in an impressive 'Mongolian' steppe landscape.

ROUTE 1: LA LAGUNA DE GALLOCANTA

35 KM, FULL DAY

The largest natural lake in Spain, rich in birds.
Located in a deserted rocky area with steppe-like plains.
Large concentrations of Cranes in winter.

Habitats: saline lake, reedbeds, cereal fields, steppe, rocky hillsides
Selected species: Crane, Montagu's Harrier, Little Bustard, Black-winged Stilt, Ruff, Gull-billed Tern, Dupont's Lark, Western Spadefoot

!

Be careful on tracks. When wet, one easily gets stuck in the mud. Weekends can be busy with visitors.

Best season
October-November and February-June
Of interest
year round

Laguna de Gallocanta in summer.

Laguna de Gallocanta is Spain's largest natural lake, atmospherically situated between mountains on the Iberian plateaux. It is famous for its Cranes, which are present between the end of October and the first week of March. Wintering birds vary in numbers between 10,000 and 20,000, but during migration (October-November and February) there may be up to 60,000. The Cranes disperse during the day to feed in the surrounding fields. Spectacular numbers flock in at dusk to roost on the lake. In winter, Gallocanta also attracts large numbers of waterfowl and during migration many waders visit its shores. Breeding Black-winged Stilt, Avocet, Kentish Plover and colonies of Whiskered and Gull-billed Terns also make this site worth visiting in spring. The surrounding fields and steppes support Stone Curlew, Calandra Lark, and a few Little Bustards and Dupont's Larks, plus an interesting flora.

Starting point: Gallocanta village.

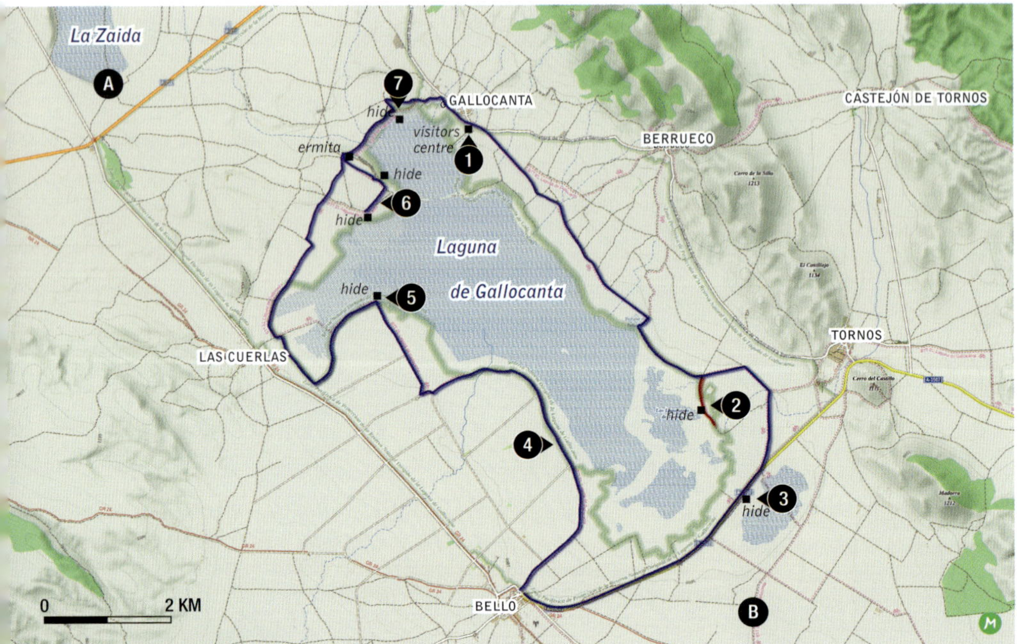

On this map and on all the others throughout the book: blue lines refer to car routes and red lines to the walks.

The visitors' centre at Gallocanta village offers excellent views over the lake from the first floor. Many of the wintering ducks and migrating waders can be seen from here.

1 From the visitors' centre, take the second track to the right (200 m) and follow the signs *Centro de Interpretación / Camino del Cid.* Drive carefully, make stops and scan the area. At a T-junction turn right. After 5 km you arrive at the hide *El Cañizar.*

2 Reeds and saltmarsh with glasswort dominate the lakeshore. Marsh Harrier, Black-winged Stilt, Avocet, Lapwing, Gull-billed Tern and Kentish Plover are breeding birds, which can be seen from here in spring and summer. In saline patches, the small Spiny Saltmarsh-grass* (*Puccinellia pungens*) is worth noting – not so much for its looks (it is a small species of grass) but because it is endemic of the Iberian Peninsula and the Asian steppes (see also account of the Relict Glasswort – page 30).

Proceed along the track, turn right twice at the next two tracks, and again right on the paved road. Park at the interpretation centre of Laguna de Gallocanta on your right.

Bird hide at Gallocanta.

3 From the rooftop lookout, you have excellent views of feeding Cranes. In spring, this is a good site for Montagu's Harrier and Whiskered and Gull-billed Terns.

Continue. In Bello village follow the direction *Las Cuerlas*. Just before exiting the village of Bello, take the track to your right. Go left at the T-junction, follow a long dirt road and after 100 m, turn right at the sign *Observatorio La Reguera*, which is the highest and most conspicuous hide of this area.

4 The fields along this track and between Bello and Las Cuerlas are, especially after the breeding season (August-October), good for Great Bustard, Stone Curlew and Pin-tailed and Black-bellied Sandgrouse. Calandra Larks breed in the fields and Rock Sparrows in the sheds.

5 The *Observatorio La Reguera* offers good views – in season – of ducks, waders and flying raptors.

Proceed. Turn right at a T-junction and after 1km, turn left and immediately right towards *Ermita de Nuestra Señora del Buen Acuerdo*, a chapel that is visible from afar.

6 Both the Ermita and the nearby hide *Observatorio la Ermita* are worth a stop. They offer the usual birdlife of Gallocanta. In winter at sunset, La Ermita is the best place to observe Cranes flying in to roost.

From the chapel, two tracks turn left. Follow the second one (leading in a northwestern direction) and take the first track right after 650m. Go right again at the next junction to make a stop at the *Observatorio Los Aguanares*.

Tens of thousands of Cranes roost at Gallocanta in late autumn and early winter (centre).

7 This hide is situated between tamarisks and gives a different view on the lake and the birdlife. Similar species as in the aforementioned sites can be seen here.

Follow the shore to the left to return to Gallocanta.

Additional site A – La Zaida lagoon

On the A-2506 about one km north of the crossing with the A-2110, there is a viewpoint on your right over La Zaida. This lagoon is artificially filled with water once every two years. In the dry year, the elderly people of the nearby village of Used are allowed to grow crops in the lagoon bed. In the years of flood, there are a lot of waterfowl in winter whilst in spring waders are attracted to the muddy shore. Just beyond the viewpoint, a track turns off to the right through the cultivations for a few kilometres, before arriving at a dam. This is another excellent place for waterfowl and for amphibians, such as Natterjack, Western Spadefoot and Mediterranean Painted Frog.

Additional site B – Torralba de Los Sisones track

Near Gallocanta lake lies an unexpected area of stony steppe where interesting birdlife is found. Black-bellied Sandgrouse, Stone-Curlew, Thekla, Short-toed and a few Dupont's Larks breed here. From Bello take the A-2506 to Torralba de Los Sisones. In the latter village follow the *Calle El Pilón* that bends to the left and then take the left one, *Calle Nueva*, and just outside the village take the road right indicated *GR-24* and *Las Blancas 9 km* (see map). Cross the Holm Oak clad sierra and explore the small fields, natural and stony steppes beyond it (some 2 km out of the village). The stony steppes are the most rewarding.

Western Spadefoot (top) is one of the few amphibians to thrive in temporary, brackish waters and are quite common at Gallocanta.
Gull-billed Tern (right) is a summer visitor to Gallocanta.

ROUTE 2: THE STEPPES OF BELCHITE

44 KM, 4 HOURS

The most intact steppe area of the Ebro basin. Impressive western landscape and very rich bird and plant life.

Habitats: table mountains, saline steppes, gypsum steppes, small reservoir
Selected species: Lesser Kestrel, Pin-tailed Sandgrouse, Black-bellied Sandgrouse, Dupont's Lark, Lesser Short-toed Lark, Black Wheatear, Spiny-footed Lizard, Spanish Psammodromus, Ladder Snake, Peganum, Esparto, Pale-leaved Rockrose* (*Helianthemum squamatum*)

!

Stay on paths and tracks – the vegetation is very delicate. Be careful when driving the tracks after rain. It is easy to get stuck in the fine mud.

Best season
April-June
Of interest
October-June

Cranes turn up in the small lagoon in El Planerón during the migration period.

The steppe of Belchite is the most intact patch of steppe in northern Spain. It is famous for its rich birdlife, which includes large numbers of the very rare and localised Dupont's Lark. The tableland landscape around Belchite village consists of dry cereal plots and natural steppe vegetation. The best steppe areas are preserved in two fairly small reserves, La Lomaza can only be viewed from a car park by the side of the road, and El Planerón (600 ha), one of the very few steppe depressions that escaped cultivation and is famous for its birds, in particular the very rare Dupont's Lark.

Starting point: Belchite village.

Take the A220 that passes along the southern edge of the village. After 700m from the junction with the A222 (so in the village) where the road bends to the right, turn sharp left, next to olive oil mill. Park a little further and walk along the fence of the old, ruined

1 The new Belchite is built next to the ruins of the old village, which was destroyed by shellfire and bombing during the Spanish Civil War (1936-1939). The buildings are left as a war memorial. The site is closed to the public, except during a guided tour (see **belchite.es**), but you can walk the path along the fence to a high point some 100 m further, from which you have good views over the ghost town. Look here for Lesser Kestrel, Black Wheatear and Blue Rock Thrush. Aizoon, one of the special wildflowers of the arid regions of Spain, flowers on the abandoned plots village.
In the new village is a good SEO/BirdLife-run visitors' centre for El Planerón reserve.

Return to the A222, turn left and shortly thereafter, go right towards Codo and El Planerón. Pass the village and 4 km further, turn left onto a track, signposted El Planerón.

2 Continue driving slowly with the windows rolled down to look and listen for steppe birds (note that learning the calls is an important

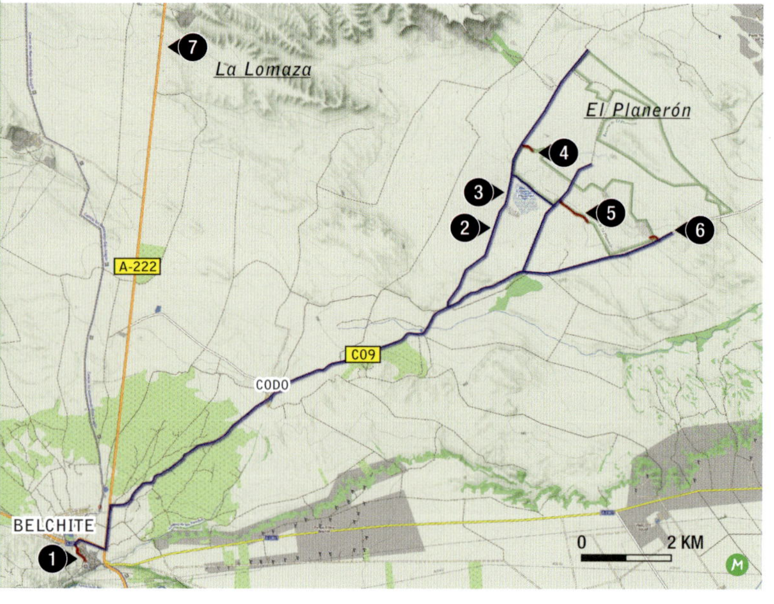

factor for success in seeing the birds). Scan for Stone Curlews, Black-bellied and Pin-tailed Sandgrouse, all of which breed here, but are, with their cryptic plumage, a challenge to find. The larks are easier. Lesser Short-toed is a common bird in the saline shallows, while Short-toed and Thekla Larks frequent the gypsum steppe on the reserve edges. Calandra Larks are most frequent on the plots of cultivation that lie scattered around.

The tamarisks around the small lagoon are migrant traps in spring, while Penduline Tit breeds in the bushes. Cranes often roost on the lagoon during migration.

3 Ignore the track to your right for now and continue to a small hide.

4 The hide overlooks a small, man-made pond where Calandra and Short-toed Larks frequently take a bath and the tamarisk vegetation attracts Iberian Grey Shrike and Spectacled warbler. Some expectation management: this is not the place where sandgrouse come to drink.

The steppes of Belchite are home to six species of lark, including Dupont's Lark (top), and Short-toed Lark (bottom).

You can continue in more good steppe habitat and then return to the aforementioned junction and turn left. At the T-junction go left and park in the car park a little further ahead (don't park here when the ground is wet!).

5 Follow the small footpath that departs from here named Sendero Rocín. Rocín is the local name for Dupont's Lark, and that is exactly what is present here. This bird is found exclusively on level steppes in the hottest part of the Ebro basin where a mosaic of patchy vegetation is the natural habitat. Listen for the distinctive, odd, whining 'choo-chee' song which, astonishingly given the open landscape, is often the only sign of the species' presence. It flies reluctantly and somehow manages to stay hidden even in the scantiest vegetation. Dupont's Larks are best looked for at dawn when they are most likely to be heard. This is also the best spot for other larks which, fortunately, show themselves much more frequently.

Go back and go straight ahead to return to the road (all this is still good steppe habitat). Turn left.

6 At kilometre post 12, a viewpoint overlooks the El Planerón plain. Scan the steppes for the aforementioned species. Then walk 300m back along the road and then take the footpath to your right.
The vegetation of El Planerón consists mostly of halophytes (salt resistant plants), but the more interesting vegetation of the gypsum hills can be explored by walking the short way-marked trail that departs from the car park at the viewpoint on the C-09 a bit further east. This trail is highly recommended to explore the steppe ecosystem from up close.

Return to Belchite and turn right on the A-222. After 11 km, park at the Lomaza reserve car park on your right.

7 There is some excellent gypsum vegetation right by the car park. Dupont's, Short-toed and Lesser Short-toed Larks breed and can be easily heard. Stone Curlew, Pin-tailed Sandgrouse, Golden and Short-toed Eagle also occur at La Lomaza, as do Ladder Snake, Spanish Psammodromus and Ocellated and Spiny-footed Lizards. While El Planerón is one of the few unscathed steppes of the valley, La Lomaza has this role on the plateaux of the tablelands. The fully natural gypsum vegetation is unique, and well worth a visit.

The Black-bellied Sandgrouse is one of the great attractions of Belchite.

ROUTE 3: MONEGROS 1 – FROM SÁSTAGO TO CANDASNOS

75 KM, 6 HOURS

Versatile route – vast plains alternate with salt and freshwater lakes, dry scrub and a river valley.
Great birdwatching route, the best for Great and Little Bustard.

Habitats: cereal fields, natural steppe, salt pans, arid woodlands, river gorge, freshwater lake
Selected species: Relict Glasswort*, Red-crested Pochard, Black-necked Grebe, Golden Eagle, Lesser Kestrel, Dotterel (winter), Great Bustard, Little Bustard, Lesser Short-toed Lark, Black Wheatear, Greenish Blacktip

!
Be careful not to get stuck on wet tracks. An early start will increase your chances of finding birds.

Best season
April-June
Of interest
October-June

The *La Playa* salt lake is a shimmering, deserted salt flat in summer.

This route runs through the southern part of Los Monegros and consists of two distinct parts. In the first half, dry steppe, cereal plots and irrigated fields dominate, whereas the second part of the route crosses more scenic scrubby river valleys with Mediterranean woodland and ends at the freshwater lake of Candasnos. A special feature here is the presence of several saline seasonal lagoons, *saladas*, which boast a unique fauna. This route offers the best chances on finding Great Bustards, which are quite rare in this part of Spain.

Starting point: Sástago.

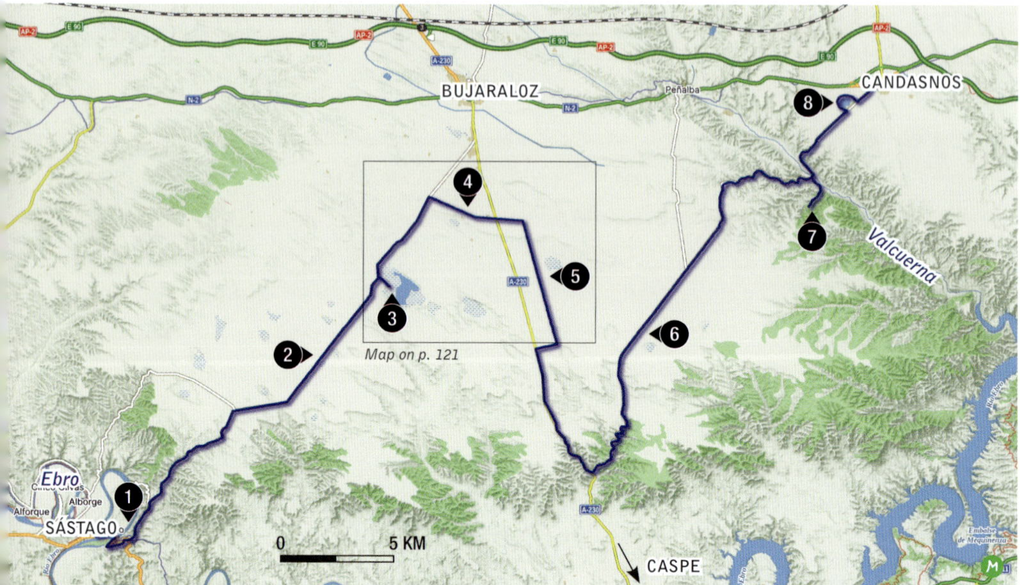

Cross the Ebro bridge and follow the A221 as it climbs out of the river gorge. After 2 km, stop at the viewpoint near the crossroads.

1 The view of the Ebro snaking through the sandstone gorges is impressive. Black Wheatear breeds at this spot and Little and Great Egret may be present on the river. During migration, there may be raptors such as Osprey. We've also seen Red-rumped Swallow, a rare but slowly increasing bird in this part of Spain.

Continue on the A-2105 towards Bujaraloz.

2 The road crosses a fine area of stony steppes. At first the terrain is still hilly, and there are plenty of places where you can stop. There may be Black-eared Wheatear, and the many stony areas have a rich reptilian fauna, with geckos (both species), Ocellated Lizard, Ladder and Montpellier Snakes.
Further ahead, you arrive on the plain, which is dry, with a mix of steppe, fallow and arable land. The small stone houses were used by workers who lived in the distant villages. There are also many piles of stones. In order to work the land, the stones were taken from the surface and placed in piles. Now, both the houses and the stone piles are occupied by Lesser Kestrel, Little Owl and reptiles. Calandra Larks are numerous in the flat plains; Short-toed Lark is also frequent.

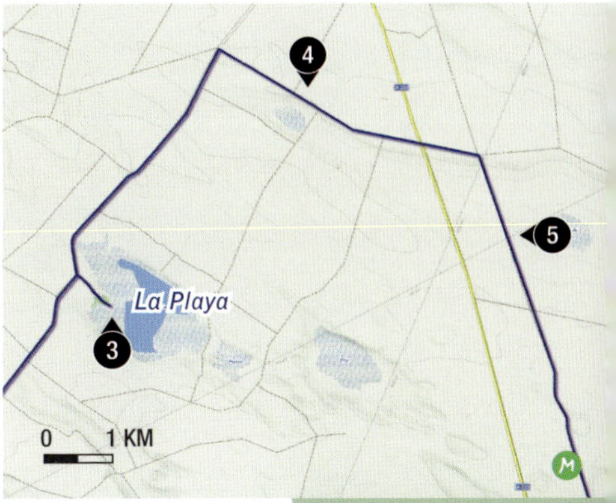

After 17 km turn right, signposted La Playa, and stop at the deserted salt works a little ahead (the plant is a conspicuous landmark).

3 Measuring 3 by 2 km, La Playa is the biggest salt lake in the area. The ruins here are a reminder of the days that the salina was used to produce salt. Salt harvesting stopped in the 1930s and the storehouse and barracks fell to ruin. Jackdaws and Red-billed Choughs are now breeding here.
From the ruins you can walk a little further to a bird hide that overlooks the salt plain. Scan the lake for waders and Shelduck on migration. Kentish Plover, Lesser Short-toed Lark and Spectacled Warbler breed along the lake margins. Also scan the fields behind the lake – sometimes Great Bustards show themselves here and Montagu´s Harrier can be around. Relict Glasswort* (*Microcnemum corraloides*) and a score of endemic invertebrates are other highlights of La Playa. It is possible to walk around the lake (11.5 km).

Continue along A-2105 and after 3 km, take the second track to the right. Scan this area carefully. Turn left at the end of this track and turn right at the next one, which will take you to the A-230, which connects Bujaraloz and Caspe.

4 The cereal steppes along these tracks and on both sides of the A-230 support good populations of steppe birds. Most of the Great Bustards of Los Monegros are here. The population is estimated at only 60 individuals but the chances of finding this magnificent bird are good. It is also a favoured spot for Little Bustard, Pin-tailed and Black-bellied Sandgrouse and various other steppe species are also present. Golden Eagle and vultures frequently visit the region. In autumn, this general area is often visited by Dotterel.

The extensive cereal fields near La Playa support the last sizable population of Great Bustard in the Monegros.

Cross the A-230 and continue. Turn right at the next crossing of tracks (near a pig farm). After 6.1 km, take the second track to the right, to return to the A230 again.

5 This section of well-maintained tracks leads through more prime Great Bustard habitat.

Look for Ocellated Lizard in the Valdecuerna valley.

Go left on the A230 and after 6km, go left onto the A2410 to Candasnos.

6 Aleppo pinewoods, steppes and arable fields dominate this arid valley. The landscape is reminiscent of that of point 2. After the open plain, the road snakes down through fine scrubland where raptors are usually present. Look for Golden, Booted, Short-toed and even Bonelli's Eagles and Griffon Vultures.

Park near the small bridge and follow the track to the right (i.e. downstream). After 200 metres, it turns away from the river and into the pine-clad hills.

7 The Valcuerna is a life line in the arid Monegros. Although the section near the bridge runs through a channel, the river is undisturbed and quiet over much of its length. This is one of the few places in the region where European Pond Terrapin occurs (although it is not easily seen). The aforementioned raptors breed on the riverside cliffs. Keep an eye open for Orphean Warbler in the open pine wood. The most remarkable inhabitant of the valley is a butterfly, the Greenish Black-tip, which is an African species with only two small populations in Spain.

Return to the road and continue the road towards Candasnos. Just before the village park at the reedy lagoon on the left and walk to the hide.

8 The man-made Candasnos lake used to be a great spot for birds, but its quality has declined dramatically. However, you may still see Marsh Harrier, Purple Heron, Reed and Great Reed Warblers and Penduline Tit. Winter brings a larger variety of waterfowl. During migration, waders and Black Terns often visit.

Candasnos lake

Continue towards Candasnos (note the Bee-eater holes in the roadside) where this route ends.

Additional remarks

Driving 9 km on the A-2214 north out of Candasnos will connect you to route 4.

ROUTE 4: MONEGROS 2 – THE ALCOLEA-ONTIÑENA-BALLOBAR TRIANGLE

65 KM, 4 HOURS

Best season
April-May
Of interest
October-June

Another fascinating steppe route, teeming with birdlife. Impressive sandstone escarpments towering over the Cinca river.

Habitats: dry fields, sandy and saline steppes, sandstone cliffs, riverine habitat
Selected species: Montagu's Harrier, Lesser Kestrel, Red-necked Nightjar, Alpine Swift, Spectacled Warbler, Great Spotted Cuckoo, Roller, Hoopoe, Ocellated Lizard

The sandstone cliffs of La Ripas (point 6).

This route visits several small areas of steppe that have escaped the irrigation frenzy due to their status as an Important Bird Area (IBA). This route is primarily described as a birding trip, but venturing into the steppes here and there is bound to yield interesting wildflowers, reptiles and insects. The contrast of arid uplands and the tree-lined river Cinca with spectacular sandstone cliffs is another striking and attractive feature of this route.

Starting point: Alcolea de Cinca.

Before you start the route, visit the beautiful church of this old village, which is full of stork's nests.

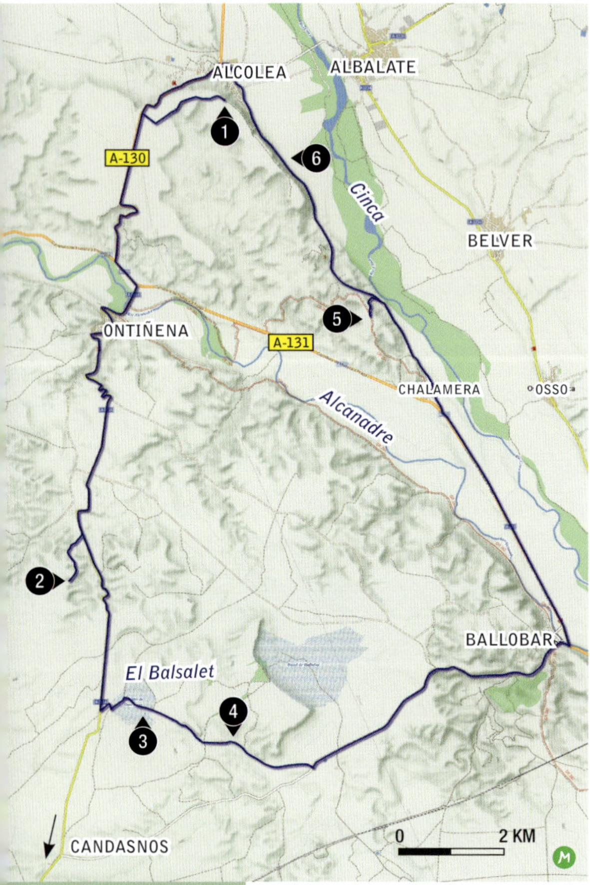

Follow the A-130 towards of Sariñena (Bee-eaters are likely here; check the wires). After 1 km turn left onto a track signposted Mirador de la Sta. Cruz-Ripas. After 350m, Follow the track to the left that leads to a viewpoint.

1 The viewpoint with a large cross stands directly above Alcolea village and looks out over the irrigated lands and gallery forests along the river Cinca. Ripas is the local name for these impressive sand cliffs, which are testimony of the softness of the sandstone of the Ebro Basin. The bedrock consists of horizontal layers – hence the flatness of the plateau – through which the Cinca has carved its river bed. With a little luck, a White Stork, Egyptian Vulture or Golden Eagle may glide past. Look below the viewpoint for Black Wheatear. A pair breeds amongst the rocks here. The fields on the way over to the viewpoint may have Pin-tailed Sandgrouse, Calandra or Short-toed Lark.

Back on the road, continue southwards to Ontiñena (more Bee-eaters here). At the T-junction, go left and 600m further right to Ontiñena. Pass through the village and follow the road up the plateau. For the first kilometres, there are a lot of irrigated fields (the dreaded regadíos – see page 54).
After you pass a bridge, turn right onto a Camino Rural and park after about 100 m.

2 This small valley escaped irrigation – the outcome of protracted negotiations. Look out for Black-eared Wheatear, Iberian Grey Shrike, Rock Sparrow, Golden Eagle and other raptors.

Return to the road and turn right. After a long, straight stretch of road, turn left at a conspicuous pig farm onto a track. After about 100m, turn right at the first opportunity and left at the T-junction.

3 This track leads through excellent steppe habitat to El Basalet, a natural, if usually dry, salt lake. In its usual state, El Basalet is a flat expanse of salt-stained mud with scattered saltworts. Birdwatching in and around the "lake" is excellent. Stone Curlew, Hoopoe, Tawny Pipit, Calandra Lark, Thekla Lark, Short-toed and Lesser Short-toed Lark, Iberian Grey Shrike and, in the low scrub, Spectacled Warbler and even Dupont's Lark are all on the cards. Until recently, even Little Bustard was recorded in the surrounding steppes. Sadly, this species is in such decline that it is uncertain if it is still present – both here in the Monegros as a whole. Pin-tailed and Black-bellied Sandgrouse are faring a little better and may be seen here. Golden, Booted, Short-toed Eagles, Montagu´s Harrier and Griffon and Egyptian Vultures hunt this area, as do numerous Black Kites.

Continue on this track, which leads down into a valley. Ignore the track that branches off to the right, but continue instead to the main road.

The Ballobar area is, together with the eastern banks of the Cinca, the stronghold of Roller in Huesca.

4 This is one of the few areas where Roller breeds. In Huesca, this splendid bird nests in old trees which are a bit away from the track, so look carefully. They are easily missed. The aforementioned raptors occur here too, as does Bee-eater and Red-legged Partridge. The whole area hosts a healthy population of Ocellated Lizards.

At the tarmac road, go left to Ballobar. In the village you come to a T-junction, where you go right. You arrive at the main road, where you go left and cross the Cinca river. After 5km, in Chalamera, go right towards Alcolea. This is quite a spectacular road with Badlands and cliffs in which many Bee-eaters breed. Unfortunately, it is not easy to stop. After 2 km, go left to Ermita de Santa María.

5 The chapel offers a fine viewpoint over the rice-fields and the Cinca riverine forests. White Storks and Egyptian Vultures may glide by, and Black-eared Wheatear can be found on the cliffs.

Continue along the road.

6 On this last stretch you pass beneath the spectacular Ripas of the start of the route. Stop at the side of the road to look for cliff-dwelling birds on the massive sandstone walls. We have found Blue Rock Thrush, Peregrine Falcon, Crag Martin, Alpine Swift and Egyptian Vulture here.

ROUTE 5: FROM HUESCA TO THE ALCUBIERRE MOUNTAINS

84 KM ONE WAY, FULL DAY

Wild-west landscape of sandstone pillars and other desert type geological formations.
Good overview of the variety of habitats of the Ebro basin.
Rich birdlife, varying from waterfowl to inhabitants of semi-desert.

Habitats: sandstone mountains, dry rocky steppes, agricultural land, rice paddies, freshwater wetland
Selected species: Egyptian Vulture, Red-crested Pochard, Eagle Owl, Black Wheatear, Bee-eater, Iberian Grey Shrike, Great Bittern, Ocellated Lizard, Dull Bee Orchid, Striped Grayling, Long-nosed Grasshopper

The beautiful shapes of the sandstone rocks of the Serreta de Tramaced remind one of the 'Wild West'.

If you want to get to grips with the landscape of the Ebro basin and see some spectacular geological features, then this is the route to take. It features a mix of natural dryland steppe, rocky hills and irrigated fields, along with some freshwater marshes. There are various stops and short walks by which you are able to explore these rich habitats. There is Red-necked Nightjar here – the closest area for this species south of the Pyrenees. This route is also excellent in winter.

Starting point: Huesca

Leave town on the A131 to Sariñena. Beyond the small village of Albero Alto, turn right on a small road to Piracés. Follow it for 3 km and park on the right where a track turns off to a hermitage.

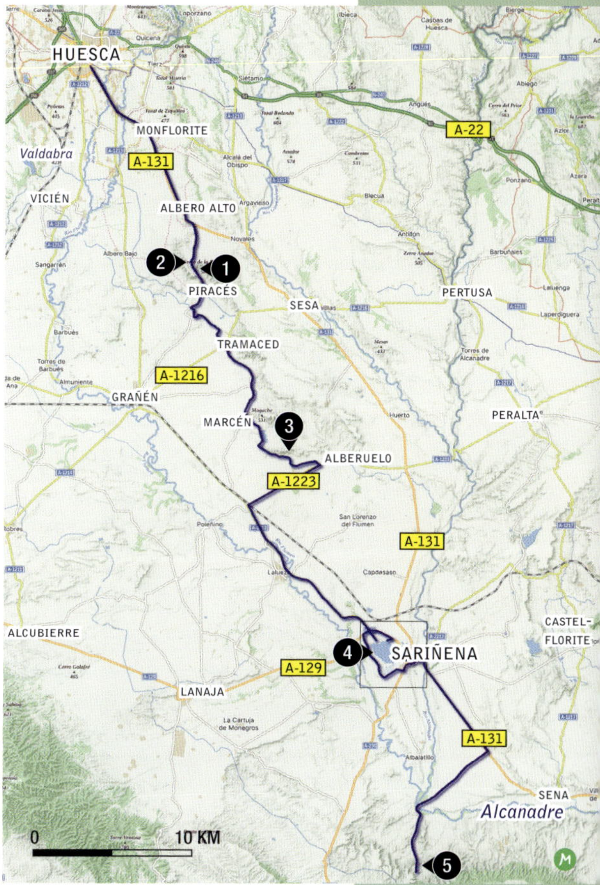

1 This is where the rolling fields suddenly give way to an impressive landscape of sandstone cliffs with boulders and pillars.
Across the road, there is an excellent natural viewpoint from a flat rock overlooking the valley and an old Olive grove. There are some beehives here upon which Bee-eaters often rest. The surrounding cliffs may yield, with luck, Eagle Owl. Blue Rock Thrush, Rock Sparrow, Black-eared and Black Wheatears are more easily found. Indeed, the latter is fairly common in this mountain range. Frequent raptors include Griffon and Egyptian Vultures, Short-toed and Booted Eagles, plus, of course, Black Kite.

Walk towards the hermitage, passing a small woodland, and proceed to a series of odd-looking man-made pillars called *"árboles como arqueología"* (trees as archaeology).

2 From here you have great views over the Serreta de Piracés, as this little range is called. It is the ragged edge of the Somontano plain of Huesca, and the lower plain of Sariñena. The erosion of the hard sandstones is far from tidy and numerous chunks of resistant sandstone remain. These are now present in the form of curiously shaped sandstone pillars and rocks, locally known as torrellones. You will encounter various spectacular ones on the way down to Sariñena. Here too you have a chance on seeing Black-eared and Black wheatears and Blue Rock Thrush. On summer evenings you can hear both European and Red-necked Nightjars. The two species have a small area where their ranges overlap, and the Serreta is precisely within that area.

Bee-eaters are very numerous along the channel of the Serreta de Piracés.

The Iberian Jerusalem-sage is a common scrubland and roadside flower in June.

Return to the car and continue to Piracés. As you enter the village, turn left and cross the irrigation channel. To the left, a road runs parallel to the channel. It is owned by hydrographic company CHE, and entrance is officially forbidden. However, local motorists have been using the road for years without the water company objecting. If you feel like a local, follow this road along the channel to Tramaced, Fraello and then on to Marcén. Beyond Marcén, it runs along a small reservoir (lots of Bee-eaters here, plus some fascinating torrellones) and comes to a T-juntion where you turn right, following the channel again. After 3.5 km, follow the track signposted Parque de Aventura Gabarda. Park at this adventure park. Alternatively, to arrive at this point following the main road from Piracés (as indicated on our map), drive to Grañén and then south in the direction Lalueza. Then turn left to Alberuela de Tubo. Before Alberuela, turn left at the sign Parque de Aventura Gabarda (note that the sign faces traffic coming from the opposite direction).

3 Walk the short, way-marked circuit that starts next to the small adventure park. It is signposted with yellow-white bars. The signposting isn't very good, but there is little risk of getting lost. This walk is an excellent way to explore the superb dry sandstone habitat of the Ebro basin, with its odd rocks. There are many interesting wildflowers, including rarities of arid regions like Small-leaved Rockrose* (*Helianthemum marifolium*). Large and Spanish Psammodromuses and Fringe-toed Lizard are common lizards here as is the beautiful Striped Grayling butterfly. This is another good site for Black Wheatear.

Continue on the A1223 and turn right onto the A131 towards Sariñena. The rice paddies here often support Black-winged Stilt and other waders. Just 1 km before the town turn right, at the sign for Zaragoza, for the visitors' centre which is behind this junction. From here you have a good view over the lake. For a better exploration follow the road to Zaragoza and, after 2.6 km, turn onto a track to the left which leads around the lake (see inset map).

4 Formerly a saline laguna, Sariñena lake was turned into a freshwater lake at the beginning of the 1980s for irrigation purposes. There are dense reedbeds and tamarisk thickets bordering the lake which is surrounded by saline patches with glasswort.
With the growth of reeds and a healthy fish stock, Purple Heron, Little Bittern, Little and Cattle Egrets and Marsh Harrier settled in. Sariñena also supports Spain's largest – but still modest – population of Great Bittern and is an important wintering site for waterfowl. The reeds and tamarisks have Penduline and Bearded Tit year-round.

From Sariñena, continue in the direction of Fraga. After some 7 km, a track signposted as the Ruta Juvierre, turns to the right. Follow this track, cross the Alcanadre river (a good spot to get a glimpse of the riverine habitat) and continue until you reach a little chapel. From here, continue on foot or by car.

Look for Black Wheatear on prominent rocks of the Serreta de Piracés.

5 You find yourself again in the very dry, desert-like hills at the foot of the Alcubierre range. The attraction of this spot are the odd-shaped torrellones, which are here mostly of soft sandstone and semi-petrified clays, shaped by wind and water erosion, and baked by the scorching sun. Several of them have names which are indicated along the track. This site is as good as any to find the wildflowers of gypsum and saline steppes, its reptiles and invertebrates, whilst Hoopoe, Iberian Grey Shrike, Booted Eagle and Black-eared Wheatear are among the birds present here.

Return to the road and turn right. In the next village, Sena, turn left to Castelflorite and go all the way straight to return to Huesca. The area around Castelflorite displays another superb desert-like landscape with table mountains.

ROUTE 6: VALDABRA RESERVOIR

25 KM + 5 KM WALKS, 4 HOURS, EASY

Easy walk in a traditional agricultural landscape.
Waterfowl and Mediterranean birds.

Habitats: open water, reeds, cereal fields and natural holm oak forest
Selected species: Purple Heron, Red-crested Pochard, Great Reed Warbler, Soprano's Pipistrelle, Orphean Warbler, Melodious Warbler, Woodchat Shrike, Wryneck, Turtle Dove, Parsley Frog

Valdabra reservoir.

This short route connects two sites close to the town of Huesca. The first is the Valdabra reservoir, built in 1983 as part of the irrigation system that was created to serve the dry hinterland of southern Huesca. This wetland is located in a beautiful landscape of cereal fields, patches of holm oak woodlands and sandstone rock. The Sierras Exteriores form a scenic backdrop throughout the route. It is via small, partially unpaved roads through this landscape that you reach the second site, the riparian woodlands along the Flumen river.
This route, rather off the beaten track and little visited, is above all attractive for its Mediterranean birdlife, especially in spring and during migration.

Starting point: Huesca

Leave Huesca via the N-330 towards Cuarte. This road runs parallel to the motorway towards Zaragoza. At the roundabout, 1.5 km out of town, go left towards Phlus (the commercial zone), straight at the next roundabout (same direction). At the third roundabout, you go straight onto an unpaved road (this is the exit after the turn to Phlus). Continue and follow the signs Valdabra and Vicién.

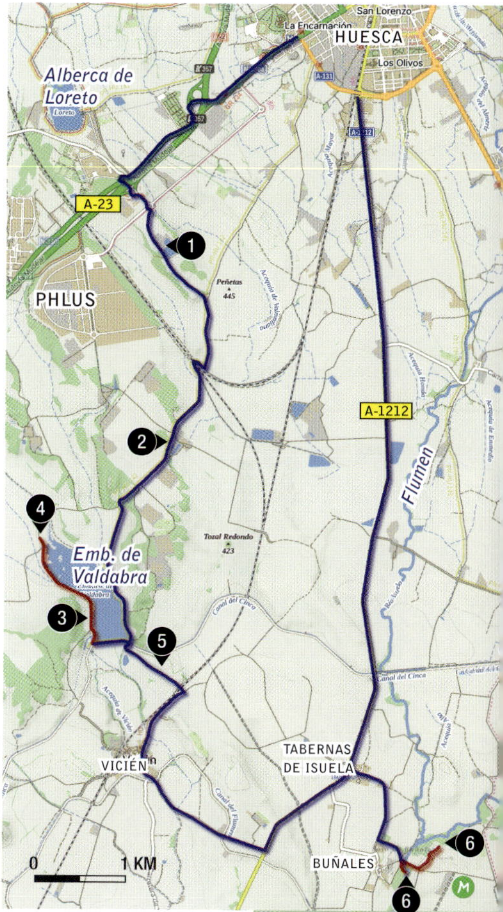

1 You soon cross the original landscape of the Somontano around Huesca, with its cereal fields (here still without irrigation) and scattered holm oaks. Raptors hunt over the fields (mostly vultures and Black Kites) and the more common dryland birds, such as Corn Bunting and Serin are present in good numbers.

You pass underneath the railway and turn left. 1.4 km beyond this point, you'll get your first views of the lake. Turn left, again towards Vicién.

2 You continue through cereal fields where Quail can be heard and Bee-eaters and Corn Buntings can be seen. Keep an eye open for Ladder Snake and Montpellier Snakes, Iberian Wall Lizard and Large Psammodromus on the track and among the rocks. Iberian hare also lives here, but tends to show itself only around dawn and dusk.

Follow the track along the lake and after 850 m turn right, onto the dam. Park on the other side and follow on foot the narrow concrete path along the blue fencing. Cross the outlet channel and follow the path along the shore of the reservoir.

3 Search here, and along the rest of the route, in the trees and reed patches for Mediterranean warblers. This can be an excellent walk and the list of potential species is long: Cetti's, Melodious, Reed and Great Reed, Sardinian, Western Subalpine, Western Orphean and Western Bonelli's Warblers are all in the cards, as are Serin, Nightingale, Woodchat Shrike, Cirl Bunting and Turtle Dove.

4 As you continue, you'll pass several viewpoints over the lagoon and its reedbeds, which become increasingly extensive as you

Purple Herons breed towards the back of the reservoir.

proceed towards the back. Scan the reeds for herons and the open water for waterfowl. A few Purple Heron breed here, Great White Egret is regular and Cattle Egret accompanies the flocks of sheep. Muddy edges often attract waders on migration. Red-crested Pochard, Garganey, Black-winged Stilt, Little Stint and Whiskered Tern regularly show up in spring. Even Spotted and Little Crakes pass through. These elusive birds have been recorded using mist nets during bird ringing projects. It is very unlikely that you'll see them, but the fact that they are found is a testament to the importance of Valdabra.

Continue for as far as you want and then turn back. Note that the track can be partly overgrown but does continue.

Back at the car, cross the dam again and turn right, again signposted Vicién.

5 The next stretch often has Bee-eaters and other Mediterranean birds like Woodchat Shrike or Hoopoe.

In Vicién, go straight, pass the church and the Ayuntamiento (townhall), turn left and go straight ahead. At the main A-1212 road, turn left, direction Huesca. In the small village of Tabernas de Isuela, turn right to Buñales. Upon entering the village, turn left onto a track and park a little further on a crossing of tracks, next to the river.
At the crossing you can follow a path along the river, or walk across the bridge and explore.

6 Of all the spectacular sites in Huesca, this thin strip of riverine forest and grassland may appear somewhat unremarkable. Nevertheless, it is of great ecological value, offering a retreat to wildlife and forming a highway for migrating birds. Marsh Harrier, Cetti's Warbler, Zitting Cisticola, Penduline Tit, Turtle Dove, Wryneck and Golden Oriole are breeding birds here. The Río Flumen holds a winter roost of several hundred Red Kites as well as a roost of Black Kites on migration.
Here, the White Poplars have breeding White Stork, the grasslands support the odd-looking Long-nosed Grasshopper Various orchids, including Dull Bee, Woodcock and Early Spider Orchids can be found flowering among the rocky scrub.

Return to Tabernas de Isuela and turn right to drive back to Huesca.

ROUTE 7: SOTONERA RESERVOIR
30 KM, 4 HOURS

Best season
February-March
Of interest
November-June

The most important wetland close to the Pyrenees. Large staging site for Cranes.

Habitats: open water, shores and marsh vegetation
Selected species: Crane, Purple Heron, Red-crested Pochard, Calandra Lark, Great Reed Warbler, Soprano's Pipistrelle, Parsley Frog

With the Sierra de Guara in the back, the Sotonera reservoir has a beautiful scenery.

This route circles around the large Sotonera reservoir, west of Huesca. The main interest of this site is its strategic position on the migration route of Cranes, with up to 40,000 birds roosting here in late February and early March. This is the closest site to the Pyrenees where steppe and Mediterranean wetland birds can be found. There are better sites further south in the Ebro depression, but if you are based in the Pyrenees, Sotonera is your best option to find some lowland birds. Being close to Riglos, it is easily combined with route 10.

Starting point: Montmesa

1 At the western end of the village, just beyond a Stork's nest, turn left and follow the signs Ruta Verde for 1 km and park your car. Walk the small circuit to explore the bushes, reeds and muddy shores. Purple Heron, Red-crested Pochard, Zitting Cisticola, Great Reed Warbler and Melodious Warbler breed, waders and passerines are seen on migration. There are raptors around such as Marsh Harrier and Red Kite. Parsley Frog, Viperine Snake and European Pond Terrapin inhabit the lake.

Return to your car and follow the track west from Montmesa, signposted as *Vuelta a la Sotonera.*

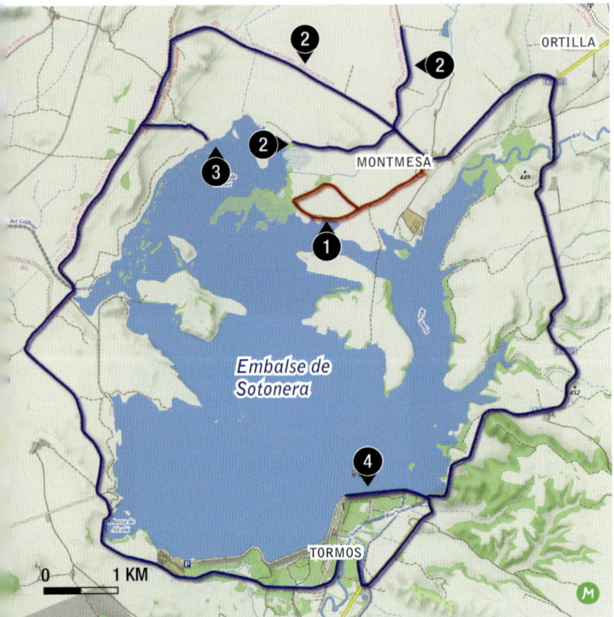

2 After 300 m you arrive at the prime site for Cranes (in February-March). The track left leads to the watchpoint (observatorio) 600 m ahead, which is good for photographers. The track right goes to La Mezquita where the largest numbers are present. Proceed 500 m along the main track where you can see Cranes crossing low over the track in the early morning. They rise up spectacularly, with their far-carrying, trumpeting calls, to ascend high into the thermals. However, if high-altitude winds are unfavourable, they may descend again and try the next day.

3 At the next junction, turn left where, after 250 m, another track leads you to farm buildings called Corral de Antonié. This point allows good views over the northern part of the lake, especially in the afternoon when the sun is at your back. Natural patches of vegetation with Holm Oak, Juniper and Mediterranean shrub are interesting for Woodchat Shrike, Dartford and Subalpine Warblers. Rush-leaved Jonquils are common here in early spring, as in many other scrublands of the Somontano.

Go back the same way to the main track, turn left and after 1.5 km you reach a paved road. Turn left in the direction Tormos / Almudévar. After 12 km you reach the junction with the A1207, where you go left for Esquedas.

4 Just 800 m from the junction you will find the eastern end of the 3 km long Sotonera dam. You can park 50 m further on the left. The dam gives the best overview of the lake and is especially rewarding in winter when up to 5000 ducks and other waterbirds may be present. On summer evenings this is a superb place for watching bats. There are colonies of Lesser Horseshoe, Natterer's and Daubenton's Bats and Kuhl's Pipistrelles, while the tiny Soprano's Pipistrelle and the large European Free-tailed Bat hunt nearby.

Continue towards Esquedas where, at the Montmesa junction, your walk is completed.

Additional sites in the Ebro valley

For locations of these sites, see map on page 108.

1 – The Ebro river and Galacho de la Alfranca

Just east of Zaragoza are a series of oxbow lakes (*galachos* in Aragonese). The most important is a 140 ha reserve, Galacho de la Alfranca. Water, reedbeds and woodlands are an oasis in the dry landscape. It is a place where Night Heron breeds, alongside Little Egret, Purple Heron, Kingfisher and Penduline Tit.

The Galachos lie just beyond the village of Pastriz, but are best reached by taking the NII from Zaragoza to Lerida and after about 10 km, in la Puebla de Alfindén, turn right at the roundabout, indicated *c/ Cortés de Aragón*. At the next roundabout, turn right again and you drive straight towards it.

If you are with children, it is worth considering a boat raft on the (gentle!) Ebro river. There are boat trips centred around birdwatching for beginners. Visit **ebronautas.net** or call +34 654898400 for more information.

2 – The Sierra de Alcubierre and more Monegros

The minor road from Osera to Monegrillo to Lanaja forms an excellent extra trip to explore the Monegros. The first part, to and just beyond Monegrillo, runs through large areas of original steppe, where most steppe birds occur and which is interesting for steppe plants. The section to Lanaja is excellent, because it crosses the arid Sierra de Alcubierre – an important ecological corridor that is otherwise difficult to access. The Sierra is clad in scrub and arid, open woodland of Aleppo Pine and Spanish Juniper. This is a good stretch for finding Booted and Short-toed Eagles, Woodchat Shrikes and the Mediterranean warblers. Many of the unique wildflowers of the Ebro basin occur in the scrub, as do the reptiles. You can stop at any place to explore.

Turning left at Lanaja you cross the Sierra again between Alcubierre village and Leciñena where there is a viewpoint at the top of the range. British author, George Orwell, best known for *1948* and *Animal Farm*, fought here in the Spanish Civil War (see box on page 48).

A boat trip on the Galacho de la Alfranca (site 1)

Eagle Owl chicks (right) and a Lesser Kestrel (bottom) with prey for its young – both species breed in the church of Valfarta.

3 – Valfarta

The small village of Valfarta (GPS: 41.557028, -0.133278) barely has five streets and would resemble any other hamlet in the Monegros, were it not for two remarkable features.
First, the large church, which hosts a vibrant colony of Lesser Kestrels and, surprisingly, a breeding pair of Eagle Owls. At the time of writing, both species were easy to watch and photograph from the small square in front of the church.
The second attraction is the small camp site just north of the village (GPS: 41.561417, -0.131083; it is signposted in Valfarta). Campsites are rare in the Monegros, and small, low-key ones like these even more so. It offers a unique chance to spend the night in the heart of this arid landscape—an experience we thoroughly enjoyed. During our stay, we were treated to the nightly calls of both European and Red-necked Nightjars, singing simultaneously. At the same time, a pair of Ocellated Lizards was showing exceptionally well—so much so that the campsite owners had even given them names.
If you're travelling with a tent or caravan, and looking to camp somewhere quiet, Camping La Estepa in Valfarta (**campinglaestepa.es**) is highly recommended.

4 – The river woodlands of the Cinca

Some of the best riverine woodlands of the region are found along the Cinca south of Monzón. The best options to explore this difficult-to-access terrain are from the bridge between Alcolea and Albate (GPS: 41.725944, 0.137028).

On the Alcolea side there is a track leading to the river. From here you can explore on foot.

Birds are the prime attraction here. Golden Oriole, Penduline Tit, Cetti's and Melodious Warblers, Zitting Cisticola, Turtle Dove and Wryneck are frequent. Some herons are regular visitors or even breed, such as Little Egret, and Purple and Night Herons. Several Otters live in the Cinca between Monzón and Fraga and a large number of bats fly over the river at night to feed.

5 – El Pas and Finca San Miguel

GPS: 41.700083, 0.274000 The Finca San Miguel with its small, marsh-fringed reservoir El Pas is protected as an Important Bird Area (IBA) and partly converted in a nature reserve. This private property is managed by SEO/BirdLife. Cattle, Little and Great White Egrets are regular visitors and in some years, Purple and Night Heron breed.

The entrance of the finca is at km. 12 at the A-1241 road north of Zaidín. Continue past the finca and follow the track to the reservoir (2 km). Rollers are common between May and September and breed in the poplars, using both old woodpecker holes and the nest boxes along the track. Red-necked Nightjars breed in the area. Their repetitive, mechanical call *(kyok-kyok-kyok)* can be heard at night.

6 – Embalse de San Salvador

GPS: 41.785583, 0.180472. This shallow reservoir of 1,450 ha (*Embalse de San Salvador*) was constructed in 2015 and is now the biggest wetland in the area. Although rather early to say for sure, but it promises to be the best for waterfowl in the region, due to its location in the southern part of the province and its long shoreline and shallow waters. Up to 8,000 grebes,ducks, herons, egrets, shorebirds and gulls were counted in 2015. You reach the reservoir from the A-140, 1,5 km west of Binaced where an unpaved road turns left (south) to 'Planta Binaced' and the reservoir. Turn left again at the reservoir to get to the best spots.

View from the Sierra de Alcubierre over the Monegros (site 2).

Routes in the *Sierras Exteriores* and *Somontano*

The Sierras Exteriores form a broad, somewhat distinct band of mountains, running parallel to and just south of the main Pyrenean range. Approached from the south, they rise steeply and dramatically from the gently undulating landscape of the Somontano. Their northern boundary is less abrupt, blending gradually into the sandstone formations that dominate the Depresión (see page 14).

Clefts and canyons divide the Sierras Exteriores into a fragmented series of ranges, which include, within the province of Huesca, the Sierras of Riglos and Loarre in the west (route 11), the Sierra de Guara in the centre (routes 9, 10 nd 12) and to the east, the Sierras de Carrodilla and Coscollá (route 8). The highest peak in these 'lower Pyrenees' is the Tozal de Guara (2,077 m) and over much of the range the peaks range between 1,000 and 2,000 metres.

The evergreen southern slopes of these sierras stand in stark contrast to both the fields and steppes of the Ebro Basin and the fresh, green alpine peaks of the high Pyrenees. The world of the Sierras Exteriores is a Mediterranean one, with thick scrub and evergreen woodlands, small fields and dramatic cliffs and rocky slopes. Only the north-facing slopes, dressed as they are in deciduous woodlands, reveal the range as the northern limit of the Mediterranean sphere The Guara's most striking feature is its many steep and narrow gorges, which have been cut out by melt water through the soft limestone (routes 8 and 9).

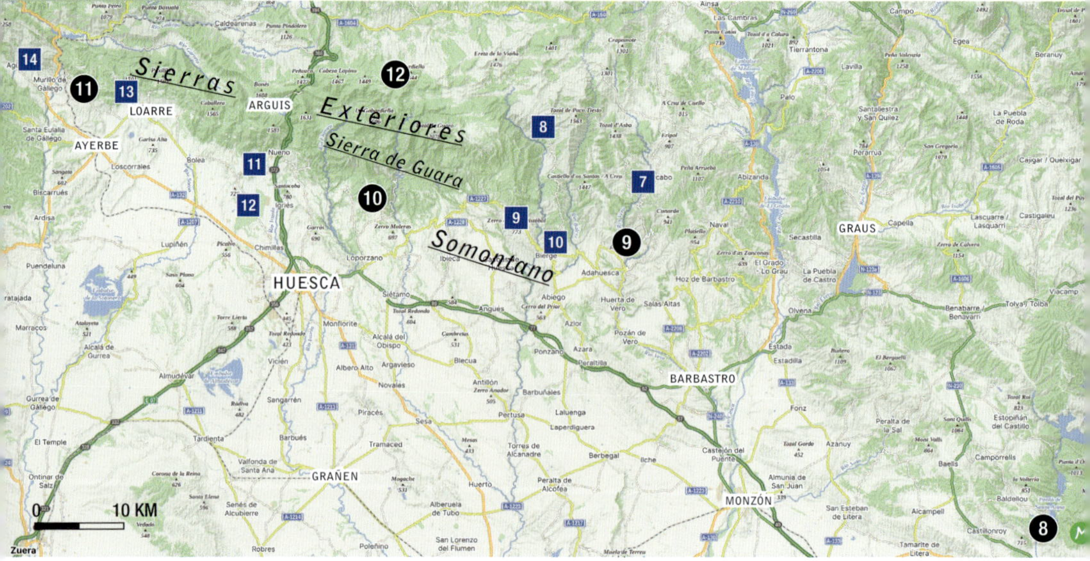

Overview of the Sierras exteriores and Somontano. In black are the locations of the routes described on the following pages; in blue are the sites described on pages 157-160.

The dry slopes of the *Sierras Exteriores.*

The rock cliffs and wild currents have made the sierra famous among some – predominantly French – climbers and canyoneers. Equally spectacular sites are found along the narrow and discontinuous belt of conglomerate rocks that mark the southern edge of the range. Erosion has sculpted spectacular vertical rock pillars, several hundred metres high, locally known as Mallos – the most famous of which are the Mallos de Riglos.

The entire sierra remains wild and largely untouched, with only a handful of settlements. The most important towns, such as Huesca, Barbastro and most villages are located along the southern foothills and provide access into the mountains.

The diversity of habitats here means that birds that favour rocky habitats (e.g. Common and Blue Rock Thrushes), Mediterranean scrub (e.g. Dartford and Orphean Warblers) and woodland (e.g. Firecrest and Bonelli's Warbler) are all typical of the Guara mountains. Both the limestone and conglomerate cliffs house large colonies of vultures. Griffons are the most common, but Egyptian Vultures and Lammergeiers are fairly common as well. Botanically, the scrub and rocky fissures offer a world waiting to be discovered, including eyecatchers like Petrocoptis (text box on page 70), Long-leaved Saxifrage, Spanish Fritillary and a score of orchids.

Travelling between sites, one passes through the pleasant landscape of the Somontano – a delight in itself. The combination of small plots, scrubby slopes, hedges and small, forest-lined rivers support a rich flora and fauna. Many raptors visit these plains to hunt, whilst birds of Mediterranean and temperate areas mix to form a rich bird community. Orchids, Beautiful Flax, and wild daffodils grace the roadside verges. Rocky spots support reptiles and lots of butterflies.

ROUTE 8: SANTA ANA RESERVOIR

15 KM, 2-3 HOURS

Mediterranean hillsides with interesting raptors, bats and rock flora.

Habitats: Mediterranean scrub, rocks and cliffs
Selected species: Bonelli's Eagle, Sardinian and Dartford Warblers, European Free-tailed Bat, Sarcocapnos, Woolly Snapdragon

The reservoir of Santa Ana, home to Bonelli's Eagle.

This is perhaps the most authentically Mediterranean of the sites described in this book, and one that lies furthest away from the other sites and human habitation. The well developed scrubland, imposing cliffs and a flora and fauna that is different from the other areas, makes it well worth the detour. In April and May there is a rich fissure and scrubland flora. The many cracks and clefts in the bedrock host a rich bat fauna, which hunts over the reservoir and river for nocturnal insects.
Santa Ana is the best place to find Bonelli's Eagle. One pair of this rare and endangered raptor breeds nearby.

Starting point: Binéfar.

Follow the A140 to Alfarrás. Turn left onto the N-230 and after 2 km, turn right road towards Embalse de Santa Ana. At the next crossing, go left and follow the road that ends at a magnificent viewpoint.

1 Explore the cliffs for raptors, which usually include Griffon Vulture. Wait a little and keep scanning the sky, and you will

have a good chance of finding Bonelli's Eagle. Golden Eagle, Egyptian Vulture and Peregrine are other possibilities.
On the road over, it is worth stopping somewhere in the Rosemary scrub. The stout Rosemary Broomrape is common here, as is Large-flowered Meadow-rue* (*Thalictrum tuberosum*), Beautiful Flax, Blue Aphyllanthes and, more locally, Woodcock Orchid.
Return to the crossing and turn left. Park at the foot of the dam where the road ends.

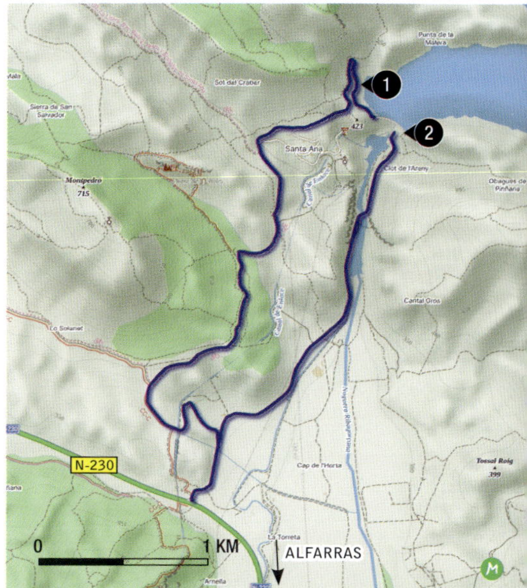

2 Walk up the flight of stairs onto the dam. Along this short stretch there is a wonderful flora, with many Mediterranean shrubs and wildflowers, including, in spring, Lavander-leaved Sage, Leuzea, Sad Stock, Pygmy Bindweed, Large-flowered Meadow-rue* and Rosemary-leaved Cistus* (*Cistus clusii*).

From the dam you have another opportunity to spot the raptors of the area. Scanning the cliffs with telescope may yield Blue Rock Thrush or Black Wheatear.
The cliffs near the tunnels you passed on your way over to the dam are worth exploring as well for wildflowers, such as Sarcocapnos, Ramonda and the pretty Woolly Snapdragon. The local Petrocoptis is *Petrocoptis montsicciana* (see box on page 70).
Bats occur in the tunnel, and come out in the evening to hunt over the river. With a bat detector, it is possible to find Kuhl's Pipistrelle and Daubenton's Bat throughout most of the year. In the hotter months the big, but very difficult to find European Free-tailed Bat may be present and Mediterranean Mouse-eared Bat is often abundant. During the day, check the river for Grey Wagtail, Viperine Snake and Large Pincertail.

Blue Rock Thrush breeds near the dam (left). In spring, Rosemary Broomrape is a conspicuous plant (right).

ROUTE 9: LAS PASERELAS DE ALQUÉZAR

4 KM, 3 HOURS, MODERATE

!
It can be extremely hot on this exposed route. Take precautions.

Best season
April-June
Of interest
year round

Superb gorge, cliffs and scrubland walk, departing from the most beautiful village of the Guara. Excellent opportunities to watch raptors and butterflies and discover the fissure flora.

Habitats: steep gorges, bare rock, evergreen scrub and trees
Selected species: Petrocoptis, Ramonda, Maidenhair Fern, Egyptian Vulture, Griffon Vulture, Blue Rock Thrush, Alpine Swift, Crag Martin, Rock Sparrow, Dartford Warbler, Wallcreeper (winter), Panoptes Blue, Scarce Swallowtail, Large Wall Brown, Southern Gatekeeper, Striped Grayling

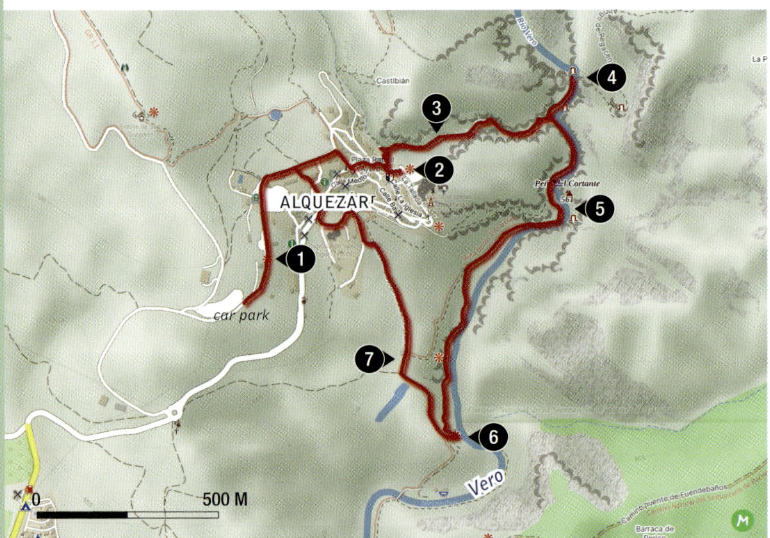

Alquézar village is undoubtedly the most touristy village of the Guara and the Pasarelas walk is the most popular in the region. And for good reason – this is a superb walk through a deep gorge and along the river Vero. Large sections of the route follow spectacular cliffside walkways, adding to the adventure. Although the scenery is the great draw of this route, there are massive colonies of swifts and martins and good views Egyptian Vultures to be had, plus a number of rare plants. After the trail, a stroll through the village and a visit to its Moorish citadel make for a fine morning's activity.

Preparations for the Pasarelas path

There are a couple of things you need to know before heading out on the Paserelas path. First is that there is a fee of € 5.00 (2025 price) meant to maintain the path and to limit the number of visitors. It is best to order in advance via **pasarelasdealquezar.com**.

Second is that it is a popular path, so it's best to avoid weekends and holidays.

Third, the trail is one way – you must follow the route as described in this guide.

Fourth, it can become seriously hot. The final stretch is the hottest and most exposed. Therefore, we advise to start the walk as early as possible, which is, at the time of writing, 9.30 AM (before this time, the trail is closed). We also advise to be a bit earlier than that, because the best views of the Alpine Swifts and (with a little luck) Egyptian Vultures is in the morning from the viewpoint next to the entrance of the trail. Especially if you are interested in photography, it is worth spending some time here before starting the walk.

Fifth, although the walk is short and there is not a lot of climbing involved, it is still demanding, as it leads through some narrow sections underneath rocks and along cliffs. You need to be a little agile and squeeze through tight spots. If this isn't you, then unfortunately, the Paserelas walk is not for you.

Finally, in the hot months, bring plenty of water.

Alquézar in march, when the Almonds flower.

Large numbers of Alpine Swifts breed on the cliffs near the village.

Starting point: Car park above Alquezar. You'll be directed to this car park when you drive to the village.

On foot, continue along the road towards the village.

1 From this elevated street, you have great views of the village, the citadel and the cliff behind it. Note that Alquezar lies on a junction of different types of bedrock. The cliff just left of the citadel (which is where the Paserelas walk starts) is cream coloured with vertical lines, and is made of limestone. So is the cliff to the right of the citadel. The darker, more rounded rocks further to the right consist of conglomerate rock (like the Mallos of Riglos; route 11). Turning 180 degrees, the rocks next to the street are sandstone.
The fortifications at Alquézar are typical of many forts built in this area by the Moors or Christians as they wrestled for control over these northern limits of Muslim Spain throughout the Middle Ages.

In the village, go right at the T-junction (to Casa Jabonero) and then left in front of Hotel Castillo. Cross the square and a little further you are at the start of the Paserelas walk.

2 Just to the right of where the walk goes down into the gorge, you have good views of the cliffs. Large numbers of Common and Alpine Swifts, Crag and House Martins breed on the cliffs and are easily visible. You also have a chance of seeing Rock Sparrow and Blue Rock Thrush, either here or further down.

3 Follow the trail down into the gorge. Large Fig and Nettle trees grow in the gorge making for a lush appearance. The rocks on your right are full of Ramonda, which flower here as early as April, much earlier than in the Pyrenees. The rare *Petrocoptis guarensis* (see page 66) also grows on the rocks, particularly on the more exposed parts.

4 Once down on the banks of the Rio Vero, you can go left to a cave which is a particularly scenic spot on this route, again with lots of swifts and martins. Note the willow trees along the river with their very narrow leaves: this is the Rosemary Willow, a species typical of southern European mountain streams.

Return and follow the Paserelas route through the gorge.

5 This is perhaps the most exciting part of the walk, with large sections of the trail suspended on the vertical cliffs. The aforementioned Petrocoptis is quite numerous here. All along the high water line of the river, grows a band of Maidenhair Fern.

6 The trail passes the ruins of an old water mill arrives at a viewing platform from which you have open views of both the river and the village. This is a good spot to look for raptors.

7 The walk then continues uphill to Alquezar (signposted). It leads through an old olive grove, where Orphean, Melodious and Sardinian Warblers can be found. This is also a good place for butterflies with (in season) False Ilex Hairstreak, Adonis Blue, Dusky Brown and Striped Grayling.

The trail down to the river leads through this beautiful gorge.

ROUTE 10: VADIELLO AND ROLDÁN – THE GREAT GATES TO THE GUARA

75 KM + 5.5 KM WALK ONE WAY, FULL DAY, EASY-MODERATE

Best season
April-June
Of interest
year round

Spectacular cliffs with large vulture colonies.
Pleasant walk through Mediterranean woodland and scrub.

Habitats: steep gorges, bare rock, Mediterranean scrub and woodland, almond groves, agricultural land, hedgehog broom scrub
Selected species Long-leaved Saxifrage, Yellow-fringed Fly Orchid*, Spanish Fritillary, Lammergeier, Griffon Vulture, Egyptian Vulture, Wallcreeper (winter), Alpine Accentor (winter), Woodchat Shrike, Alpine Swift, Rock Thrush, Subalpine Warbler, Scarce Swallowtail

The large conglomerate rocks and turquoise reservoir of Vadiello make for a surreal landscape.

Two spectacular rock formations, that of Vadiello and Roldán, form the backdrop to this magnificent route in the Sierra de Guara. At both sites, but particularly at Vadiello, there are excellent hiking options. One of these walks is described in detail here. Due to the rugged terrain, these two sites can only be reached by minor roads through the lovely and green *Somontano*. The scenery and the birds of prey are the most spectacular feature of this route, but there are plenty of wildflowers, reptiles and butterflies to please the all-round naturalist. From Roldán it is easy to photograph vultures in flight (photo on page 32).

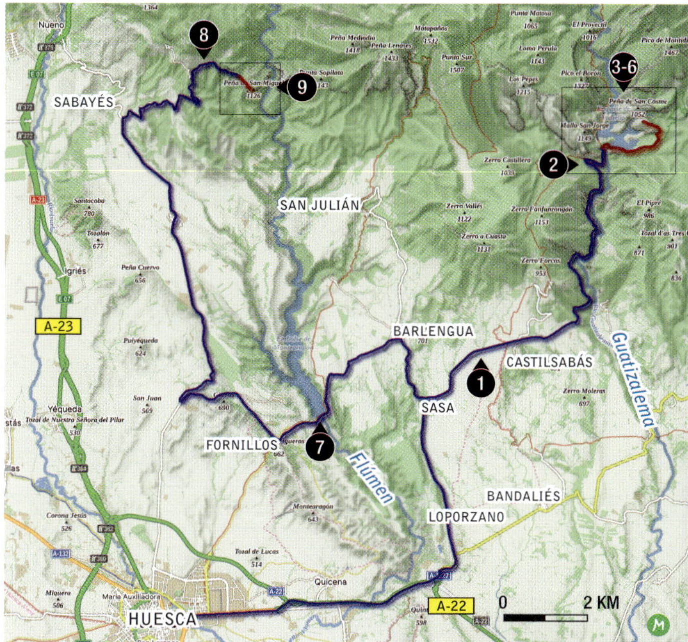

Starting point: Take the N-240 east of Huesca and turn left after 4 km, in the direction of Bandaliés and Loporzano.
Follow the road through Loporzano, Sasa de Abadiado and Castilsabás.

1 This is typical *Somontano* country: fields, little areas of scrub, isolated trees and Holm Oak wood and Almond Groves. Many Black and a few Red Kites scout the fields. In May, the bright blue Beautiful Flax (p. 156) lines the roadsides. Make some stops here and there to explore the countryside. A wide variety of Mediterranean song birds breed in this landscape. One scenic stop is above the village of La Almunia del Romeral, which is the gateway into an entire different landscape: that of the Guara mountains. Look for Rock Thrush and Dartford Warbler.

Continue and park at the car park by the only hairpin on the road and walk up the small trail along the secluded stream.

2 Western Spectre and Common Goldenring can be seen from the trail. The grassy glades host Weaver's Fritillary, Southern Grizzled and Lulworth Skipper. Wallcreeper winters on the steep cliff to your right. This is also the start of a strenuous, but excellent, circular trail through pine woodland scrub and along cliffs.

Continue to the dam and park. From here starts a 4 hour circular trail (easy-moderate difficulty) which is highly recommended. Follow, on foot, the signs San Cosme y San Damián.

3 Scan the sky and cliffs here and along the entire trail for raptors. Griffon Vultures are numerous and Egyptians are frequent, but this is also a very good site to see Lammergeier (although it is far outnumbered by the other species). In winter, the south-facing cliffs are

another site for Wallcreeper. You will likely encounter some feral goats which, having been abandoned, now live a free life in the scrub of the Guara.

4 In May, just beyond the dam, many of Long-leaved Saxifrages flower. The scrub and woodland ahead supports Rosemary Broomrape, Laurel-leaved Cistus, Strawberry Tree, Grass-leaved Buttercup, Liverleaf and various other interesting wildflowers. Large Psammodromuses are frequent, whilst birds include Bonelli's and Subalpine Warblers, Firecrests and Crested Tits.

The massive rock of Roldán has a large breeding colony of Griffon Vultures, which can be seen from up close.

5 A trail turns off to the left (again signposted for *San Cosme*), passed a small chapel, and down into a more damp Mediterranean wood which is good for fern species. On the other side of the valley, you come to a track which you follow to the right, signposted to *El Huevo*. Your route winds uphill, through more interesting Mediterranean scrub habitat.

6 A small detour can be made to *El Huevo* – an egg-shaped rock pillar. The end point of this linear walk may be something of an anticlimax, but the mature and tall Holm Oak forest is quite special as these trees usually remain small.

Return to the car. For the second part of the route, return by car over the same road until after Sasa de Abadiado, and then turn right to Barluenga. Beyond this village, turn left to the small reservoir of Montearagón.

7 From the dam you have unimpeded views of the next site: the impressive cliffs of the Salto de Roldán. Legend is that the courageous

Roland de Roncevaux and his steed jumped over the walls in one fantastic leap to escape his enemies.
Continue and enjoy good views of the scavenging birds, such as Red Kite and Raven, exploiting the Huesca rubbish dump which, thankfully, is hidden behind the hills at your left. At the next junction turn right, pass Apiés and after 2 km take the road to Santa Eulalia.

8 Keep a sharp lookout on this narrow and winding road as Thekla Lark, Rock Thrush, Tawny Pipit, Black-eared Wheatear, Subalpine and Dartford Warblers all breed in the Mediterranean scrub. At the next junction, take the small road to the right. Park at the Salto de Roldán.

9 There are various trails to the cliff of Roldán. We found the very rare Yellow-fringed Fly orchid* *(Ophrys subinsectifera)* on the left one, together with Spanish Fritillary, Dull Bee Orchid and masses of Rush-leaved Jonquils. The best views of the Griffon Vultures and Red-billed Choughs can be had on the right where you overlook the plain of Huesca. With luck you may see Golden and Bonelli's Eagles, Lammergeier and Egyptian Vulture. In winter, there are Wallcreeper and Alpine Accentor here.

Feral goats roam the cliffs of Vadiello.

Additional remarks

Beyond Roldán, a track leads deeper into the mountains through a vegetation of Yellow Hedgehog Broom* (*Echinospartum horridum*). It is passable by car, though very narrow and rocky. Consider continuing on foot! For photographing vultures at Roldán, the best light conditions are in the evening.

Vadiello has a rich cliff bird community which includes, in winter, Wallcreeper.

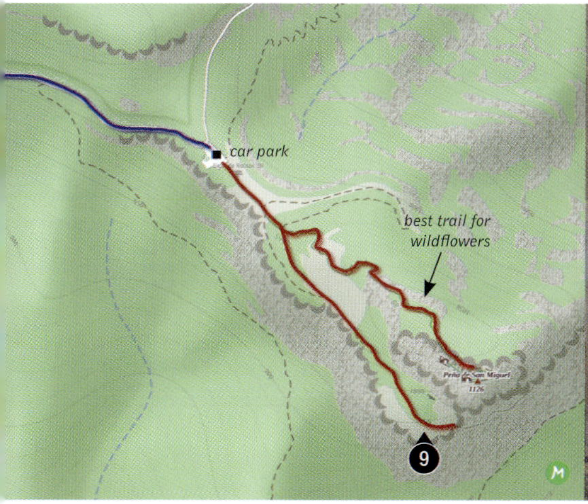

ROUTE 11: LOS MALLOS DE RIGLOS

27 + 7.5 KM WALK, 5 HOURS, MODERATE

Spectacular rock pillars.
Great views of vultures and other cliff and scrubland birds.

Habitats: high cliffs and Mediterranean scrub
Selected bird species: Griffon and Egyptian Vultures, Lammergeier, Blue Rock Thrush, Rock Thrush, Rock Bunting, Rock Sparrow, Dartford Warbler, Wallcreeper (winter), Alpine Accentor (winter), Silver Spotted Skipper, Chapman's Blue, Dark Green Fritillary

The magnificent cliffs (Mallos) of Riglos.

The most spectacular mallos are those of Riglos: vertical rock pillars that rise up several hundred metres, dwarfing Riglos village at their feet. For a brief period in the 12th century this was an independent Kingdom, therefore it is still called El Reino de los Mallos, loosely translated 'the kingdom of the cliffs'.
Riglos offers first class birdwatching, amidst dramatic scenery. The route consists of a fairly strenuous circuit around the rock pillars and a much gentler walk further away from the cliffs. Additionally, there is a viewpoint for a vulture colony a short stretch away by car.

Starting point: Public parking just before Riglos village

Walk to the village and go straight onto the Calle del Peñon below the cliffs. At the end of the road, a marked trail (yellow-and-white) leads up between the rock pillars.

1 This strenuous climb leads through a scrubland with breeding Dartford and Sardinian Warblers. The surrounding cliffs are home to noisy Red-billed Choughs, Kestrels, Crag Martins and Blue Rock Thrushes, while Griffon and Egyptian Vultures fly around the cliff tops. At the highest point of the walk, the terrain is more level and there are a few fields. Look for Common Rock Thrush, Green-winged and Dull Bee Orchids. The trail down is gentler and allows you to look for butterflies. Ilex Hairstreak, Silver-spotted Skipper, Dusky Heath, Great Banded Grayling and Spanish Gatekeeper are common.

2 A much gentler walk nearby leads through some orchards to another set of Mallos, which are less busy with tourists and free of climbers. These cliffs harbour a big Griffon Vulture colony. Egyptian Vulture, Peregrine Falcon and Alpine Swift can be seen here too.
To get there from the car park and walk towards the village and take the first right (*Calle Lavadero*) towards Loarre and Linas de Marcuello. Turn right at the plaza. A track continues through the orchards and through rosemary scrub and continues beneath the vulture colony. The scrub is home to Dartford, Sardinian and Subalpine Warblers, while Blue Rock Thrush can be seen on the cliffs.

3 The visitors centre Arcaz (*Centro de Interpretación de aves ARCAZ*) is strategically situated on a hilltop that offers great views of the Peñas de Riglos and is surrounded by Mediterranean scrub. To get there from the car park, drive 200m back, away from the village, and go left onto a steep road. After 600 m you arrive at the visitors centre.

Dartford Warbler (bottom) and Griffon Vulture (right) are both common around Riglos.

The 'official' viewpoint over the Griffon Vulture colony lies close to the path described under point 2, but can only be accessed by driving to Ayerbe, continuing to Loarre and then turning to Sarsamarcuello. In this village, follow the signs *Mirador de los Buitres*. A 7 km dirt track (be careful here after rain) leads over a scrubby mountain to the viewpoint.

4 Stop at the castle ruin on your left, about 1.5 km before the viewpoint. A word of warning here: this track has deteriorated in recent years and we've heard of many flat tires (including our own). This track will likely be patched up again at some point in the future, but if you don't trust the conditions – don't attempt this track.

Explore the rocks and walls of the castle for Common Rock Thrush and Black Wheatear. The latter used to breed much more widely in the area, including at Riglos, but is disappearing. In 2025, however, a pair was still present. In the scrub, Tawny Pipit and Ortolan Bunting can be observed, while in winter, this general area often has Alpine Accentor.

5 Continue on to the hide at the end of the trail to see vultures flying by at close range. The views over the Mallos de Riglos are stunning.

Additional remarks: The impressive Castle of Loarre (site 13 on page 159) is just a little further to the east and and can easily be combined with a visit to Riglos.

ROUTE 12: THE WILD NORTHERN GUARA
102 KM, 6 HOURS

Wild mountainous landscape with abandoned villages.
Superb butterfly fauna.

Best season
May-mid August

Habitats: rocky, dry sandstone ravines, hedgehog broom scrub, small fields, open forests, calcareous marsh
Selected species Robust Marsh-orchid, Woodcock Orchid, Wild Boar, Red-backed Shrike, Short-toed Eagle, Lammergeier, Apollo, Cinquefoil Skipper, Forster's Furry Blue, Weavers Fritillary, Spanish Heath

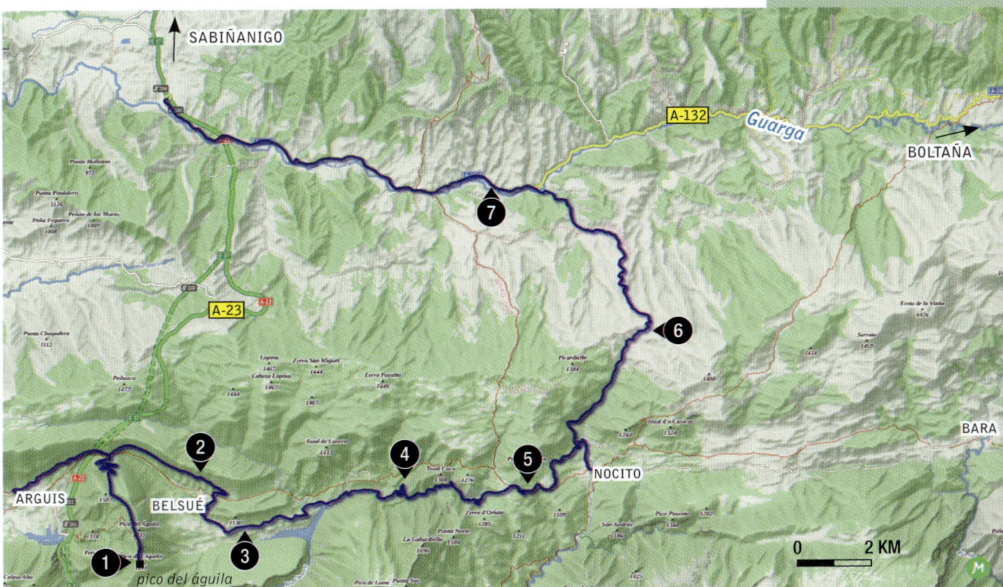

This is the best route to explore the remote northern part of the Guara. By car you follow little travelled roads that connect half abandoned villages. The woodlands, scrub and overgrown fields are home to a wealth of plants and animals. We describe several easily recognisable points along the way, but pretty much any spot along the road is likely to produce something of interest. During the afternoon, butterflies are abundant: we once found 70 species in a single day! An evening trip may be productive as well: Wild Boar, Roe Deer, Fox, Beech Marten, or, with luck, a Genet or Wild Cat may cross the road.

The beautiful landscape around Nocito with the Guara peak in the background.

Starting point: Arguis

Take the old road towards Belsúe. Pass the A-23 motorway and at the junction, turn right towards the Pico del Águila (not signposted).

1 The Pico del Águila is the highest point that can be reached by car in the Guara. On the way up, keep an eye open for Crossbill, Rock and Cirl Buntings, which frequently look for food in the roadside. At a height of 1,640 m you have superb views over the Guara, the *Depresión* and, on clear days, even up to the snow-covered Monte Perdido. Lammergeier can be seen here, just like along the rest of this route. Butterflies frequent on the peak include Apollo, Spanish Gatekeeper, Swallowtail and Violet Copper.

Return to the junction and turn right towards Belsué and Nocito. The narrow tarmac road passes various small hamlets which were nearly deserted but have recently revived with the aid of small-scale rural tourism. The whole stretch is of interest, with partially abandoned plots, scrub, oak and pine woods and rocky escarpments. The rough, flowery grasslands here are excellent for butterflies. All Guara raptors are present, with the snake eating Short-toed Eagle relatively common, indicating a rich reptile fauna. We recommend the following stops.

2 At the curve just before Belsué village, there is a small gully on the right hand side. This is the type of sunny, wind-sheltered place where butterflies are easily found. Walk around and find, besides butterflies, White Flax, Brown Bluebell, Blue Aphyllanthes (p. 34), Fragrant, Pyramidal, Woodcock and Bee Orchids.

3 Beyond Belsué, there are many small plots lined with old pollarded oaks and areas with scrub. About 1 km past Belsué there is a farm ruin. A little further, a track descends towards the river on the right. This one is worth walking down. Frequent birds include Red-backed Shrike, Cirl, Corn and Rock Buntings.

4 Continue and, after crossing the river, park on the left and follow the track to the ruins a little further ahead. You cross two shallow rivers. In flowery spots and wet mud, look for butterflies, like Ripart's Anomalous Blue, Dusky Meadow Brown, Southern and Spanish Gatekeepers, Spanish Purple Hairstreak, Lesser Marbled Fritillary, and Southern White Admiral. The rivers are lined with thin patches of calcareous marsh, where Robust Marsh-orchid and Common Twayblade grow.

5 Between Lusera and Nocito you traverse a wild gorge with cliffs, scrub and pine woods.

Just before Nocito, you come to a fork. The route continues left towards Molino de Villobas (green sign). Alternatively, continue to Nocito for coffee (only in summer) or to further penetrate the northern Guara. The road continues through excellent habitat to Bara, which is with its surroundings of flowery fields a very good area for butterflies.

6 Winding up the Sierra, you arrive at a cattle grid next to the river. In summer, there is Robust Marsh-orchid and Marsh Helleborine, growing in a calcareous marsh with Yellow Sedge. The

Old pollarded oaks remind of the days that this nearly deserted area was inhabited.

same stream can be explored when you drive further up. You can park at the mountain pass where, at 1,215 metres, you are in the middle of the Hedgehog Broom scrub and have excellent views of the *Depresión*, Oroel and San Juan de la Peña (Route 12).
The route continues as a rough, but well maintained, track down to the river Guarga. The track is safe to drive except after heavy rain or snow. Turn left once you reach the main road.

7 After about a km, you arrive at Molino de Villobas. Turn left at the bend of the road (just beyond the sign Molino de Villobas, but before the houses), and park on the side of the track. Walk over to the River Guarga and its wide pebble strewn floodplain. This is again an excellent point to look for butterflies and dragonflies such as Copper Demoiselle, White Featherleg and Small Pincertail.

Continue along the road, making stops to check the river, until you come to the E7. Turn left to return to Arguis.

The banks of the small rivers that drain the Guara mountains form a special habitat of damp chalk grasslands (left). The Robust Marsh-orchid (top right) and Marsh Helleborine (bottom right) are two of the orchids to be found here.

Other sites in the *Sierras Exteriores* and *Somontano*

For locations of these sites, see map on page 138.

7 – The Río Vero gorge

4 hours – moderate

This adventurous yet well-maintained trail offers dramatic views, rich birdlife and an abundance of wildflowers, butterflies, and dragonflies. The hike begins at a large, unshaded parking area along the A-2205 road (GPS: 42.219632, 0.045380), 13.3 km north of Colungo. Be aware that there's another car park at 11.6 km from Colungo — don't mistake it for the trailhead.

From the car park you follow the signs for the Ruta de Las Escalateras. The trail first leads into the gorge where you'll wade through the river twice — about knee-deep — before reaching Las Escalaretas, a steep ascent over well-maintained boardwalks and steps that lead to caves adorned with prehistoric drawings. From here, you can either return the way you came or continue walking along a well-equipped but slightly exposed via ferrata — a climbing route with metal fittings, manageable for most hikers with a head for heights.

The dry, sun-baked plateaux contrast sharply with the gorge's cool, lush microclimate. Up on the plateau, there are various species of warblers and Short-toed Eagles, while Griffon and Egyptian Vultures, Rock Martins and Alpine Swifts soar along the cliffs — especially visible at las escalaretas, where they often pass at eye level. The walk is great for wildflowers. In May, we found Woodcock Orchid, Blue Aphyllanthes, Beautiful, Upright Yellow and White Flaxes, White Rockrose and Large-flowered Meadow-rue grow here, drawing many butterflies, such as Provence Orange-tip, Black-eyed Blue, Red-underwing Skipper and Glanville Fritillary.

In the gorge below - a true oasis - Southern White Admiral and many Blues gather at the water's edge, while Common Goldenring dragonflies patrol the stream. The rare Robust Marsh Orchid and Marsh Helleborine also grow here.

Reserve half a day for this walk. Although you have to wade through the river and follow a trail that clings to the bare rock, we consider this an easy to moderately difficult walk.

Long-leaved Saxifrage, a common and conspicuous endemic of the Pyrenees and nearby mountains.

The Mirror Orchid is a rare species that grows close to the road at Bierge (site 8).

8 – The Mascún Gorge and Otín heights

8 hours, strenuous

The ancient name Mascún indicates that demons and mythological creatures live in this deep, spectacular valley. Today, chances are higher of an encounter with those equally strange creatures, climbers, and demonic looking feral goats.

This spectacular, but strenuous walk takes you deep into the Guara mountains. From the village of Rodellar, you first descend into the gorge, cross a stream twice (which can be a problem when the water level is high) before arriving at a junction of ravines. Take the left ravine and follow the signs to Otín. This abandoned hamlet lies at 1050 metres amidst the Yellow Hedgehog Broom* *(Echinospartum horridum)*, flowering in abundance in late June and July. From Otín follow the red-white signs of GR 1, until it turns to the north and you need to follow the trail to the southwest towards Rodellar.

9 – The Somontano road

The serpentine road that connects the sites at Roldán and Vadiello (route 10) with Alquézar (route 9) and Bierge (site 10 below) is an experience in itself. It runs through a patchwork terrain of wild sandstone hills clad in scrubby Holm Oak woodland alternating with small fields and almond groves. It is great for birdwatching, with Hoopoes, Bee-eaters, Corn, Cirl and Rock Buntings, Short-toed Eagles, all vultures (including Lammergeier)... basically anything is possible. Orchids are frequent along the roadside, and any stop and stroll into the scrub may yield interesting wildflowers, butterflies and reptiles.

If you wish, continue along this road beyond Alquézar towards Colungo and up to Boltaña as it just remains spectacular.

10 – Along Río Alcanadre at Bierge

1-4 hours, easy-moderate

This linear route follows yet another river gorge, but is a much easier walk. It stands out for its wealth of wildflowers and Mediterranean songbirds. From Bierge, drive in the direction Aguas and after 1.5 km, park on the large car park beneath the restaurant next to the river. The trail leaves from the car park and first follows the east bank. Further on, it climbs up to follow a ridge above the river. The itinerary ends after 5 km at a well, called *Fuente la Tamara.*

Dartford, Subalpine, Sardinian and Orphean Warbler all occur, and there is a chance of Lammergeier, Egyptian Vulture, Booted and Short-toed Eagles. Plants include Silver-lined Broom* (*Argyrolobium zanonii*; a small, yellow, clover-like plant), Round-leaved Restharrow, Rosemary Broomrape and various orchids. For the latter, walk the short track from the bridge down to the river on the west bank. On this perhaps 200 metre stretch, we saw Dull Bee and Early Spider Orchids, Violet Bird's-nest and, although only few plants, the rare Mirror Orchid (at the beginning of the trail on the right side).

11 – Las Gorgas de San Julian

1.5 hours, easy

The small canyon of Gorgas de San Julian is one of those spectacular 'secret places' in the *Sierras Exteriores.* It is a deep and narrow gorge of reddish sandstone. Peregrine and Red-billed Chough breed, but it is the sublimity of this confined scenery that is the real attraction.

From the Huesca – Sabiñánigo road, take the exit to Arascués, 12 km north of Huesca, and turn right just before entering the village. Proceed to the other end of the *urbanization Guara Golf,* park and follow the signs *San Julian.* A 45 minute walk through Mediterranean scrubland brings you to the gap in the cliffs, which marks the beginning of the gorge.

Beautiful Flax (left) and Spanish Chalkhill Blue (top) are both common around Agüero (site 14).

12 – Holm Oak forest *Carrascal de Nisano*

The original vegetation of the *Somontano* and parts of the Monegros consists of a more or less open Holm Oak forest, patches of which can be found all over the *Somontano*. The greatest area of original Holm Oak forest lies just northeast of the city of Huesca. This *carrascal*, as the Spanish call it, is about 4 × 1.5 km and gives an impression of what the landscape looked like centuries ago.
From Bastarás village it is 2 km to the southern limit, walk to the right following the sign *Campamento de Igriés*. It is another 2,5 km to the northern limit, where a track crosses the road to a farmhouse to the right. To the left stands, isolated in the field, a huge Holm Oak, which is officially catalogued for its size.

13 – Loarre Castle

GPS: 42.32766, -0.61113. The impressive Loarre Castle, strategically located on the southern slopes of the Pyrenees (1,278 m), overlooks the Ebro Valley. Being the best preserved Romanesque castle in Spain, it receives more than 100.000 visitors a year. The natural surroundings are also impressive. Many birds hide in the crevices of its walls and in the nearby rocks and scrub vegetation, unnoticed by most visitors. Crag Martin, Red-billed Chough, Black Redstart and Rock Sparrow breed in the castle walls. Explore the immediate surroundings of the castle to find Rock and Ortolan Buntings, Red-backed Shrike and Rock Thrush. Alpine Accentor often visits in winter. The warm mountain slope forms a conveyer belt of hot air, along which Lammergeier, Egyptian Vulture and Short-toed Eagle glide effortlessly. Along the tracks that run east and north from the car park, butterflies as the Apollo, Silver-washed Fritillary can be found in late spring and summer.
Loarre castle is reached from a junction near Loarre village and is well signposted. An entrance fee is charged (see castillodeloarre.es). A visit is easily combined with a walk around the Mallos de Riglos (route 11).

Mallos de Agüero.

14 – Mallos de Agüero

GPS: 42.35309, -0.79319. GPS: 42.35309, -0.79319. The village of Aguëro is away from the usual bird and wildlife routes, on the edge of the uninhabited Sierra de Santo Domingo. Its reddish pinnacles of conglomerate rock (*Mallos*) are impressive, although not as spectacular as those of Riglos (route 11). The vegetation and the species are similar to those of Riglos, and with Agüero being much less visited, this may well the more rewarding of the two, if you want to look for wildlife peacefully. The birdlife is one of Agüero's attractions, with lots of Griffon Vultures and both Egyptian Vulture and Lammergeier being frequent. Wall Creeper winters, and Dartford Warbler, Blue Rock Thrush, Rock Sparrow and Red-billed Chough are frequent.

In spring and summer there are many butterflies to be found, especially near the streams that flow around the Mallos. The Mediterranean Two-tailed Pasha lives here thanks to the presence of Strawberry Trees. This spectacular species is here at the edge of its range and not common in Huesca. Look for it along the road to the abandoned village of San Felices. Other frequent species are Spanish Chalkhill and Adonis Blues, Spanish Ilex Hairstreak, Cleopatra, Spanish and Southern Gatekeepers, Western Marbled White and Southern Admiral. Botanically, Coris, Leuzia, Stehellina, and Pyramidal, Southern Marsh and Dull Bee Orchid stand out.

There is a trail that loops around the Mallos (3.1 km; 225m altitude gain), on which most of the above can be found. Note that the slope is south-facing and that there is little shade. Just west of the village is a small stream that is worth checking out, whilst the dirt road that continues to San Felice (3 km) is where Pasha is most often seen.

Agüero is reached from a junction on the A-132, 9 km north of Ayerbe.

Vulture watching in the Sierras Exteriores

One of the most spectacular wildlife activities in the Sierras Exteriores is witnessing vultures as they are being fed. There are several places where you can watch this. For more information, see page 233.

Vulture watching at Santa Cilia.

High Pyrenees and *Depresión*

The high Pyrenees stretch out all along the French-Spanish border. The range looks somewhat like a spinal cord running west to east. To extend that metaphor, various ranges run like ribs in a north-south direction, and often curve to the east or west when reaching the spine of the mountains. The 'ribs' end in the hilly *Depresión*, where most of the major (but still small) towns are located (e.g. Jaca, Sabiñánigo, Fiscal, Aínsa and Campo). Here lies the only east-west road link, the N-260 or *Eje Pyrenaica* – the Pyrenean axis.

As a direct result of this topography, a visit to the Pyrenees always departs from one of these north-to-south valleys. Travelling from one valley to another is not always easy, because you always need to return to one of these towns, before taking the N-260 to the next valley.

Each valley offers at least several excellent day trips, so assuming you have a limited number of days at your disposal, making a choice as to which valleys to visit, is unavoidable.

This choice is not easy, since all of the valleys sport excellent mountain

Top: on the edge of the Ordesa canyon (site 25 on page 210).
Below: Overview of the high Pyrenees. In black are the locations of the routes and in blue are the sites described on the pages that follow.

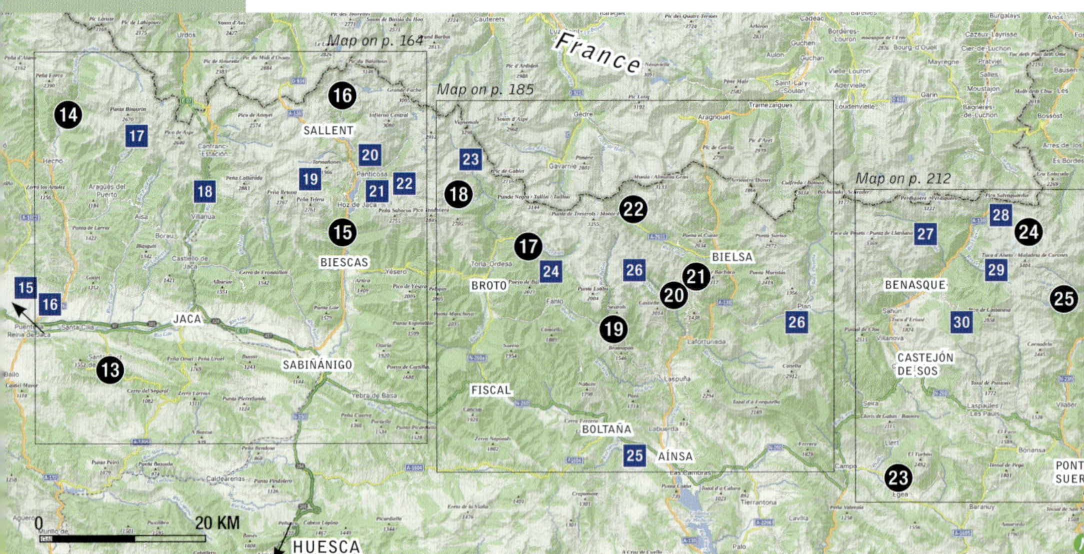

Choice of Starting points

To give an idea of which area of the Pyrenees to focus on, here is a description of routes / sites can be easily accessed from the four major starting points in the Pyrenees in Huesca.

Western valleys of Jaca / Sabiñánigo – facing page
San Juan de la Peña (route 13): sub-Mediterranean orchids, butterflies; birds of old forest.
Hecho Valley (route 14): green valley in original state, large old forests, good birdwatching, many orchids.
Tena Valley (route 15): Access to high areas (see also sites 19-22), many orchids.
Las Sarra (route 16): strenuous but spectacular walk, great for wildflowers and butterflies.
Not far to Mallos de Riglos, northern Guara and Roldán (routes 10-12).

Ordesa – western part from Torla – page 185
Ordesa valley (route 17): The most famous and spectacular of all the glacial gorges, excellent for all flora and fauna, including mammals like chamois, rather busy in summer.
Bujaruelo valley (route 18): Open, glacial U-shaped valley, excellent birdwatching.
Ara valley (sites 23 and 25): the most natural of the larger rivers in the area.
Bus trip to Ordesa's high plateau (site 24 on page 209): butterflies, birds and wildflowers of high altitudes, stunning views.

Ordesa – eastern part from Aínsa – page 184
Añisclo Gorge (route 17): superb, narrow gorge, great wildflowers, busy in summer.
Escuaín and Revilla (routes 20 and 21): slightly wider but equally spectacular gorge. Best place to see Lammergeier.
Bus trip to Ordesa's high plateau (site 24 on page 209): butterflies, birds and wildflowers of high altitudes, stunning views.
Pineta (route 22): splendid alpine scenery of glacial cirque, good for butterflies, busy in summer.
Plan (site 26, page 211): Original valley, subalpine forest, rich in butterflies and amphibians.
Turbon (route 23): Mediterranean habitat of the *Depresión*, great for butterflies and wildflowers.
Not far to Colungo road (site 7 on page 157) and Alquézar (route 9).

Benasque – Castejón de Sos – page 212
Benasque valleys (route 24 and sites 27-30): Great alpine habitat of all altitudes, excellent for hiking, wildflower watching and searching for butterflies.
Llauset (route 25): highest possible area to be reached easily. Great for birds, butterflies and wildflowers of high altitudes.
Turbon (route 23): Mediterranean habitat of the *Depresión*, great for butterflies and wildflowers.

habitat. They all start as broad, lowland valleys with fields, Mediterranean type scrublands and evergreen woodlands of Holm and Portuguese Oak. Subsequently there are pine forests, beech-fir forests, subalpine heathlands and stands of Pyrenean Pine, which give way to alpine meadows above the treeline, with mountain lakes (*Ibóns*) and rocky areas. There are rivers, gorges and cliffs at all possible altitudes. As for which valley(s) to explore, as so often, the devil is in the detail. Our aim in this book is to present the information to allow you to explore maximum diversity of habitats and wildlife. This will make your choices clearer, if not always easier (see box on page 166).

Broadly, there are three different areas to explore. First, there are the western valleys situated above Jaca and Sabiñánigo, which are green and moist due to Atlantic influences. Then there is the central limestone area of Ordesa-Monte Perdido, with its impressive gorges. And finally, there is the eastern section which is dominated by the giant massifs of Posets and Aneto – the highest peaks of the Pyrenees.

Apart from these three sections of the Pyrenees, there is another area outside the main Pyrenean range. Towards the south, between the high Pyrenees and the *Sierras Exteriores* lies a broad area of lower mountains. This area is known as the *Depresión* and is somewhat comparable to the *Somontano*, being covered by open Oak forest and scrub. With a few exceptions, the land does not rise over 1,300 metres. Two routes explore this region: route 12 to San Juan de la Peña in the west, and route 21 at the foot of Turbón in the east.

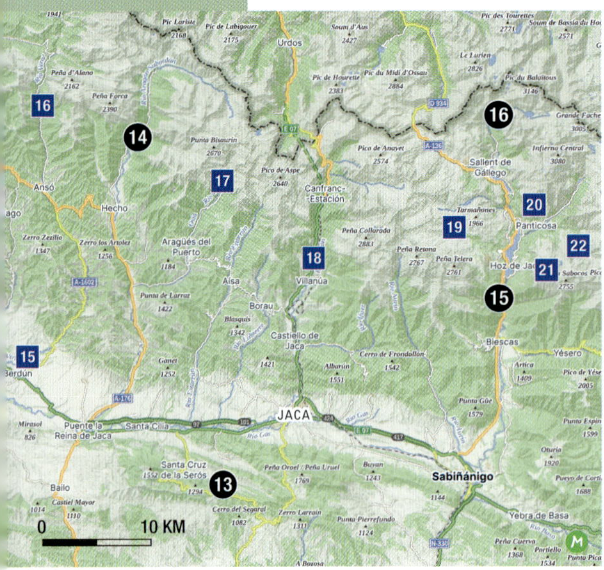

Overview of the western valleys. In black are the locations of the routes described on the facing page and further; in blue are the sites described on page 181-184.

The western valleys

The wide valley of Jaca and Sabiñago offers the widest range of options in the Pyrenees. Travel through the lowlands is easy, which makes it possible to visit various valleys from a single starting point – from Ansó in the west (see site B on page 181) to the Tena valley in the east (route 14). It is also just as easy to go down south to explore the more Mediterranean influenced nature of the *Depresión* and even the Guara (route 11) and Riglos (route 10).

In the following pages we describe several routes and suggest several more options to explore the mountains.

ROUTE 13: SAN JUAN DE LA PEÑA AND OROEL
64 KM + 11 KM WALK, 6 HOURS, EASY-MODERATE

Best season
June-July
Of interest
April-September

Forested isolated mountain in the centre of the Depresión. Good site for the flora and fauna of woodlands, high altitude scrub and for observing raptors.

Habitats: Scots pine and mixed forest, rock walls, hedgehog broom scrub
Selected species: Black Woodpecker, Crossbill, Lammergeier, Griffon Vulture, Citril Finch, Spanish Moon Moth, Apollo, Lady Orchid, Grass-leaved Buttercup

The isolated, flat-topped mountains of San Juan de la Peña and Oroel, just below Jaca, are a particularly resistant chunk of conglomerate rock. Although officially part of the *Depresión* between the two Pyrenean ranges, San Juan de la Peña and Oroel are with 1546 and 1770 metres respectively serious mountains.

San Juan de la Peña is well-known because of the old monasteries on the top of the mountain which attract visitors all year round. But the mountain is equally worth visiting for its splendid natural attractions. The top and the north slope are covered in mature Scots Pine forest (in places mixed with Beech) which were protected as early as 1927. No wonder that this area is excellent for birds of old forests, such as Black Woodpecker and Crossbill.

Another attraction is the hedgehog broom scrubland, with its many

The plateau of San Juan de la Peña with Oroel in the back.

butterflies, and the dazzling views from the isolated mountain tops – excellent too for watching vultures.

This route comprises a car drive with stops over the mountain of San Juan de la Peña and a 3 hour walk around the monasteries.

Starting point: Jaca.

Drive west along the N-240 towards Puente la Reina and turn left for Santa Cruz de la Serós and San Juan de la Peña. Beyond Santa Cruz (look for Lady Orchid at the roadside near the village) the road climbs up the mountain. Stop at the viewpoint half way up.

1 Beside a splendid vista over the Pyrenees, look out for flying Lammer-geier, Griffon and Egyptian Vultures, Short-toed and Golden Eagle and Honey Buzzard. Look too at vultures breeding on the ridges below. On your left you see a typical feature of the Pyrenees: Beech forests on the shady north slopes of the mountain.

Continue and park at the designated car park at the monastery.

2 The forest at the car park and further along the route has breeding Black Woodpecker, Crossbill, Short-toed Treecreeper, Bullfinch and Coal and Crested Tits.

Take the broad footpath on the right side of the monastery towards the *Balcón de los Pirineos.*

3 The *Balcón de los Pirineos* is yet another excellent viewpoint, a bit higher still, with similar birds as the previous, with addition of Alpine Swift. Grass-leaved Buttercup, Yellow Hedgehog Broom* (*Echinospartum horridum*), and Long-flowered Valerian flower on the cliff edge.

The trail continues to the left. At a crossroads, follow the signs *San Voto,* crossing the paved road and turning right to reach the small San Voto chapel, with yet another viewpoint overlooking the old monastery.

San Juan de la Peña is a Mecca for butterfly enthusiasts. Apollos are frequent on the plateau.

4 The mixed forest contains a fair amount of dead wood, making it suitable for forest birds mentioned in point one. This is also the habitat of the superb, but extremely rare, Spanish Moon Moth (p.171), for which there are only few records in this region. Citril Finch may be seen near the forest edge.
Turn left at San Voto to reach a small paved road closed to traffic. It leads to San Salvador and the radio tower at the highest point of the San Juan de la Peña mountain.

5 This is an excellent area for butterflies, even though the spiny Hedgehog Broom vegetation makes venturing away from the road a precarious undertaking. Keep your eyes out for Apollo butterflies, Wood White, Cardinal, Queen-of-Spain Fritillary and Piedmont Ringlet.

At the radio tower, turn left and walk along the cliff edge back to the car park.

6 The views from the radio tower and along the trail downwards are breathtaking. In clear weather you see the *Depresión* all around you with the *Sierras Exteriores* to the south-east and the high Pyrenees in the north. The cliffs of Riglos should just be visible to the south. This is the best spot to get an accurate appreciation of the general geology of the Spanish Pyrenees. Wild Tulip grows along the trail and similar butterflies can be expected here as on the way over to the radio tower.

The last bit of the route crosses the grassy area surrounding the new monastery. Keep your eyes open because it is often here that some last minute excellent sightings are being made. The flowery forest edges are good for butterflies and there are a few Green-winged Orchids here

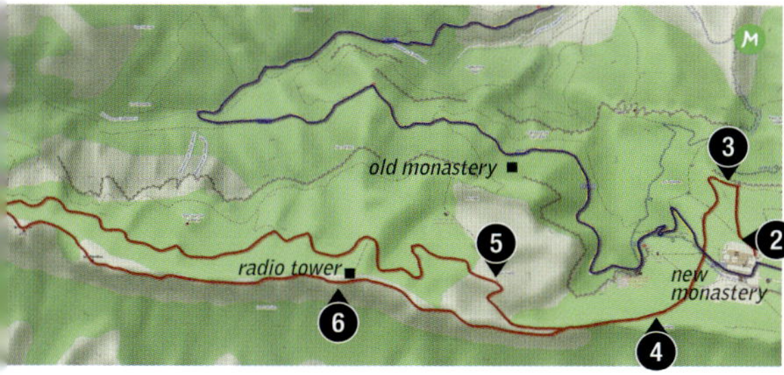

Common Spotted-orchid with Wood White at Oroel.

in May. Citril Finches are not uncommon, while Black Woodpeckers or Crossbills may pass over from one woodland to the next.

Continue by car until you come to the junction near the village of Bernués where you turn left.

7 Along this road there are many tempting places to stop and stroll along the road or venture into the open woodland. There are plenty of butterflies here, and numerous orchids. A little searching should unveil, in season, Lady, Early Spider, Woodcock, Fly, Fragrant, Pyramidal and Greater Butterfly Orchids.

Beyond the mountain pass *Puerto Oroel*, turn right onto a small, potholed road after 2 km beyond the pass, signposted Parador de Oroel (easy to miss though, as the sign is placed to be viewed when coming from the other direction). Stop at the restaurant Parador Oroel.

8 From the Parador a long and strenuous trail heads for the top of Oroel mountain. This climb is for another day, but it is worth walking it for a short distance to get a taste of the area. Being heavily wooded with pines, this is another good area for Black Woodpecker, Crested Tit and Crossbill. The acidic conglomerate soil means that the flora is limited, but there are plenty of Common Spotted Orchid, Common Columbine, Round-leaved Bedstraw and, between the mosses, Serrated Wintergreen.

The extremely elusive Moon Moth is a rarity of the pine forests.

Continue by car over the small road through more excellent pine forests, with windows wound down to hear more birds. At the junction, turn left to return to Jaca.

ROUTE 14: THE HECHO VALLEY

43 KM ONE WAY + 1.9, 2.7 AND 7.4 KM WALKS, FULL DAY

The most densely wooded and most verdant of the Pyrenean valleys. One of the better routes to find Lammergeier and Wallcreeper.

Habitats: mountain slopes with mixed forest, gorges and alpine meadows
Selected species: Elder-flowered Orchid, Pyrenean Dragon's-mouth, Trumpet Gentian, Bird's-nest Orchid, Brown Bear, Chamois, Alpine Marmot, Lammergeier, Black Woodpecker, Wallcreeper, Red-backed Shrike, Citril Finch, Marbled Skipper, Purple Emperor, Alcon Blue, Provencal Fritillary, Mountain Ringlet, Piedmont Ringlet, Pyrenees Brassy Ringlet

Best season
May-July
Of interest
May-October

The upper part of the Valle de Hecho

The Hecho Valley is, along with the side valley of the Ansó (site B on page 181), the westernmost valley described in this book and and, compared to the other valleys, has a distinctly Atlantic character. This expresses itself in the presence of the impressive old beech and silver fir forest of Selva de Oza. Just beyond this forest lies a wide glacial (U-shaped) valley, which is one of the more unspoilt and wild valleys of the entire Pyrenees. The grazing of cattle, which is disappearing throughout the mountains, is still important here and, as a result, the meadows are orchid and bird rich. Hecho is one of the best valleys to see three of the most sought-after Pyrenean birds: Wallcreeper, Lammergeier and Citril

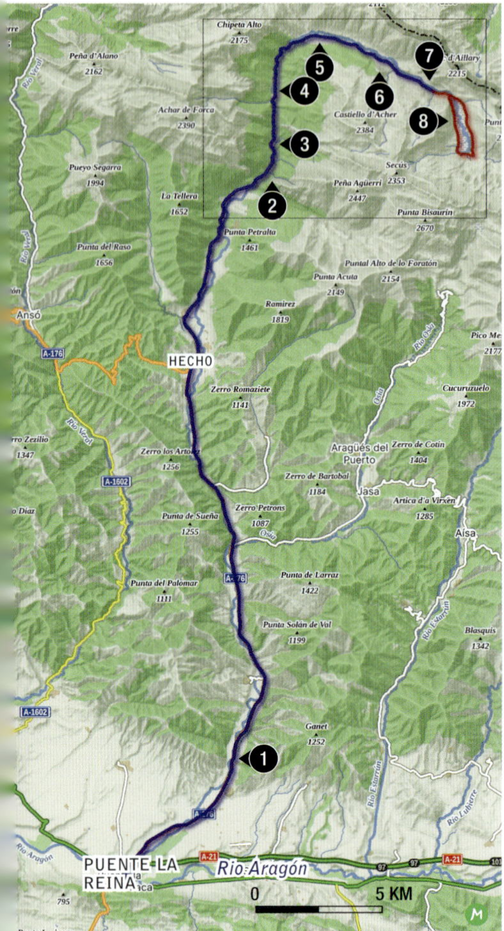

Finch. One can spend several days in Hecho and its side valleys. Here, we describe the best spots as a single day trip, and recommend other walks and sites for those who make the wise decision to spend more time here.

Starting point: Puente la Reina. Go north in direction Hecho.

1 The valley begins gently with fields and wooded hills. Black and Red Kites are frequent, but look out too for Honey Buzzard and Booted Eagle. Lady Orchid is frequent along the roadside. To the left, there are good examples of the silk-like blue clay with its typical erosion gullies (see geology section on page 16).
Beyond Hecho, keep an eye open for Red-backed Shrike, which breeds in the hedgerows. Five km beyond Hecho, just after the Natural Park entrance sign, turn right to Gabardito and follow the winding road up.

2 The bar Gabardito is situated in a pasture meadow and surrounded by forest and rocky cliffs. Citril Finch, Crossbill and Black Woodpecker occur in the woodland right around the building.
Follow the trail that goes right from the refuge. Walk on for about 20 minutes (approx. 800m) through the forest until you reach a bare rock face, currently the best place to see Wallcreeper during the breeding season.

Return to the main road and turn right.

3 After 1.5 km, you reach the Boca el Infierno (Hell's Mouth), an impressive gorge. This used to be the place to find Wallcreeper could be found but the bird seems to have disappeared here. It is nonetheless a beautiful spot for a stop, with Grey Wagtail and Dipper breeding along the river, and Long-leaved Saxifrage (p. 165) growing on the cliffs on the other side of the tunnel.

Continue along the increasingly spectacular road. A few kilometres further into the valley you cross the river. Park on the other side. From

The odd, silk-like blue clays are soft sediments brought down by the Pyrenean rivers. They occur in broad Pyrenean valleys such as near Puente la Reina.

here you can make a short (2-3 hour, moderately demanding) walk through the Selva de Oza.

4 The 'primeval' forest of Oza is probably the best preserved large woodland expanse of the central Spanish Pyrenees, extending westwards all the way into the Ansó valley. It is a refuge for the Brown Bear in the Spanish Pyrenees and the only place in the Aragonese Pyrenees where there is a remote chance of finding the old-growth forest specialist, the White-backed Woodpecker (better sites in Ansó valley). Forest dwelling bats include Greater and Common Noctules, Savi's Pipistrelle, and Leisler's and Barbastelle Bats. Chances of finding (let alone identifying) these species without a bat detector are remote, to put it mildly, but they are the 'quality mark' of the ancient Beech and Fir forest of Selva de Oza. Black Woodpecker is a much likelier species to encounter amongst the ancient trees, and there are a number of interesting wildflowers, including Bird's-nest Orchid and Small-leaved Helleborine. On open spots, look out for butterflies like Purple Emperor, White Admiral, Camberwell Beauty and Silver-washed Fritillary.

Of the various hiking options in the Selva de Oza, we recommend the circuit

The Elder-flowered Orchid has two very distinctive colour forms, which is why, in some languages, it is called Adam and Eve. The red form is the rarest, but in the upper Hecho valley, both occur in abundance.

Boca del Infierno (right).
The Ortolan Bunting (bottom) is a fairly rare breeding bird of shrubby terrain around the tree limit.

starting at the picnic spot at the river and following the direction Castillo de Archer. After about half an hour, in a bend to the left, take the small path to the right, signposted Oza (Small-leaved Helleborine flowers on this trail in July). Crossing some excellent streams, this path eventually brings you back to the road. Turn right to return to the picnic spot. Allow 3 hours for this moderately demanding walk.

Continue (either by car or on foot) further up the valley.

5 You go through a thick beech and fir forest, which gradually opens up when you go around the bend. The meadows here are full of orchids between mid-May and early July. There are Elder-flowered, Greater Butterfly, Early-purple, Burnt, Common Spotted, Frog and Fragrant here. In the scattered bushes, look out for Red-backed Shrike, Yellowhammer and, less commonly, Ortolan Bunting.
Park at the barrier and continue on foot (an easy walk of about 3 hours or more if you wish).

6 At the barrier and beyond, keep your eyes open for Lammergeier. A pair breeds nearby and they very often cruise along the valley here. Further ahead, Red-billed Choughs breed in the conspicuous rocky 'mount' in the middle of the valley. Marmots are frequent in rocky areas throughout the walk.

7 At the end of the valley the track winds up a cliff (it remains an easy walk, though). This area is excellent for wildflowers. Pyrenean Lousewort, Pyrenean Dragon's-mouth, Pyrenean Honeysuckle, Parsley Fern and Trumpet Gentian are a few of the more eye-catching species here. Perched on the rocks are Linnet, Common Rock Thrush, Dunnock and Black Redstart. Keep looking up for Lammergeier.

8 By the cliff sits the last farm in the Hecho valley. Beyond it a trail continues through a very wide and level valley through which a river quietly meanders. This is the Valle de las Aguas Tuertas, or 'Valley of the twisted Waters'. The river has taken advantage of the broad plain valley bottom, which is typical of glacial valleys. The river twisted and meandered over the entire valley, depositing a peaty soil. There are large numbers of Broad-leaved Marsh-orchids here, and the landscape is superb, with birdlife similar to that at points 6 and 7.
You can continue along the trail for hours, but if you made all the stops described in this route, you probably ought to be heading back.

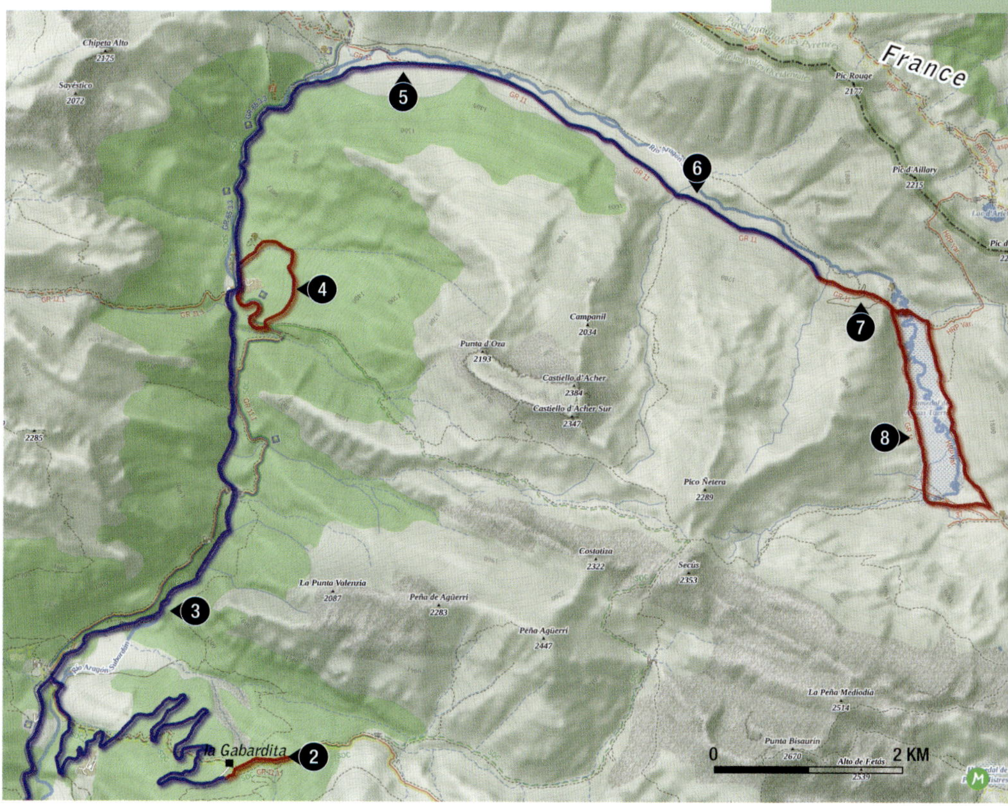

ROUTE 15: THE TENA VALLEY AND EL PORTALET

68 KM + 2.6 AND 6.5 KM WALKS, EASY-MODERATE

Best season
May-July
Of interest
May-October

A diverse valley, with excellent alpine pastures and hay meadows. Some of the best places for butterflies and wildflowers, including many orchids.

Habitats: alpine and hay meadows, lakes and rivers, forests and rocky outcrops
Selected species Dragon's-mouth, Pyrenean Fritillary, Pyrenean Honeysuckle, Vanilla Orchid, Lady's-slipper, Marmot, Chamois, Red Kite, Common Rock Thrush, Black Woodpecker, Dipper, Red-backed Shrike, Alpine Chough, Ortolan Bunting, Asp Viper, Glandon Blue, Eros Blue, Purple Emperor, Western Brassy Ringlet, Piedmont Ringlet

Ibón de Piedrafita (top), home to the Pyrenean Brook Newt (facing page).

The Valle de Tena stretches from the town of Sabiñánigo up to the French border. The main attractions are the alpine meadows, flowery hay-meadows and bushy terrain. Further down are extensive pine and mixed forests. The main river, the Río Gállego, has its source near the French border.
The Tena valley is, with the exception of the Canfranc valley (which we do not describe in detail), the most developed of the Aragonese Pyrenees. The sizable communities of Biescas, Panticosa, Sallent de Gállego and

Formigal are based around extensive ski slopes and the Gállego river (in the main valley) is dammed at various points.
In spite of these scars on the landscape, there is a lot to discover in the Tena valley. Moreover, the infrastructure that comes with these developments makes access to higher areas much easier. In comparison with the other valleys, the Tena valley is distinguished as an area for wildflowers and butterflies. In late May and June the number of orchids is amazing and includes one of the few Spanish populations of Lady's-slipper. The Tena valley is also a good place for amphibians and reptiles, including the endemic Pyrenean Brook Newt in clean and cold brooks and the Pyrenean Rock Lizard in the highest ranges.
There are many excellent day walks in the valley, like the ones we describe under sites 19-22. The main route, which we describe in detail here, gives an excellent overview of what the area has to offer.

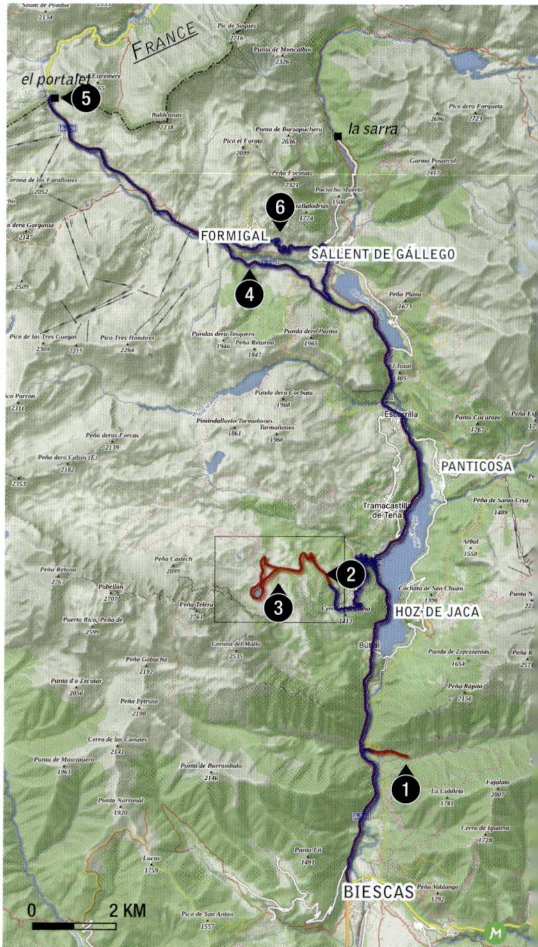

Starting point: Biescas

Follow the A136 northwards. After 4 km turn right towards Dolmen de Santa Ana. Park at the barrier near the Dolmen and walk the track into the forest.

1 The pine forest supports Firecrest, Black Woodpecker and Bullfinch (here at the edge of its range). Along the track you can find Black Pea and Lange's Orchid – an orchid species that is endemic to the Iberian Peninsula. Deeper in the forest, the track turns into a trail and gradually becomes more difficult to follow.

Return (by car) to the main road and continue up the valley. Beyond Bubal, turn left towards Piedrafita. Continue through the village, park at the Lacuniacha animal

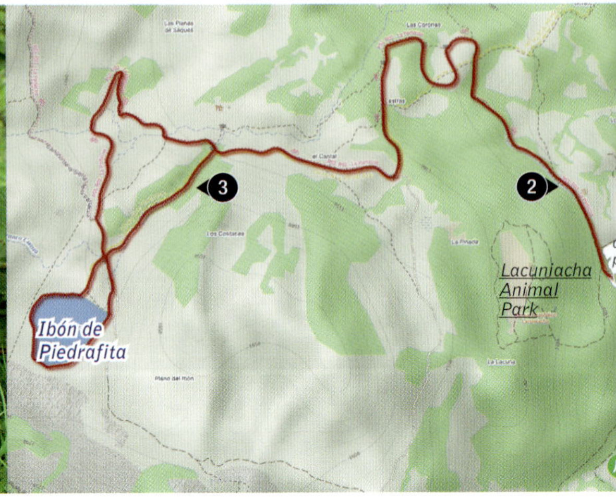

Lady's Slipper is very rare in the Pyrenees. One of the few places where it grows is near Formigal (point 4).

park (parking costs are € 5.00 in 2025) and continue the track beyond the barrier on foot. This gentle walk should take about 3-4 hours including stops for observation.

2 The walk starts in a well-developed Scots pine forest and continues through flowery meadows with juniper scrub. In May and June there is an enormous number of orchids here, primarily Common Spotted, Fragrant, Elder-flowered, Early-purple and Greater Butterfly Orchids. In June and all through summer, this is an excellent area for butterflies, with species including Mountain Clouded Yellow, Purple-shot and Purple-edged Coppers, Turquoise Blue, Alcon Blue, Eros Blue, Dark Green Fritillary and Twin-spot Fritillary.

Follow the signs for Ibón de Piedrafita. After 2.6 km, turn left at the fast-flowing stream and follow the small path to get to the mountain lake.

3 Look along the stream for Pyrenean Brook Newt. The mountain lake is overshadowed by a massive mountain range – a spectacular site. There are Marmots here and, with luck, you may see Chamois. The lake and surroundings are also home to Spiny and Midwife Toads (look for tadpoles), Grass Frog, Wall Lizard, while Asp Viper and Smooth Snake are present in the Alpine meadows.

Walk around the lake, crossing the stream and following the path and after 200 m turn right on the junction with the little peatland filled with Bogbean. The track returns to the car park.

Return to the A136 in the Tena Valley and turn left.

4 The entire road between Formigal and the French border is excellent for wildflowers of alpine meadows (with many orchids, including Pale, Fragrant, Frog, Vanilla, Burnt, Broad-leaved Marsh, Greater Butterfly, Elder-flowered and Heath-spotted). At km 20, opposite Formigal, there is a car park, from which, between mid-May and June, there are short, free guided botanical excursion to find, amongst others, the Lady's-slipper Orchids (highly recommended!).

5 At the El Portalet pass, park and follow the trail to the right which starts at the border. The alpine meadows above El Portalet support enormous numbers of generally rare, and often endemic, wildflowers such as Pyrenean Fritillary (by the thousands), Pyrenean Dragon's-mouth, Pyrenean Lousewort, Narcissus-flowered Anemone, Pyrenean Honeysuckle, Vanilla Orchid, Spring Squill, Gouan's Buttercup, Clasping Buttercup* (Ranunculus amplexicaulis), Alpine and Spring Gentians and many more. Apollo is frequently seen and Water Pipit, Black Redstart, Rock Thrush, Ortolan Bunting, Whinchat, Yellowhammer and Alpine Chough breed here. There is also a large population of Asp Viper.
In winter, El Portalet is frequented by birds of the highest reaches of the Pyrenees, such as Snowfinch and Alpine Accentor.

Pyrenean Fritillary grows in large numbers on the Col de Portalet (top). The solitary Peña Foratata is a conspicuous landscape feature in much of the Tena valley (bottom).

Return through Formigal and take the old road to Sallent de Gállego.

6 Flowery hay meadows make this a lovely stretch, excellent for butterflies such as Marbled Skipper, Apollo, Geranium Argus, Glandon and Eros Blue and De Prunner's, Spanish Brassy and Piedmont Ringlet. If you have the time, you can visit La Sarra, where one of the finest butterfly walks in the entire Pyrenees starts (see point E on page 182).

Return to Biescas via the same road.

ROUTE 16: THE VALLEY OF LA SARRA

6.8 KM ONE WAY, 6 HOURS, MODERATE-STRENUOUS

Long but rewarding walk up to a high mountain valley
Superb butterflies (especially near the starting point)
Rich route for wildflowers.

Habitats: hay meadows, pine wood, beech forest, subalpine heath
Selected species: Marmot, Citril Finch, Bullfinch, Pyrenean Iris, Pyrenean Lily, Globeflower, Pyrenean Columbine, Pyrenean Rampion, Alpenrose, Adonis Blue, Meleager's Blue, Pearl-bordered Fritillary, Piedmont Ringlet

The Rospumosa reservoir.

La Sarra is a side valley of the Tena Valley (see previous route). A beautiful, long walk can be made from the reservoir just above the village of Sallent de Gállego (1460m) all the way up to the reservoir of Respumoso at 2100m, which is known for its stunning blue colour.
This walk leads through an increasingly wild Alpine landscape with a superb flora and many butterflies.
Note that you can tailor your walk according to your interests. If you come to look for wildflowers, the scenery or simply because you enjoy a nice walk, the route as described is perfect. If your interest lies primarily with the butterflies, you may want to consider a much shorter walk towards the first bridge and back via the other side since this area holds the greatest butterfly diversity.

Starting point: La Sarra Reservoir

As you drive into the village of Sallent de Gállego along the main road, turn sharply left at a small chapel, where the road bends to the right. Among the many trails signposted here is Refugio de Respumoso. Continue for 1 km and in a hairpin bend to the left, go straight ahead. Continue for another 3km and park at the fat end of the reservoir.

On foot, continue and cross the river and follow the trail to the right. From now on, keep following signs to Refugio de Respumosa, ignoring all side trails.

1 The first section of the walk follows the river along now largely abandoned meadows with some woodland. The flowery grasslands are already excellent for butterflies. Purple Emperor, Rock Grayling, Lesser Marbled, Provencal and Meadow Fritillaries, and Eros, Alcon,

Meleager's and Osiris Blues are just a few of the species present here. The best spot is where the track passes directly alongside the river. many butterflies gather to suck up minerals from damp ground and dung patches. Plants at this spot include the large lousewort Pedicularis foliolosa, Great Masterwort and Globeflower. Orchids in this general area include Fragrant, Burnt-tip, Broad-leaved Marsh, Early Purple, common Spotted and Greater Butterfly Orchids.

A little further you pass a narrow footbridge. If you only want to do the short loop, this is the way to walk back. However, even then it is worth continuing a bit further, through a swing gate to more flowery grasslands with lots of butterflies.

Adonis Blue (top) and Pyrenean Lily (bottom) are just two of the highlights along this walk.

2 After the meadows, you continue through a forested section, first with pine and then later with Beech. In a few places, small rivers thunder down from the slopes. The forest is not continuous; many open patches provide habitat for different wildflowers. New wildflowers keep appearing, such as Bird's-nest Orchid, Small Wintergreen, Pyrenean Rampion (with large, pale-blue flowers) and the stout, yellow Vetch Lathyrus laevigatus.

3 After the large waterfall, the track bends to the east and enters a steep gorge. This is a particularly attractive part of the route. In open areas, check the nearly vertical slopes as it is here that the rare and very beautiful, yellow-flowering Pyrenean Lily grows. A few of them grow directly along the trail, but for the larger numbers, you need to look up. In the woodlands, Pyrenean Hyacinth and Pyrenean Squill grace the forest floor in spring.

4 The forest gives way to a wild landscape of scree and a subalpine 'heathland' with Alpenrose (Rhododendron) and Bearberry. Along the Wood Crane's-bill plants, look for the Geranium Argus, a butterfly that depends on crane's-bills.

5 The dam of the Respumosa reservoir now comes into view. The last kilometre or so before arriving there, the vegetation and its butterflies change once again. This is an Alpine meadow, with near the dam a few scattered pines. This is a good area to look for Citril Finch, as well as Chamois and Alpine Marmot. There are many butterflies here, including Piedmont Ringlet and Glandon Blue.

Return via the same path.

Additional walks and sites in the western valleys

For locations of these sites, see map on page 162.

15 – Berdún, Veral river

GPS: 42.609030, -0.858310. Close to the picturesque hilltop village of Berdún flows the Río Veral. Its crystal-clear meanders are hidden behind the foliage of a verdant riparian forest. It is a difficult-to-access and rarely visited place and therefore a small gem. The riparian forest forms a ribbon in the cultivated fields and unstable blue clay 'badlands' called Marga in Spanish.

The area holds an abundance of raptors and Mediterranean birds such as Tawny Pipit, Bee-eater, Rock Sparrow, Golden Oriole and European Turtle Dove. Groups of Red-billed chough come in winter from the high mountains to feed on the fields. The other wildlife is bound to be attractive too. Roe Deer, Otter, Badger, Red Fox, Montpellier Snake, Ladder Snake and Ocellated Lizard are known to occur in the area, but it must be good for Aesculapian Snake, whilst the habitat looks attractieve for Copper and Western Demoiselles, Western Spectre and Large Pincertail.

To get to the river turn off the main N240 onto the A1602 (direction Ansó). A bit further in the bend of the road, turn left between industrial warehouses. After crossing a Marga slope it arrives at the Veral river, park somewhere behind the bridge and explore the area.

A little further east, between Puente La Reina and Jaca, the road to Alastuey is also worth exploring, especially for those interested in birds, butterflies and dragonflies. The first kilometre of this road is the most rewarding.

16 – Ansó valley

From the village of Hecho, you can turn left towards the beautiful village of Ansó. In comparison to Hecho (and all other valleys in this book), the Ansó valley is more densely wooded and you can walk endlessly in old mountain forests comparable to those of Selva de Oza (point 4 of route 13). In the Ansó valley, the last indigenous Pyrenean Brown Bears roamed, and today it is one of the valleys where the bears from the French reintroduction project frequently turn up. If you want to explore the Ansó valley, we can recommend a drive up to Zuriza at the northern end of the valley and walk from there. In Ansó village is an interpretation centre devoted to the Brown Bear.

The Valley of Ansó was the last place of the Spanish Pyrenees where Brown Bears occurred. Now it is the first place where new animals are seen from the reintroductions in France.

17 – Aragües del Puerto

Up to full day, easy-strenuous

The pristine valley of Aragüés del Puerto (map on page 172) is an excellent place to enjoy mountain flowers – not in the least orchids. Their abundance is quite overwhelming around the Refuge of Lizara, situated at 1,540 m at the far end of the valley. In the last twists of the trail, before reaching the Refuge, there are a lot of Man and Lady Orchids by the roadside. In the meadows around the refuge Field Gentian is very common and there are about 10 species of orchid, including many Elder-flowered, Burnt and Fragrant.

We advise the walk up and to the right, towards the Bernera mountain pass (2,230 m), which sports a spectacular scenery and rich birdlife with Lammergeier, Wallcreeper and Snowfinch. Butterfly enthusiasts may expect, in season, Prunner's and Piedmont Ringlets, Berger's Clouded Yellow and Apollo.

18 – Las Guixas cave

Las Guixas, ('The Witches') is one of the few caves that can be visited in the Spanish Pyrenees. It is full of fanciful stalactites and stalagmites, formed during the glaciations of the Quaternary period, which are still evolving and changing due to the action of water. The remains of an old human habitation has been found. An important colony of bats inhabits the deeper parts. A path and steep steps have been constructed to give access to the first part of the cave. A guided visit takes about 30 minutes (€ 5.00 daily from July-September, otherwise at weekends only) and can be booked in the visitors' centre situated at the entrance of the cave at Villanúa.

19 – Ibon de Tramacastilla de Tena

Up to full day; easy

The mountain lake (Ibón) of Tramacastilla de Tena lies at almost 1700 metres in a superb area of Alpine meadows. The bedrock is acidic here, which translates into a mix of mountain heathlands, meadows and peaty slopes. The outflow of the lake is dammed, enlarging the original ibón, although its shores have remained largely natural and unspoiled. The flora is very attractive and somewhat similar to that of Piedrafita (route 15) which lies just across the valley from here. Catsfoot, Koch's Gentian, Elder-flowered, Greater Butterfly, Fragrant and Heath Spotted Orchid are all numerous. Scarce Copper, Piedmont Ringlet and Dark Green Fritillary may be found here.

The Ibón de Tramacastilla can be reached by car, which makes it a convenient starting point for hiking deeper into the mountains. Several

Ibón de Tramacastilla (site 19).

easy trails, remaining more or less level, allow you to explore the treeless Alpine meadows just below 2000m.
You reach the Ibón over a toll track (€9.- in 2025). Go north from Biescas in the direction of Col de Portalet (French border). After 12km from Biescas, turn left to Tramacastilla de Tena. On the main road in the middle of the village, next to the park / children's playground is the vending machine for tickets (next to Calle Navero 28; GPS: 42.715806, -0.316472). After buying the ticket, continue. At the roundabout 300m outside of the village, go left and through the barrier. Note that you also need the ticket for your return journey and that it is only valid on the day you bought it.

20 – Panticosa ski slopes

3-4 hours, moderate

The Panticosa ski lifts operate in July and August (€ 22.50 for a return ticket in 2025), and provide a rare possibility to start your walk at a high altitude of 1,800 m. Of the various walking options, we advise to follow the signs *Ibón Los Asnos* (2,060 m.) and from there, continue to *Ibón Sabocos* (1,905 m.). The area of Panticosa supports a large population of Alcon Blue, in addition to Mountain and Shepherd Fritillaries and Mountain and Pyrenees Brassy Ringlets.

21 – Balneario de Panticosa

Full day, strenuous

A fantastic but demanding walk, rich in flora and butterflies, starts at Balneario de Panticosa. The *Balneario* (thermal springs) became a popular tourist destination early on. The current, huge hotel complex dates from the late 19th century. The Ash trees here host a population of Spanish Purple Hairstreak, and the general area supports Apollo, Purple-shot

Copper and Esper's Marbled White. The trail that starts here leads to the Blue Lakes (*los Ibónes Azules*) and passes through scrub and rocky areas rich in wildflowers and butterflies. The trail begins with a 500 metre climb over a length of 2 km, before arriving at a more level high mountain landscape with mountain lakes.
The *Balneario* lies some 8 km from Panticosa. The trail starts at the north side behind the refuge *Casa de Piedra*. The trail is part of the GR-11 and marked with red and white bars.

22 – Ripera valley by tourist train

5 hours, easy

From the town of Panticosa, a tourist "train" (actually an ill-disguised tractor pulling two wagons) brings you to the secluded valley of La Ripera. Although sitting in an open carriage listening to trivialities about the route through the speakers may not sound like a promising start of a wildlife excursion, it is actually well worth it, because it provides effortless access to a high-altitude valley, from where a gentle track leads further into the mountains. The wildflowers and butterflies are particularly attractive, although Marmot, Chamois, Lammergeier, Griffon Vulture, Northern Wheatear, Rock Bunting, Yellowhammer, Red-backed Shrike and Alpine Chough are present too. There is a good selection of orchids (including Frog and Vanilla Orchids) and a large population of Cross-leaf Gentian and its butterfly, the Alcon Blue. Additionally, we found Piedmont Ringlet, Glandon, Eros, Escher's and Turquoise Blues and a surprisingly large number of Swallowtails.
The Ripera Valley is not even that high (1600-1800m) but it is surrounded by high mountains to the south, giving you the feeling of a much higher area. The crystalline bedrock allows for many small rivers and a truly Alpine landscape.

The Ripera Valley can easily be accessed with the tourist train from Panticosa.

The "train" is operated everyday from late June to late August, and in the pre- and post season only on weekends. For tickets and more information, see **trendepanticosa.com**. It leaves from the the ski lift car park. You can book either one-way or return tickets; return fares are only slightly more expensive. Taking the early train gives you the opportunity to stay either 3 or 6 hours in the valley.

National Park Ordesa and Monte Perdido

Ordesa and Monte Perdido form the heart of the Pyrenees. Together with the French Gavarnie area (which lies right on the other side of the border) it is the most spectacular, most famous and most visited part of the entire range.

The Ordesa Massif consists of a massive chunk of limestone. The Monte Perdido is its highest point and, at 3,355 metres, it is also the highest limestone mountain of Europe. The combination of great altitude and soft bedrock is at the root of the dramatic landscape of Ordesa. During the ice ages, glaciers cut out huge U-shaped valleys, which end abruptly in a *cirque* – a circular rock face that marks the end of the valley. *Cirques* are typical of glaciated mountains and the best examples in the world are found here and across the border in France (Cirque de Gavarnie).

Hence, Ordesa's most characteristic feature are the dramatic vertical rock walls, many of which are hundreds of metres high and many kilometres long. At altitude, the mountains become relatively flat and form large, unbroken expanses of alpine habitat which are a vital refuge for high mountain species.

Ordesa was the last area to host the now extinct Pyrenean Ibex (see text box on page 81). It was the awe-inspiring scenery that motivated the preservation of the area. As early as 1918, the central Ordesa Valley

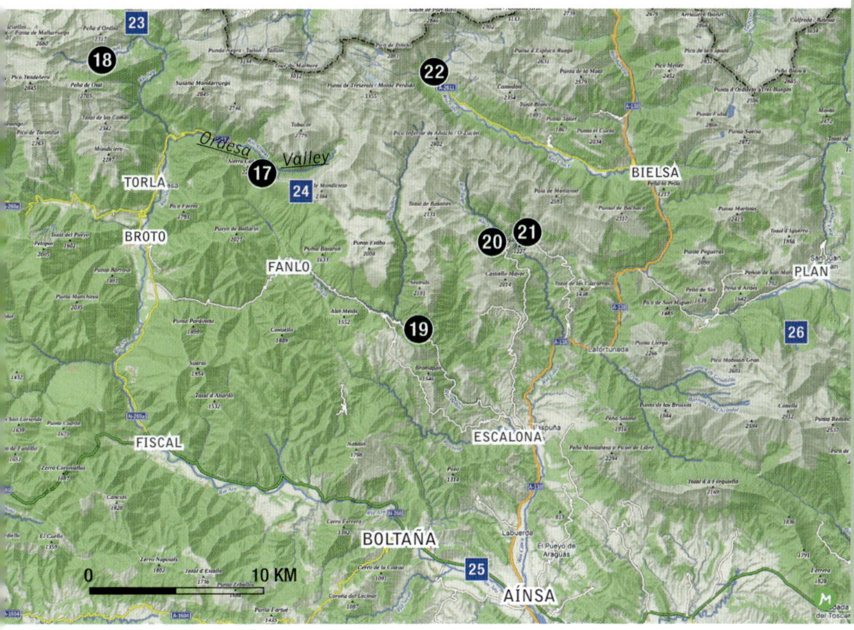

Overview of the Central Pyrenees and Ordesa valley.
In black are the locations of the routes described on the following pages; in blue are the sites described on pages 209 - 211.

(route 15) was declared a National Park. From 1982 it is known as the *National Park of Ordesa and Monte Perdido* and includes the area of the Añisclo Gorge (route 17), Escuaín (site C on page 202) and the upper Pineta Valley (route 18) and all of the Spanish side of the massif of Monte Perdido. The Park area covers 15,608 ha, with an additional peripheral buffer zone of 19,679 ha. The area of wildlife habitat available is even higher, since there are so many vertical or near vertical surfaces. Were it to be ironed flat the actual area would be much greater! Human activities in Ordesa are limited to nature tourism and traditional, low impact farming. Once, tens of thousands of sheep grazed the alpine meadows in the summer months, but their numbers are reduced to a few thousand. Cows still graze on the middle and lower mountain meadows from May to October.

The visitor will notice that Ordesa encompasses two very distinct landscapes, separated by Ordesa's immense cliffs. The easiest to access are the valleys which are clothed in flowery hay meadows and in dense deciduous forests. At lower elevations the latter consist of Hazel, Maple, Ash, Box and Portuguese Oaks, but on higher ground Beech forests, mixed with Silver Fir and Pyrenean Pine, occur.

High over the canyon walls lie the alpine and subalpine pastures with Yellow Hedgehog Broom* (*Echinospartum horridum*), dominant to an altitude of up to 2,000 metres. This is the realm of the Marmot, Alpine Accentor, Alpine Chough, Ptarmigan, several high altitude butterflies, Edelweiss and a score of other alpine wildflowers.

Marmots occur throughout alpine meadows of the Pyrenees.

Large-flowered Butterwort (top) and Edelweiss (bottom) are just two examples of the beautiful plantlife of the Ordesa.

We advise you to make the effort to visit both types of ecosystems. The canyon bottom is easily visited by following either route 15, 16 or 17, but for the upland pastures, you will need to work a little harder. Route 15 enters this habitat at the refuge at the end of the walk. For a more extensive trip you need to spend a night in the refuge, or – an easier alternative – take the National Park bus service in Torla or Nerín (see site B on page 202).

Eastern and western starting points

Because of the rugged terrain, it is not possible to visit the entire National Park conveniently from a single point of departure. Torla (and nearby Broto) is most used as a base. There are plenty of hotels and campsites. Torla allows access to the Ordesa (route 15) and Bujaruelo valleys (route 16), and you can take a bus drive to the high slopes (B on page 202). Also Añisclo (route 17) can be reached from here.

Access to the eastern parts of the National Park, such as Pineta (route 18), Escauín (site C on page 203) and also Añisclo (route 17) is easiest from the Aínsa-Bielsa valley, where there are also many hotels and campsites. Also a bus service from Nerín to the alpine pastures of Ordesa (B on page 202), is possible from here. The Aínsa-Bielsa valley is best to access the remote valley of Plan (site D on page 203). If you are staying in Aínsa or Boltaña, you can also reach the Sierra de Guara to the south and cross over to Turbón (route 20) in the east.

!

Rain and thunder are frequent at the end of summer days.

This route can be busy; avoid weekends

Best season
June-July
Of interest
year round

ROUTE 17: THE ORDESA CANYON

19.1 KM, FULL DAY, STRENUOUS

The classic walk in the Pyrenees – a must see.
The largest canyon of the Pyrenees makes for breathtaking scenery.
Wide variety of birds, butterflies and wildflowers.

Habitats: mixed and pine forest, rock walls, alpine meadows
Selected species: Leafy Lousewort, Long-leaved Butterwort, Green Wintergreen, Chamois, Alpine Marmot, Lammergeier, Golden Eagle, Black Woodpecker, Alpine Chough, Citril Finch, Ring Ouzel, Spanish Argus, Large Blue, Duke of Burgundy, False Dewy Ringlet, Gavarnie Ringlet

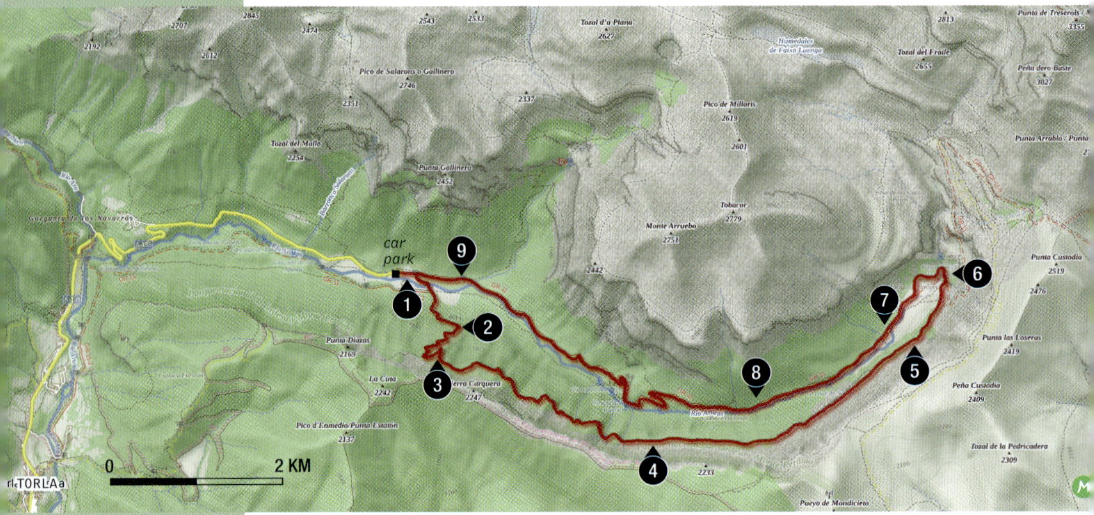

Many areas have a top hotspot, a singular attraction to which all other attractions can be compared. For the Spanish Pyrenees, this is the Ordesa Valley. The 20 km long valley was carved out by a glacier and then further deepened by the thundering river Arazas. The 400 metre high sheer rock cliffs dominate the valley over its entire length, creating a sublime, dramatic landscape (see photos on page 31 and 185).
The flora and fauna of Ordesa matches the superb landscape. Apart from the large number of rare wildflowers, birds and butterflies, this is also one of the best places to see Chamois and Marmot. You have to work for it though. Most of the valley's treasures lie in the far end of the valley – an 11 km walk (and that's just one way).

Tackling Ordesa Valley

The Ordesa valley Seen from the mirador at point 3.

The Ordesa valley can be covered in three ways: the easiest is to follow the main track on the north side of the river which climbs modestly, making it an easy walk were it not for its length. For this route, follow the signs *Gradas de Soaso*, or *Circo de Soaso*.

A more demanding, but also more rewarding journey, is to climb the *Senda de Cazadores* (the hunters' trail) on the north-facing slope and then continue into the valley, taking the 'easy' track back. Be aware, though, that this route starts with a non-stop steep ascent of 700 metres! Tackling it the other way round, seems superficially more attractive, but coming back over the *Senda de Cazadores* means a dangerous descent at the end of a strenuous day. We strongly advise against this.

The route we describe here starts with the steep ascent up the *Senda de Cazadores*. But if you read point 5-8 in reverse, you have the description for the first option.

You can also opt for an overnight stay. Walk to the end of the valley (either by de *Senda de Cazadores* or directly) and then continue to the refuge of Góriz. This is another tough climb once you are at the end of the valley, but it brings the great advantage of getting to high altitude in an area with some of the finest alpine meadows of the entire Pyrenees (Góriz lies at 2,200 m). The area around Góriz is splendid for birds, plants and butterflies. Staying overnight at Góriz allows you time to explore the alpine habitat of Monte Perdido – at which foot you now find yourself. In the summer season, book well in advance (**goriz.es**).

Another piece of sound advice is to start early. In the summer months and in spring weekends (if you can, avoid the weekend anyway) there are many people about. The best chance for a close encounter with birds and mammals is attained by getting at the front of the inevitable 'troop' of hikers.

Starting point: Torla. Drive or, in summer, take the free bus up to the car park in the Ordesa canyon. Directly after the car park, go right following the sign *Senda de Cazadores.*

1 The first few metres lead through a willow wood in the river basin. This general area is good for tits, including Marsh Tit which scarcely penetrates further south into Iberia. At the bridge, look for Dipper, which is frequent along all rivers in the valley. Look out too for Large Admiral, Large Tortoiseshell and Nettle-tree Butterfly. Just across the bridge you enter an old Beech forest, where Bird's-nest Orchid is frequent.

2 At this point starts a seemingly endless row of hairpins on a small and, when wet, slippery track. All the climbing occurs right here at the start of the route. There are a few interesting wildflowers, but all of them show in better numbers further ahead, so we advise (something we do not often do) that you don't stop, but walk steadily on. After what seems an age of trudding uphill you come to a small clearing with a large cliff in front of you. The end of the ascent is on top of this cliff, but at this clearing, have a look at Thore's Buttercup, Yellow Mountain Violet and Alpine Pasqueflower.

3 At the end of the climb, you arrive at the large viewpoint (photo opposite). Pause here, enjoy the superb views and look for Alpine Swifts, Crag Martins and, with a little luck, passing Golden Eagle or Lammergeier.

The spectacular cirque *Circo de Soaso* at the far end of the valley (point 6)

4 From the viewpoint on, the trail is easy going with breathtaking scenery, alternating with areas of woodland and mountain heathland, dominated by Alpenrose. Pause to look for wildflowers, especially around the areas with rocks. You will find Parnassus-leaved Buttercup, Alpine Toadflax and Entire-leaved Primrose here. Goldcrest and Crested Tits are frequent in the pine forest.

Eventually, depending on how easy you resist the temptation to stop and your level of fitness, you will arrive at a mountain hut. After this point, a long section of thickets starts which is of lesser interest so we advise to move on to reach the more interesting habitat of scattered Pyrenean Pines that lies ahead. (Although do look out for the rare Alpine Leek which flowers in the thickets in July).

5 This last section before reaching the *Circo de Soaso* is, perhaps, the most rewarding of the whole walk. At the time of writing, a pair of Lammergeier bred on the cliffs to your right. So look up regularly to see if they fly over. A little closer, on the rocky upper pastures to your right there are often Chamois. The best area for them is a little further ahead, where the scatter of pines gives way to open meadows. Use your binoculars to scan the grassy patches and rocks since they are often surprisingly easy to overlook. On and in the pines look for Citril Finch and Ring Ouzel. Close to the track there is a rich flora with Edelweiss, Alpine Bartsia, Bird's-eye Primrose, and, on wet rocks, Alpine Butterwort. All four butterworts found in the Pyrenees are present on this walk. Large-flowered has been a faithful companion so far and will continue to be so further on. The other two species are further ahead.

6 When you finally arrive at the *Circo de Soaso*, take the time to scan the area for wildflowers and butterflies, which include Mountain Fritillary, Purple-edged Copper, Spanish Argus and Pyrenees Brassy Ringlet. There are generally similar plant species to those mentioned at 4. Wallcreeper breeds on the rock face here, but you need a little luck to see them.

7 Your descent goes through a meadow grazed by cows. Along the margins of the rivers that you cross (where Dipper breeds), there are Broad-leaved Marsh-orchid, Bird's-eye Primrose and Common Butterwort. A striking flower in the grazed meadows is the Ashy Crane's-bill* (*Geranium cinereum*; p. 66).

Chamois is quite common in the upper part of the valley.

8 Once the descent starts in earnest, you encounter the first pines and Green Alders. There is a great splash of wildflowers here. Lesser Butterfly Orchid, Globeflower, Pyrenean Hyacinth, Pyrenean Iris, White Asphodel and the big Leafy Lousewort (p. 214) are common here. This indicates that this area was once grazed (these species, unpalatable to cattle, are typical of enriched soils).

9 Soon you enter a beech-fir forest that will accompany you throughout your descent. This lengthy stretch of forest is a superb, unscathed old-growth (primeval) forest, something which is now rare in western Europe. Only the Carpathians and Rhodopes in eastern Europe have sizable stretches of this primeval mountain forest left. Black Woodpecker, all the tits and other forest birds are present. Because of the deep shade, the flora is poor, though Liverleaf, Bird's-nest Orchid and Green and Serrated Wintergreen do well. At several points you come across spectacular waterfalls. You pass two wet cliffs where Long-leaved Butterwort grows in abundance.

Additional remark

In October, the Beech leaves turn yellow and red, and the valley looks its most gorgeous, yet then few people are around to appreciate the Ordesa's finery. In winter, only the main track is open to the public – the Senda de Cazadores is too dangerous (avalanches!). The snow lies thick in winter when no-one is around and birds are few, and Ordesa is a magically serene place.

Thore's Buttercup (top), one of the botanical delights of the Ordesa valley, grows along the track close to the 'balcony'. Superb old-growth mixed forests cover the wide bottom of the Ordesa valley, close to the car park (bottom).

ROUTE 18: BUJARUELO AND THE OTAL VALLEY

10 KM, 5 HOURS, EASY-MODERATE

The alternative route in Ordesa that leads through an open valley. Great birdwatching and lots of butterflies.

Best season
mid May-mid July
Of interest
April-September

Habitats: river, mixed forest, gorges, alpine meadows, bushy terrain
Selected species: Narrow-leaved Helleborine, Martagon Lily, Alpine Flax, Lammergeier, Golden Eagle, Red-billed Chough, Alpine Chough, Citril Finch, Ortolan Bunting, Chamois, Alpine Marmot, Pyrenean Brook Newt, Clouded Apollo, Purple-shot Copper, Yellow-spotted Ringlet, Shepherd's Fritillary

The Otal valley in spring.

The valley of Bujaruelo lies just next to the popular Ordesa valley, but is much less visited. The valley starts out as a narrow gorge, but at the *Mesón de San Nicolas de Bujaruelo* (which is the old customs post of an ancient road to France), the valley splits into the Otal valley to the west and the much longer Ara valley to the north. We have chosen to describe a walk in the Otal valley because it is the exact opposite of Ordesa (the Ara valley is briefly described on page 202). Otal is wide, open, with clear views to all sides, and with a gently meandering river. It is, therefore, excellent for viewing birds of prey whilst the rose bushes attract a large number of songbirds. The many wet patches draw many butterflies and the gorge entrance is very attractive for wildflowers, particularly orchids.

Starting point: Torla.
Drive north in the direction of Ordesa and at the roundabout, turn left to Bujaruelo.

1 Before starting the walk, it is worth making a few stops. The first is about 1.5 km beyond the roundabout where there is a small car park underneath an overhanging cliff from which water drips. This habitat of permanently wet, calcareous rock is home to the curious Long-leaved Butterwort which carpets the cliffs here. Walk a few metres back along the road to see the big Robust Marsh-orchid – the southern counterpart of Southern Marsh-orchid.

2 Once on the other side of the river, notice the young pine forests and the clearings made for the powerlines. There are many orchids here, with Narrow-leaved Helleborine, Burnt and Greater Butterfly Orchids most in evidence.

3 Park your car near the *Mesón de San Nicolas de Bujaruelo* (1,388 m). This is one of the few places in the high Pyrenees where there is a noticeable autumn bird migration. On favourable days in August thousands of Swifts pass through, followed by similar numbers of House Martins and Swallows in September and Chaffinches in October.

4 The first stretch follows the river, where Dipper and Grey Wagtail are usually about. To the left of the track there is an east facing flowery slope which receives sunlight early thus seeing the first active butterflies of the day.

Burnt-tip Orchid (right) and Pyrenean Rampion (left) can be found along the route.

At the crossing, go left and follow the winding track up to the pass to the Otal valley.

5 The bushy terrain, especially higher up, is home to many birds. All species of tit are present here, as is Blackcap, Garden Warbler and Red-backed Shrike. Higher up, keep an eye out for Citril Finch (which is common in Otal), Rock Bunting, Crossbill and Ring Ouzel. The flowery margins remain excellent for butterflies.

6 Once over the pass, the grand Otal valley opens up before you. Check carefully the sky near the cliffs to the left and right. Golden Eagle and Lammergeier breed nearby and often fly along the cliffs. Continue through the valley and look for Citril Finch, Ortolan Bunting, Yellowhammer, Water Pipit, Northern Wheatear, Red-backed Shrike and other birds in the pasture or on the rocks and bushes. Quail breeds in the meadows and Pyrenean Brook Newt and Midwife Toad can be found at the river. In wet patches on the track there are drinking groups of Blues. Scan the rocky areas to your right for Marmots and Chamois – the first, especially, is common here.

7 The barn marks the end of the route. However, you can continue a little further along a trail that leads further up the mountain. When gaining altitude, the terrain becomes rockier, which is more attractive for Marmots, Chamois and houses still more wildflowers.

Oopposite page: Red-billed Choughs occur together with the (yellow-billed) Alpine Choughs in the Otal valley.

ROUTE 19: THE AÑISCLO GORGE

31 KM + 16.5 KM WALK, FULL DAY, MODERATE

!
Beware that in winter the road may be covered with snow and ice, and the paths too.
Roads are one way in summer.

Best season
mid May-late July
Of interest
April-October

A spectacular, narrow gorge with a humid environment.
A rich fissure flora.

Habitats: steep rock walls, riverine, mixed and pine forest, small-scale farmland
Selected species: Long-leaved Butterwort, Sarcocapnos, Ramonda, Short-toed Eagle, Golden Eagle, Dipper, Cinquefoil Skipper, Wood White, Cleopatra, Amanda's Blue, Escher's Blue, White Admiral, High Brown Fritillary

Añisclo is much narrower than the other great gorges in the Ordesa National Park. It is carved out by the River Bellos.

The Añisclo gorge is perhaps our favourite walk in the Pyrenees. Unlike Ordesa, which was carved by a glacier, Añisclo was shaped by a powerful river, making it much narrower and more enclosed. Within the confinement of the cliffs, the climate is humid and the vegetation exuberant. Añisclo is like a natural botanical garden only without the convenient labels. You pass a dazzling diversity of wildflowers in your walk up in the gorge. The first part of the walk is easy going, but an hour in, the trail begins to climb steeply.
But the experience extends far beyond the walk itself – the access road is equally scenic and full of interest.

Next page: Long-leaved Butterwort is an insectivorous plant common on wet rock faces (point 1).

Starting point: the village of Puyarruego

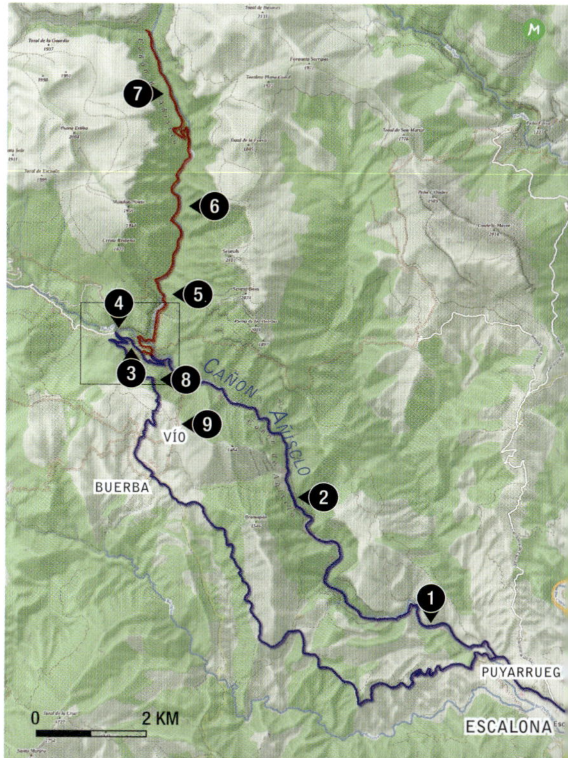

From Aínsa, drive north in the direction Bielsa / France and turn left after 10 km to Puyarruego. After 2 km ignore the turn to Puyarruego and continue straight to Cañon de Añisclo.
1.6 kms further, park on the left side of the road. If you reach a car park with a building just after a small bridge, you've gone about 150 metres too far. Simply park and walk back.

1 This first short stop is attractive in May primarily, when among the many orchids, the otherwise rare Bug Orchid is here among the most common species. Chalkhill and Adonis Blues are among the butterflies.

Continue. Note: authorities are currently considering closing the road ahead to public traffic. If it is closed, you should return to Puyarruego and take the high road to Añisclo, via Valle de Vió / Buerba.

2 Presuming the road through the gorge is open, you continue on a route that becomes increasingly spectacular. The cliffs tower over you on both sides of the road and you pass several tunnels. Fortunately, there are small spots where you can park (only outside the busy season) and walk along the road. The wet cliffs are hung with the curious, insectivorous Long-leaved Butterwort with its flypaper-like leaves. Ramonda, Maidenhair Fern and Sarcocapnos are frequent as well.

Further ahead, you arrive at the lower car park near San Úrbez. If approaching from Buerba, you'll need to park above the gorge and walk down (map on next page).

3 The area around the car parks is exposed and sunny. Look for butterflies and Ocellated Lizard. Scan the cliff edges above you with binoculars, both here and further ahead. Golden and Short-toed Eagles and all three vultures are regular.

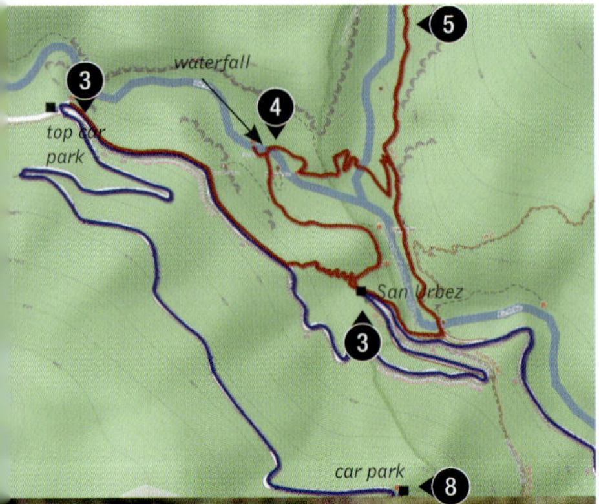

Ramonda is a common wildflower on the cliffs of Añisclo.

The walk in the Añisclo gorge

Take the small path at the end of San Úrbez car park that turns right and takes you down to the Cascada de Aso. Be careful when the path is wet as it can become slippery.

4 After passing through a boxwood forest with abundant Ramonda growing on the rocks, (flowering in May and June), you reach the spectacular waterfall near the old mill named Aso. Look for Dipper. Black-eyed Blue is a common butterfly here.

Cross the metal bridge over the Aso river and further on, cross the Bellos river that has shaped the Añisclo gorge. At the T-junction, turn left.

5 Soon, the gorge becomes narrower and the vegetation on the side of the trail shows an ever-changing palette of species: Ramonda, Pyrenean Germander, Fairy Foxglove and a variety of ferns grow on the moist rocks whilst Long-leaved Saxifrage, Sarcocapnos, Yellow Woundwort, Alpine Calaminth and Sticky Flax are present on drier, more exposed sites. Wet, nutrient-rich areas have the big Pyrenean Valerian and Pyrenean Rampion, amongst others. Where the trail crosses the river, it enters a damp gorge forest. This forest, dominated by Elm, Ash and Maple trees, has a thick, jungle-like cover of mossy Box bushes. At regular intervals, water seeps out of the rocks – a habitat that is home to Long-leaved and Large-flowered Butterworts, Robust and Early Marsh-orchids – and this really is just a small suggestion of what can be found here.

6 After about 1.5 hours you reach an open spot by the river, signposted as Cumáz. Roughly at this point, the landscape starts to change. The gorge sheds its Mediterranean character and an increasingly wild and mossy cliff forest of Beech and Fir takes over. The diversity of plants decreases. Pyrenean Saxifrage and Sanicle are among the frequent species here.

7 A hairpin bend marks the start of a new section. Thus far, the trail was easy, but a series of steep climbs makes the next section a lot more difficult. However, when you arrive at the viewpoint of Selva Plana, the worst is over. From here it is not much further on to La Ripareta, another level area at the river. The scenery along this section remains roughly the same (thus, excellent), but there is little extra to see, although Common, Green and One-flowered Wintergreens can be added to the list.

Our description ends at La Ripareta, but there are several hours of hiking ahead, if you wish.
On your return, skip the waterfall and instead follow the path via the Hermitage of San Úrbez. After the bridge take the small path to the right, back to the car park of San Úrbez.

Drive towards Vió.

8 After 1.9 km, make a short stop at the Mirador de Añisclo, which offers great views into the gorge and and scan the skies for soaring raptors – especially vultures.

Continue another 700m and turn left to Vió.

9 Vió and its surroundings form an old, small-scale agricultural enclave in this mountainous area and may offer some interesting birdwatching. Drive slowly through the area and look out for species such as Common Rock Thrush, Red-backed Shrike, Wryneck, Short-toed Eagle, and Hobby. If you pass by here after nightfall on a warm day, drive slowly. We have seen Nightjar here on several occasions, sitting on the tarmac, resting on the warm tarmac before heading out for a night of insect hunting.

Views over the Bellos River from point 5 of the walk.
Black-eyed Blue (can be seen drinking on wet spots on the trail (bottom).

Continue to return to the A 138 that connects with Aínsa.

ROUTE 20: ESCUAÍN

16 KM CAR ONE WAY AND 10.1 KM WALK, 5 HOURS, EASY

Superb views of Griffon Vultures and Lammergeier

Habitats: limestone cliffs, limestone grassland, Downy Oak and Pine forest
Selected species: Lammergeier, Griffon Vulture, Egyptian Vulture, Black-eyed Blue, Yellow-fringed Fly Orchid (*Ophrys subinsectifera*), Lesser Butterfly Orchid

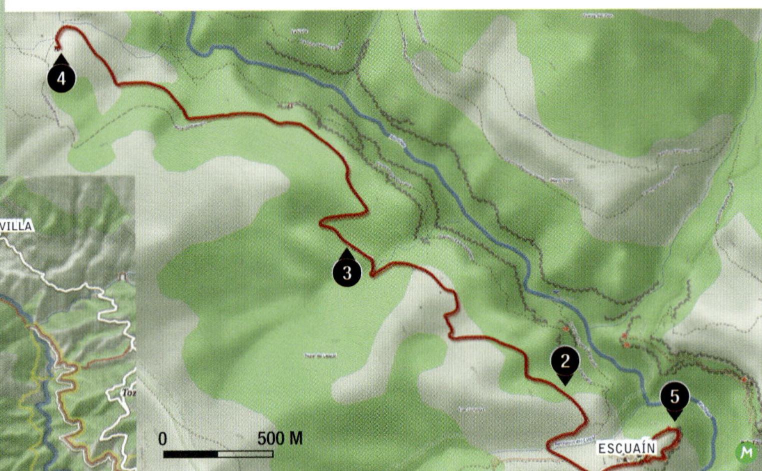

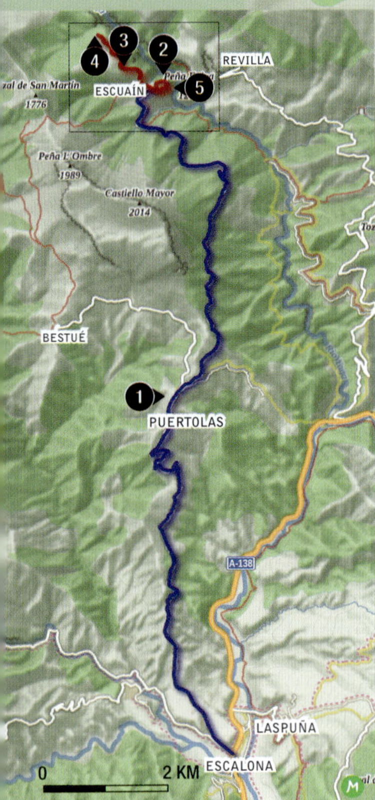

The abandoned hamlet of Escuaín clings dramatically to an escarpment between the mighty cliffs known as Castillo Mayor and the depths of the Escuaín gorge. As the crow flies, Escuaín lies only 1.3 kms from Revilla (next route), but to get from the one place to the other by car, you need to drive 35kms – the gorge makes a shorter trip impossible!

It may come as a surprise that Escuaín is very different from Revilla, because the slopes are facing to the north, making the woods and fields much lusher. There are extensive limestone grasslands full of orchids and butterflies on this route, that are missing on the Revilla-route. The gorge of Escuaín is known for its many Lammergeiers and they are the main theme of this route.

This route consists of one 3.5 km linear walk to a hide that overlooks a feeding site for vultures, and a 1km circular route that offers views of the gorge. Both walks are easy.

Lammergeier are almost guaranteed at Escuaín.

Note that the hide overlooks a site where carcasses are laid out for vultures (see page 233). This happens at regular times (at time of writing – Tuesdays and Fridays at 10.30 AM) and is an ideal moment to see the birds. However, there are nearly always vultures here that 'hang around' or fly low over the fields, so a visit at other times is worthwhile too.

Starting point: Aínsa.
Drive north in the direction of Bielsa / France and after 10km turn left to Puyarruego. Directly thereafter turn right to Belsierre and Garganta de Escuaín (going straight on this turn would bring you to the Añisclo gorge; route 19). At the next junction, go left to Puertolas.

1 You drive up through fine Holm Oak woodlands and fields to the village of Puertolas. Here are a few things of interest (either here or on your way back).
First is the little village of Puertolas itself – isolated in a stark mountain landscape but still inhabited. More importantly, the fields are still grazed and the hay is still cut. Egyptian Vultures frequently circle around the village and come down to feed amongst the cows. Just beyond Puertolas lies a junction where you can park. This area is often good for birds, including Red-backed Shrike and Cirl Bunting. We've even encountered Tawny Pipit here. The landscape is beautiful, with to the west the village of Bestué with jagged cliffs of los Sestrales, which form the edge of the Añisclo Gorge. Ahead lies the mighty limestone chunk of Castillo Mayor, behind which Escuaín lies, to the southwest is the conspicuous peak of La Peña Montañesa – all of them are limestone peaks and their odd appearances the result of millions of years of erosion.

Continue towards Escuaín. Park in the car park just before the village.

Walk 1 – To the vulture hide

Follow the track that leaves at the far end of the car park.

2 Even after your first few steps you'll realise that this walk is much more than just the route from the car park and the vulture hide. The flowery grasslands are lined with hedgerows and dotted with Downy Oaks and Ash. At various places, small brooks flow over the track, where butterflies come down to drink. Among the many species to be found here are Heath Fritillary, Marbled White, Cardinal, both Cleopatra and Brimstone and a good collection of blues. There are plenty of orchids, with Pyramidal, Common Spotted, Fragrant and both Lesser and Greater Butterfly Orchids the most numerous.

3 The second part of the walk leads through pine woods with Crested and Coal Tits and Bonelli's Warbler. Orchid enthusiasts should look for Helleborines – White, Red and Narrow-leaved all occur, although not in high numbers.

The limestone chunk of Castilla Mayor, seen from Escuaín village.

After 3.5kms from the car park, go right on the sign that points to the 'Observatorio de Aves'. Don't continue along the track; it may seem on the map that it reaches the hide as well, but access from this side is prohibited to protect the vultures.

4 From the hide you look out over the pasture where carrion is laid out for vultures. This is done to support the population that struggles to find sufficient food now that the livestock numbers have reduced (see –> history). You can enter or leave the hide at any time you want and there are no costs involved. Sometimes the area around the hide is just as good, or even better for viewing and photography. No access signs clearly state the limit of where you can go.
On days when birds are being fed, the Griffon Vultures come down first, followed by Lammergeier and Egyptian Vultures. Around 200 Griffons, 30 Lammergeier and 5-10 Egyptian Vultures were present when we were there. Outside feeding times, there are fewer birds of course, but all three species regularly fly by low, touch ground or fly off, so there is always something to see.

Return via the way you came.

Walk 2 – The gorge

Walk to Escuaín. Where the road turns left, go straight on (following *Circuito miradores*) and pass the small National Park information centre.

5 You pass through some abandoned fields to a junction of paths. Taking the left brings you in a few metres to the first viewpoint and the right makes a small loop past two other viewpoints back to the village.
The first viewpoint is arguably the best as it looks down a long stretch of the gorge. The view is majestic, with the dramatic cliffs on either side and the river deep down below you. Take your time here and watch the vultures glide along the gorge (best in the second half of the morning).
This little circuit offers more than views and vultures. Along the path are many wildflowers including large numbers of Turkish Lily in early summer. In spring we have found the very rare Yellow-fringed Fly Orchid here (although only few specimens).

Yellow-fringed Fly Orchid

ROUTE 21: REVILLA – THE LAMMERGEIER TRAIL

4.1 KM, 3 HOURS, EASY-MODERATE

Short walk to a spectacular gorge
Superb views of Griffon Vulture and Lammergeier

Habitats: limestone cliffs, scrub of box and hedgehog broom, limestone grassland
Selected species: Lammergeier, Griffon Vulture, Egyptian Vulture, Long-leaved Saxifrage, Black-eyed Blue

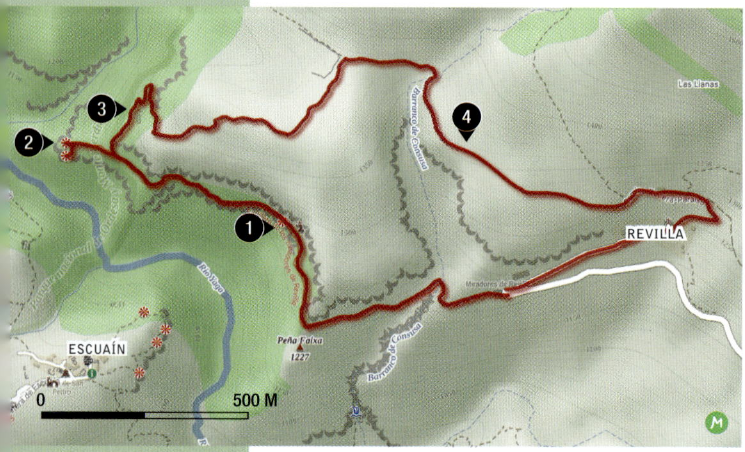

The gorge of Escuaín separates two tiny abandoned villages, that of Escuaín in the south (route 20) and that of Revilla in the north. Whereas the gorge is an unpassable barrier for people, it is the home of what might well be the highest concentration of Lammergeier in the world. This short route follows the ridge of the gorge on the Revilla side to a dramatic viewpoint. The return walk crosses some shade forest and an exposed plateau where wildflowers and butterflies are the main attraction.
The main reason for visiting this remote part of the Pyrenees is for watching Lammergeier. In order to see them, you'd best be at the viewpoint in the middle of the morning, when the air is warming up and the birds start to fly. Reaching the viewpoint takes approximately 45 minutes.

Starting point: the small car park in the switchback just before the hamlet of Revilla.

From Aínsa, drive north in the direction of Bielsa / France. After 17 km, well after the turn to Laspuña and 2 km before Lafortunada, turn left to Tella. In Cortalavina, continue towards Tella and a little further, at a Y-junction, go left to Revilla. Park after 6 km in a sharp U-turn, just before the hamlet of Revilla (where the road ends).

1 The first part of the walk leads over a narrow but more or less level stretch through Box scrub and woodland with Downy Oaks and Montpellier Maples. Although you are high up in the mountains, the south-facing, warm slopes and the porous, dry soils support many Mediterranean species. On cliffs, there are Long-leaved Saxifrages.
The first viewpoint over the cliffs is impressive, but don't linger here too long. The better spot is ahead.

Continue and ignore the track to your right heading to Revilla (this will be your way back).

2 After the junction mentioned above you arrive at the miradores (viewpoints). There are two, both of which are excellent, but the one on your right gives the wider views. Lammergeier, Egyptian and Griffon Vultures all cross the valley regularly, as do Ravens, Alpine Swifts and Red-billed Choughs. It is worth taking your time here to enjoy the views and the birds.

Return and go left to Revilla.

3 The ascent is steep, but short and shady. Liverleaf and the endemic Ramonda (with its wrinkly leaves and pretty purple flowers) are common in the woods.

On the plateau, follow the trail (marked by cairns) towards the cliff. At the junction, go right to Revilla.

4 The plateau has a mix of bare rock, box scrub with the yellow-flowering Hedgehog Broom, plus some woodland and now abandoned hay meadows. There is a range of wildflowers and butterflies to be found, including Heath Fritillary, Cardinal, Black-eyed, Adonis and Little Blues. Take your time here as you stroll back, also for birds. Crested Tit and Bonelli's Warbler are frequent, all the raptors can regularly be seen flying overhead. Since a few years, it seems a small population of Red-billed Leiothrix (an exotic species from East Asia) has established here.

Follow the trail all the way down to the village. Its only street brings you back to the starting point.

View into the gorge from the viewpoint of Revilla.

ROUTE 22: THE PINETA VALLEY
8.5 KMS, 5 HOURS, MODERATE-STRENUOUS

!
Until the end of June there is a risk of avalanches close to the mountain slopes.

Best season
June-July
Of interest
May-October

Dramatic landscape of a valley cut out by glaciers.
Meadows full of butterflies.

Habitat: Beech and pine forest, alpine meadows, hay meadows
Selected species Lammergeier, Black Woodpecker, Alpine Accentor, Citril Finch, Marmot, Chamois, Pyrenean Iris, Pyrenean Lily, Purple Emperor, Turquoise Blue, Western Fritillary, Provençal Fritillary Sombre Goldenring

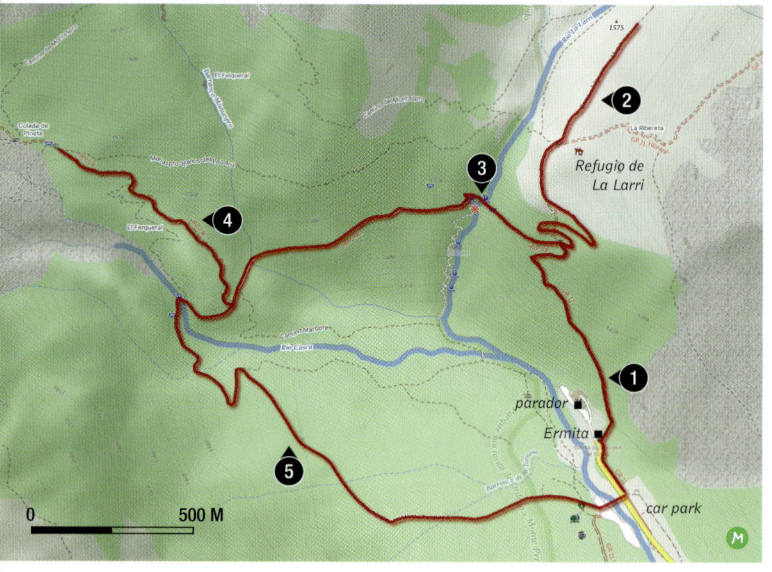

The 12 km long, U-shaped glacial valley of Pineta ends in a dramatic cirque, at the bottom of which a series of walks can be undertaken. The flora here is not as rich as in most other Pyrenean valleys, but the flowers that do occur, grow in profusion and attract scores of butterflies. The best walk is up to Marboré lake and its rapidly vanishing glacier, where all of the species of the high alpine habitats can be found (e.g. Snowfinch and Ptarmigan). Unfortunately, this means a steep ascent of 1100 metres, which makes it only suitable only suitable for people in above-average physical condition. Instead, we describe a walk here to the valley (Llanos) of La Larri and several great butterfly sites close to the car park.

Starting point: Bielsa.

Take the road towards the Parador de Bielsa / Pineta. Notice the large peatland just beyond the reservoir at the start of the Pineta Valley. Continue all the way to the car park at the end of the valley, just before the hotel Parador de Bielsa. At the reception of the hotel you can see the skull of a male Pyrenean Ibex (Bucardo in Aragonese), one of the very few of this extinct species on public display.

From the car park walk on along the road and go right just before the Ermita onto a trail that goes up steeply to Llanos / Cascadas de La Larri.

1 The first part of the route leads through a comfortably shady beech forest. There are some spectacular old trees here. Note the elongated holes of Black Woodpeckers. In summer, there are Bullfinches and in June, you may find Bird's-nest Orchid here.

You arrive at a track. This will be your return route, but first turn right to the Refugio de La Larri and continue from there some 1.5 kms.

2 Above you have great views of the La Larri plains, another U-shaped, glacial valley. The valley is grazed which is the reason for the profusion of Pyrenean Irises, which put on a fabulous display in July: the Iris is inedible and is therefore able to spread in the heavily grazed terrain. Marmots and Chamois are frequent in the rockier terrain towards the edges of the valley. Search the crests for raptors, like Egyptian Vulture, Lammergeier and Golden Eagle.

The beech forests at Pineta in October.

The La Zinca river, a site for Dipper, Sombre Goldenring Dragonfly and Large Tortoiseshell.

Return and follow the track towards the Cascadas de La Larri.

3 From the bridge over the cascade you can see Broad-leaved Marsh-orchid, Tofield's Asphodel, Yellow Mountain Saxifrage and Large-flowered Butterwort are frequent.

Continue through fine Beech forest.

4 Just before crossing the Cinca river, a trail turns off to the right, signposted Lago de Marboré. It is worth following it upwards for about half an hour. After the thick Beech forest you arrive at a clearing dominated by Bracken, a large number of the superb, yellow Pyrenean Lily (p. 62) flower in June to mid-July. There is also Leafy Lousewort (p. 214) and the endemic Horned Pansy* (Viola cornuta) here. The views into the Pineta Valley from here are especially impressive.
Should you continue for another hour or so on a very steep and strenuous path, you arrive in rocky terrain where Alpine Accentor and White-winged Snowfinch live.

Return to the main path and turn right.

5 After crossing the Cinca river you pass through flowery meadows with hedges and rose bushes. These meadows are superb for butterflies. Large Skipper, Small, Turquoise and Mazarine Blues, Purple Emperor, Duke-of-Burgundy and Meadow and Glanville Fritillaries are among the species we have seen here.

The track ends near the river Cinca, which is already very broad here. The car park is at the other side of the bridge.

Additional things to do in Ordesa

For locations of these sites, see map on page 185.

23 – Walk through the Ara gorge

Full day, easy-moderate

The trail through the Ara gorge, a continuation of the Bujaruelo valley, forms somewhat of a mix between the great Canyon of Ordesa (route 15) and the open landscape of Otal (route 16). You can spend a full day here easily. There are many sun-soaked flowery slopes to satisfy your butterfly wishes. In comparison to Ordesa, there is more acidic bedrock here (though not exclusively), which makes for a different flora. About an 1.5 hours from Bujaruelo (the starting point), just beyond the high cliffs on the other side of the valley, there is a waterfall to your right. This is an excellent site for butterflies, and one of the few places where the rare Pyrenean Lily (p. 62) and Yellow Garlic grow.

Yellow Garlic, endemic to the Pyrenees and Iberian Peninsula.

24 – Bus to the alpine pastures

An absolute highlight for its scenery, birds, wildflowers, butterflies, is the bus trip to the alpine meadows south of the Ordesa canyon. It is your only option to get to high altitude habitat without having to make long and strenuous walks. You can take the bus

View into the Ordesa gorge from the end-point of the bus (site 24).

either in Torla or Nerín. This is not a regular bus, but a four wheel drive version that services for tourists between June and September. You'll need to make a reservation, either on **monteperdidobus.com** / phone: 974 489 024 (service from Nerín) or **ordesataxis.ordesa.com** / phone: 630 418 918 (service from Torla). Ask your hotel or camp site to help you to book. A ticket costs € 30.00 (2015 prices).

The bus makes four stops at different viewpoints over the Ordesa canyon, allowing you time to look around. At each of these points the scenery is breath-taking. Scan woodland edges down in the valley for Chamois and look around for Marmots around the viewpoints. Lammergeier, Golden Eagle, Egyptian Vulture, Alpine Accentor and Citril Finch are not uncommon. Snowfinch is sometimes seen at the easternmost viewpoint. Plants of interest include Long-leaved and Livelong Saxifrages, Edelweiss and the rare Pyrenean Yam (p. 63). Look for these (with care!) at the cliff's edge and in places with loose rocks. Apollo, Mountain Clouded Yellow, Western Brassy Ringlet, Glandon and Eros Blues are a taste of the butterflies here.

The warmth-loving Knapweed Fritillary flies along the banks of the Ara river (site 25).

The bus ride takes about 4 hours. If it is not too busy, and you speak some Spanish, it is worth trying to negotiate to be dropped off at one of these points and to be picked up again by another bus later in the afternoon. This allows you more time and freedom of movement.

25 – River Ara between Boltaña and Aínsa

GPS: 42.43304, 0.08448

The Ara River runs its course freely for 70 km before joins the River Cinca in the town of Aínsa. It is thereby the only major river in the Spanish Pyrenees that is free of dams. Between Boltaña and Aínsa the wide riverbed and its natural vegetation gives shelter to a Mediterranean birdlife that is common further down in Spain, but rather rare in the Pyrenees. In spring and summer attractive birds include Bee-eater, Woodchat Shrike, Scops Owl, Melodious Warbler, Golden Oriole, Nightingale, Wryneck and Turtle Dove. Booted Eagle is common in the surroundings. Grey Wagtail, Dipper and Otter live in the river all year round. The area is bound to be attractive for dragonflies, but has, as far as we know, never been surveyed. We found 'southern' butterflies like Knapweed and Spotted Fritillary. Green Lizard, here at its southern edge, also occurs.

There are various options to explore. From the village of Margudgued (just southeast of Boltaña) is an easy 6.2 km 'Via Verde' cycling/walking path in the valley. Park at Margudgued, leave the tiny village by Calle Mayor and just continue. Alternatively or additionally, you can turn left just after passing a small stream and follow the dam along the river. This site is easily combined with a visit to the historic town of Aínsa.

26 – The valley of Plan
6 hours, moderate

The valley of Plan is perhaps the most isolated of all the central Pyrenean valleys, being completely surrounded by mountains and only accessible through a single narrow gorge. In the few villages the local patois, Aragonese, is still the principal language. Outside the summer months, few people visit the area and wildlife then finds the tranquillity that it needs. The extensive pine forests support rarities such as Tengmalm's Owl, the vulnerable Capercaillie and a large population of Chamois.

Most way-marked walks depart from the Viados refuge at the northern end of the valley. We very much recommend going up from the village of Saravillo at the beginning of the valley to the Ibón de Plan. With a good car (preferably 4x4) and with suitable care, a large part of the track can be driven. The *Basa de la Mora* or *Ibón de Plan* is home to Pyrenean Brook Newt and the surroundings support many butterflies, Ring Ouzel and Citril Finch. It is a marvellous butterfly area with many ringlets (e.g. De Prunner's, Spanish Brassy and Piedmont Ringlets).

The Ibón (mountain lake) of Plan.

Benasque – the eastern valleys

The valley of Benasque lies tightly squeezed between the two highest massifs of the Pyrenees: the Posets (3,371 m) to the west and Aneto (3,408 m) to the east. In comparison with the wide, gentle green western valleys and the Ordesa region with its typically rugged topography, the valley of Benasque exhibits the most archetypical high mountain landscape.

The village of Benasque is the ideal starting point to explore this part of the Pyrenees. More than other Pyrenean villages, Benasque is reminiscent of alpine tourist resorts as there are lots of restaurants, bars, shops and other services. Thanks to the development of the Cerler Ski Resort, Benasque has grown a lot in the last few decades.

From Benasque, various side valleys can be reached and each of them is attractive. Route 19 is one of many good routes that can be undertaken from Benasque. See page 215 for other walks in the area.

Some 15 km south of the village of Benasque lies Castejón de Sos, which sees fewer tourists but is a little more strategically placed to explore the massif of El Turbón (route 20). This mountain range is decidedly more influenced by the Mediterranean. Castejón de Sos also lies closer to Llauset (route 21), a high altitude reservoir, which is arguably the easiest place in the entire Spanish Pyrenees to reach high altitude habitats.

Overview of the Ebro basin.
In black are the locations of the routes described on the following pages; in blue are the sites described on pages 224-225.
Alpenrose (right).

ROUTE 23: EL TURBÓN

50 KM + 4.8 AND 5.4 KM WALKS, 6 HOURS, EASY-MODERATE

Best season
June-July
Of interest
May-September

An isolated limestone mountain in the Pyrenean Depresión.
A rich flora and butterfly fauna of the warm south-facing slopes of the lower Pyrenees.

Habitats: riverine habitat, fields, oak forest, pine forest, Mediterranean scrub, hedgehog broom scrub, holm oak forest
Selected species: Short-toed Eagle, Red-rumped Swallow, Alpine Swift, Orphean Warbler, Montpellier Snake, Large Psammodromus, Fragrant Bug Orchid, Robust Marsh-orchid, Marsh Orchid, Woodcock Orchid, Woodland Grayling, Weaver's Fritillary, Alcon Blue, Blue-spot Hairstreak, Spanish Heath

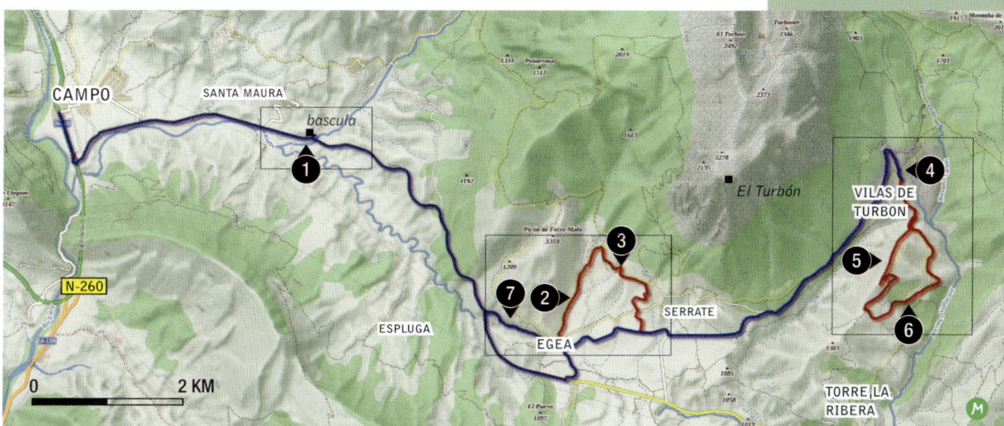

The grey, bald-headed limestone mountain of El Turbón (2,492 m) is the southernmost high peak of the Pyrenees. To the south lies the friendly valley of Lierp, a forgotten and largely deserted area. The population of its eight villages amounted to only 51 inhabitants in 2020. The valley might lack the grandeur of the high Pyrenees and the Guara, but for the nature-minded visitor, there is a lot to see. Moreover, this area is way off the beaten tourist track and almost completely ignored by visitors.

The flora and fauna have a distinct Mediterranean touch, with many species that are absent higher up in the Pyrenees. The landscape is a mix of hay meadows, (partially abandoned and partially still in use), scrubland and wild barrancos and open woodland, with holm and downy oak and pine. The hay meadows are interesting since they form a quickly disappearing habitat in the Pyrenees.

The route starts at the small town of Campo (691 m) and gradually climbs up to 1,500 m to the base of the Turbón. It consists of a stop and two short and fairly easy walks at different altitudes. Note that shade is sparse and that it can be very hot in summer.

Starting point: Campo. Take the HU-V-960 towards Vilas del Turbón. Ignore the turn to Santa Maura and a little further, just before crossing a bridge, turn left to Llert and directly thereafter, turn left onto a large parking near a building 'Bascula'.

1 A bascula is a scale to weigh crops and hay, hence the large space for parking. Explore the scrubland behind the building. Walk a little further along the road and then walk down to the river to explore. We also recommend to walk back along the road to Campo for 100m and then go left on the minor road to Espluga. In 2025, there was a nest of Red-rumped Swallow underneath the first bridge (a rare but gradually increasing bird in this area) and a little further, there is another track that leads down the river to your right.

This is the kind of site you won't find covered in other guidebooks because the habitat found here is usually ignored. Yet this area is extremely rich in plants, birds, insects and reptiles. On our visits, we found many butterflies (e.g. Weaver's Fritillary and Short-tailed Blue), Yellow-veined Ascalaphids* (*Libelloides longicornis*) and various orchids (e.g. Woodcock, Fragrant Bug, Fragrant, and Pyramidal), Montpellier and Viperine Snake, plus Griffon Vultures, both kites, Short-toed Eagle and the droppings of a Genet.

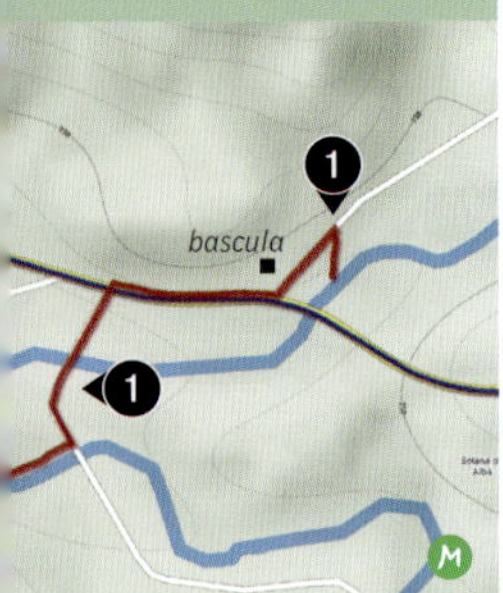

El Turbón is a massive limestone massif in the *Depresión* of Campo.

Continue along the main road to Egea and Vilas del Turbón. After 5.5 km, go left to Egea. At the T-junction, go left and park near the church.

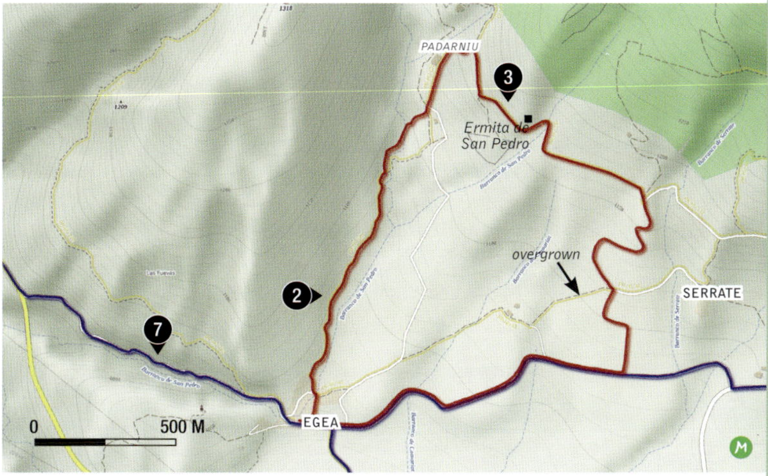

Walk 1 – Egea (4.8 km, easy-moderate)

Follow the street to the right side of the church. Directly after the barranco, go right, following the signs to Padarnín, Ermita de San Pedro and the yellow-white flashes. Waymarking is generally good, though overgrowth may obscure the path in some places. However, the first part of the walk more or less follows the left bank of the barranco and you can't get lost here.

Yellow-veined Ascalaphid* (*Libelloides longicornus*) flies in summer over the limestone grasslands.

2 With the scenic El turbón ahead of you, you follow a rocky limestone path on the edge of a Holm Oak forest with Nettle Tree. Along this track there are 4 species of Flax: the yellow-flowered Bellflower Flax* (*Linum campanulatum*; p. 73), the blue Beautiful Flax (p. 156), the White Flax and the rose-coloured Sticky Flax. Blue Catananche, Common Globularia and Pink Rockrose are other conspicuous species. Towards summer, there are many butterflies to be found, such as Spotted Fritillary, Provence Chalkhill Blue and False Ilex Hairstreak, All the reptiles are possible and from the trees, you can hear the songs of Bonelli's and Orphean Warblers and Cirl and Corn Buntings. In short, this is a Mediterranean mountain ecosystem with plenty to discover.

Opposite page: The warm south slopes of the mountains create a microclimate perfect for insects. Weaver's Fritillary (top) and Provence Orange-tip (centre) are frequent. Sticky Flax is one of four flax species common in the scrub of El Turbón (bottom).

Eventually, you arrive at a tarmac road where you go left to a still functioning farm. Just after the farm houses, you go right in the direction of the Ermita de San Pedro.

3 This next section leads through a much more open countryside with a mix of fields and low scrub with scattered Holm Oak. You have wide views over the valley; ideal for watching raptors. We found this section to be excellent for birds, with Orphean and Sardinian Warblers, Woodlark, Tawny Pipit, Red-backed and Iberian Grey Shrikes and Stonechat all present. Check the power lines here, as this is where some of the afore-mentioned often perch.
There are Woodcock and Fragrant Orchids among a score of other wildflowers, including Jerusalem-sage and Wild Lavander. There are still plenty of butterflies, including Moroccan Orangetip.

After passing the Ermita, you arrive at a tarmacked country road. Go right here and follow this road down through more excellent habitat to the main road. Turn right here and follow the road back to Egea.

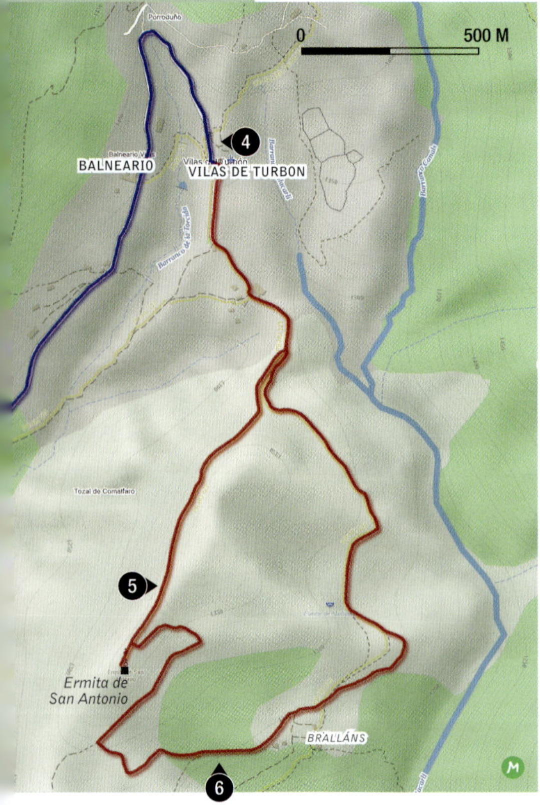

Take the car and continue to Vilas del Turbón. At the T-junction, turn left towards Vilas. Continue all the way, past the Balneario and the following switchback and park near the church.

4 A couple of things before you start the walk. First is the fact that you've now entered the zone where Yellow Hedgehog Broom dominates the vegetation. It flowers in profusion in June and early July. Also note the deep purple Marsh Orchids that grow in wet spots between the hairpin curve and the church. This is a rare orchid throughout most of its range, including in Aragón.
Finally, Vilas del Turbón itself. It is hardly a village; rather a scatter of farm houses and a Balneario. The latter you'd now translate to a wellness centre, but it is in fact already very old. The water from Turbón, that springs at this place, is perfect for bathing and is considered to be very healthy. It is also collected for drinking water.

Walk 2 – Vilas de Turbon (5.4 km, easy-moderate)

Continue on foot along the road. Ignore the route to Egea but follow the signs 'Brallans' and 'San Antonio'. Where the latter two split, follow the signs to San Antonio.

5 Due to the nearby spa (Balneario), this second walk is a bit busier. At on average 1300m only 200m higher than the previous, but the landscape is quite different. This walk leads in part through the margas azules — the pale blue clay badlands characteristic of this area.
Additionally, there are cultivated fields with hedgerows, open pine and downy oak woods and low scrub with Yellow Hedgehog Broom* (Echinospartum horridum). This walk has splendid views and large numbers of butterflies.
Bonelli's Warbler, Crested Tit and Firecrest are present in the pine forests and we've seen all three species of vultures cruising overhead. The flowery roadsides (there are masses of Fragrant Orchids here, and various other species in May) boast an enormous number of butterflies between May and mid-August. Lesser Spotted, Knapweed, Dark Green and Heath Fritillaries, Spanish and Pearly Heaths, Marbled White (en masse), Provence Chalkhill, Adonis, Little and Green-underside Blues, Grayling and the owlfly Libelloides coccajus are some of the species we've found.

After enjoying the views from the San Antonio Ermita, go back and then right, following the track towards Brallans.

6 This walk down leads through scrubland and open woodland of Downy Oak, again with large numbers of butterflies and many Orchids. Near the farm of Brallans is an impressive old Downy Oak tree.

At Brallans, go left and follow the tarmac road back to the car.
Drive back to the church of Egea (starting point of the first walk) and go straight ahead.

7 You now follow the old road down from Campo. This narrow, one direction road follows a beautiful, narrow gorge. Park in the gorge and scan the cliffs. There is a small colony of Alpine Swifts here that regularly swoop down to feed their young.

Continue and at the junction, go right to return to Campo.

Best season
June-July
Of interest
May-September

ROUTE 24: BENASQUE
5.8 KM, 5 HOURS, MODERATE

Beautiful high mountain walk right underneath the highest peak of the Pyrenees. An excellent area for wildflowers and butterflies.

Habitat: alpine meadows, subalpine heath and pine forests, fast flowing rivers
Selected species: Water Saxifrage, Vanilla Orchid, Chamois, Dipper, Citril Finch, Ring Ouzel, Snowfinch, Small Whiteface, Clouded Apollo, Apollo, Large Blue, Chestnut Heath

The plain valley on the far end of the Benasque valley is, with its meandering river, an enchanting place. Look here for Dipper and Small Whiteface (a Dragonfly).

This beautiful walk has everything one may expect from a visit to the high Pyrenees: superb scenery to all sides, a score of wildflowers and butterflies, some challenging climbs to altitudes where you have a good chance of Chamois and other alpine wildlife. The mix of open Pyrenean pine wood, subalpine heathland and high altitude meadows sport a very high diversity of wildflowers and butterflies, whereas the plain of the Ésera river has a good number of dragonflies.

Starting point: Benasque. Take the road north out of the village to the La Besurta car park (1,940 m.), from which, in the summer months a bus (€ 6.10 return, 2025) takes you to *La Besurta*, some 4 km further up the valley (this is also an easy and attractive walk, with lots of wildflowers and butterflies).

From *La Besurta*, Follow the signs *La Renclusa*. This important refuge (2,140 m.) is open all year for those wanting to spend the night (phone 974 344 646).

Ring Ouzel breeds in the open pine forests.

1 Through open pine woods and subalpine heath and meadows you climb to the refuge. Keep your eye out for Citril Finch and other birds of the subalpine pine forests. In summer, the trailside heaths are very rich in wildflowers, with Wolfsbane, Common Monkshood, Burser's St. John's-wort* (*Hypericum burserii*), Mountain Avens, Elder-flowered Orchis, Wood Saxifrage and Narcissus-flowered Anemone among the more conspicuous species.

2 The Renclusa refuge offers good views over the largest glacier of the Pyrenees, the Maladeta. Just around the refuge birds often come down to look for food. Citril Finch and Alpine Chough are among the possibilities while in front of the cliffs towards the south, the odd Golden Eagle or Lammergeier may pass by.

Follow the trail that turns left behind the refuge and climbs another 150 m to a pass over the mountains. The walk up to there passes through more stunning scenery with a combination of old subalpine pine forest and heath, again with excellent wildflowers and butterflies, Ring Ouzel and Citril Finch.

Alpine meadow with Pyrenean Iris (left). Beautiful old Pine trees grow on the slopes above the Renclusa mountain hut (right).

3 Beyond the pass you look down into the Esera river plain. Your descent passes excellent alpine meadows again. On this stretch, keep an eye out for Alpine Marmot and Chamois, Vanilla Orchid, Yellow Betony. The stout, Pyrenean endemic Water Saxifrage grows near a small stream here. Further down, there are masses of Pyrenean Iris. Look for highmountain butterflies, such as Shepherd's Fritillary.

4 The path enters the valley on the far left side of the river plain, but to return to *La Besurta*, you need to cross the Esera river on the far right. An easy walk loops around the river plain. Look for Dipper in the stream. This is also one of the very few places in Spain where the Small Whiteface – a northern dragonfly – occurs.

You leave the flat valley bottom through a small gorge that brings you back to your point of departure.

ROUTE 25: THE HIGH MOUNTAIN LAKE OF LLAUSET

8 KM WALK, 5 HOURS, MODERATE

The easiest route in high altitude habitat.
Flora and fauna of the upper alpine zone.

Habitats: mountain lakes, scree, cliffs, alpine meadows
Selected species Parsley Fern, Leafy Lousewort, Vanilla Orchid, Frog Orchid, Alpine Marmot, Chamois, Golden Eagle, Wallcreeper, Alpine Chough, Alpine Accentor, Snowfinch, Pyrenean Brook Newt, Mountain Clouded Yellow

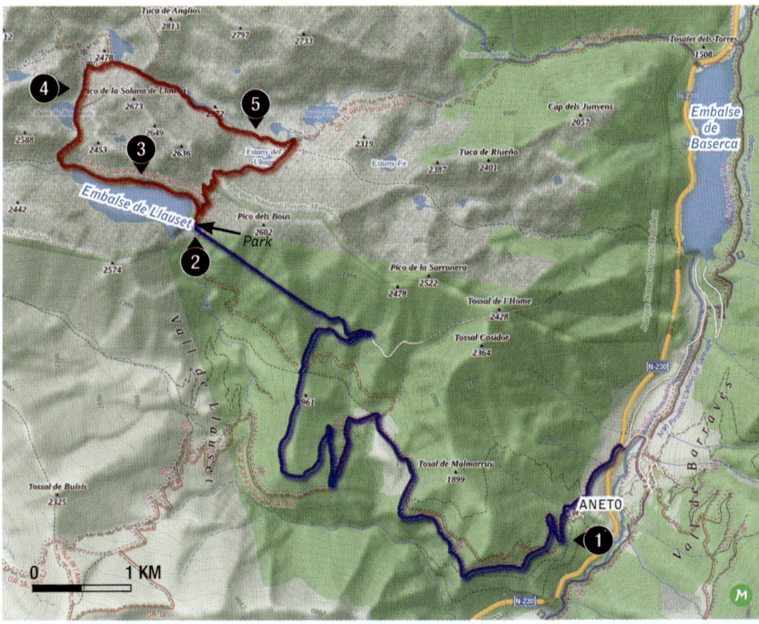

It is difficult in the Pyrenees to reach truly high mountain habitat without making a considerable effort. Thanks to the well-maintained road to a reservoir, the *Embalse de Llauset* (2,200 m), this lovely route in the far north-eastern end of the region is an exception. This is an excellent opportunity to get acquainted with the specialist flora and fauna of the highest regions. There are various hiking options at Llauset, of which we describe the most obvious route. The description below relates to a summer visit.

!

This is high altitude habitat. Walking is more demanding here, due to the lower oxygen concentration, very high solar radiation and changeable weather. Take precautions.

Best season
June-mid August
Of interest
May-September

Starting point: Aneto village, 20 km north of El Pont de Suert. From the village, continue along the slightly potholed road.

1 In the hedges and hay meadows around the village there are Red-backed Shrike and Yellowhammer. Higher up, you come to extensive subalpine hay meadows with sheep. Linnet, Northern Wheatear, Rock Bunting and Common Rock Thrush may be present here.

After passing several large hairpins, you arrive at the ridge where some buildings and a large car park mark the start of the route.
From here, follow the GR 11 to the dam of the Llauset reservoir, where there is another small car park. Note that many hikers (and even official route descriptions) start at this car park next to the reservoir, which is easily reached through a tunnel owned by hydrographic company CHE.

White-winged Snow-finch (top) and the Leafy Lousewort (*Pedicularis foliolosa*; right) can be found on the trail along the Llauset reservoir.

2 At the car park, check the dam, the cliff near the tunnel and any other sheer rock wall for Wallcreeper. Here, and during the entire walk, keep an eye on the skies for passing Lammergeier, Griffon Vulture, Golden Eagle, Kestrel and Alpine Chough.

Follow the GR 11 alongside the lake until, at the far end, you turn right to Botornés, a crystal-clear mountain lake at 2,300 m.

3 In summer, this whole stretch is excellent for butterflies (e.g. Mountain Clouded Yellow, Shepherd's Fritillary) and wildflowers. Orchids include Broad-leaved Marsh, Heath-spotted, Dark Vanilla, Frog, Burnt-tip, Greater Butterfly and Fragrant. Burser's Spring and Field Gentian grow in various places, as do Grass-of-Paranssus, Edelweiss the stout Leafy Lousewort, Yellow and Water Saxifrages, Martagon Lily and many more. Water Pipits, Northern Wheatears and Black Redstarts are fairly common, but look out too for

White-winged Snowfinch, Alpine Accentor and, of course, Marmot and Chamois.

4 Explore the *Botornés* lake, particularly for Pyrenean Brook Newt. Between the boulders, the high altitude specialist Parsley Fern is fairly easy to track down. Snowfinch and Alpine Accentor breed in the area and with luck you may find Ptarmigan (best chance in autumn).

5 If you have the time, you can continue the trail up to the next plateau, where the *Cap de Llauset* mountain lake (2,400 m) is situated. Before this lake, a trail heads off to the right, leading up to a pass (*Collado de los Ibóns* – 2,500 m) and then down to a peaty plain with a scatter of large and small lakes. From here, turn right to another pass (*Collado de Anglios* – 2,450 m) before descending to the car park (see map on page 213). Many of the aforementioned plant and butterfly species can be seen here, plus Alpine Pasqueflower, Alpine Gentian and Trunpet Gentian.
This entire walk is superb, but strenuous. Consider the weather, whether you have suitable equipment (stout boots, raingear, etc) and your fitness before deciding to go for it. Otherwise, return from *Botornés* lake by the same route.

The reservoir Embalse de Llauset.

Additional walks and sites near Benasque

For locations of these sites, see map on page 212.

27 – Valley of Estós
Full day, moderate

GPS: 42.628889, 0.541028. Some 4 km north of Benasque lies, to the west, the valley of Estós. Leave Benasque and just after crossing the river, turn left to Valle de Estós. After a few bends in the road, you arrive at a car park. Continue on foot. After an initial short climb, you enter the gentle Estós valley, with its meadows and woodlands where Short-toed Eagle, Golden Eagle and Ortolan Bunting can be found. As can be expected from a high mountain area (the valley lies at 1500 metres), there is a score of interesting wildflowers and butterflies.

The upper part of the valley is the best and from here various trails lead higher up into the mountains. You may consider spending the night in the mountain hut Refugio de Estós (1850m) and continue from there higher up into the mountains. This is a wild and remote area, home to Chamois and some of the rarest birds of the Pyrenees, like Capercaillie and Rock Ptarmigan.

Alpine Accentor is found in the highest parts of the mountains.

The trail in the Vallibierna valley.

28 – Hospital de Benasque

GPS: 42.681917, 0.604056. The old ruins of the Benasque hotsprings at the start of the Benasque Valley (the starting point of route 24) are home to a thriving population of Western Whip Snake. Look around the buildings and surrounding bushes for this rare and generally difficult to find snake. Here you make a fair chance.

29 – Valley of Vallibierna

Full day, moderate-strenuous

GPS: 42.641361, 0.563944. Some 6 km north of Benasque, turn right at the far end of the reservoir to the *Senarte* camp site (recommended to those in search of basic, quiet and beautiful camping spots). From the first weekend of July until the last weekend of August a bus takes you up 8 km along a steep gravel track to the refuge of Vallibierna / Las Coronas at almost 2,000 m (€ 18.50 for a return ticket in 2025; reservations are not needed). This is an excellent way othe to get into higher mounains. A lovely landscape awaits you there with old pines, flowery meadows, fast flowing streams and rocky summits. Rock Bunting, Common Crossbill, Black Redstart, Citril Finch, Ring Ouzel, Dipper, Grey Wagtail, Tengmalm's Owl and Lammergeier are present here. There are several walks to various mountain lakes, all of which are interesting.

Golden Eagles breed throughout the Pyrenees, *Sierras Exteriores* and Ebro lowlands.

30 – Ski resort of Cerler

GPS: 42.561944, 0.569583. This ski resort can be reached turning right 1 km north of Benasque. A scenic road winds through the green alpine pastures up to the resort (1,500 m) and the ski lifts at 2,630 m. Snowfinch, Alpine Accentor and Alpine Chough come down to the ski lift area in winter and there is a chance to see them in summer if the ski lifts are running to take you up to higher elevations.

TOURIST INFORMATION & OBSERVATION TIPS

Travel

Travelling to Huesca

Most visitors to Huesca come by car from the west via the valley of Canfranc (i.e. the road between Pau and Jaca), or the east from Montréjau to Vielha. There are two other approaches on smaller roads via Col de Portalet (connecting with Sabiñánigo) and Bielsa (connecting with Aínsa).
There are good connections by train from Paris (via Irún and Zaragoza). Another good option, if a bit more hassle, is to take the train to Pau and subsequently the bus connection to Canfranc, from which the train continues to Huesca.

Travelling in Huesca

By far the easiest way to travel in Huesca is by car. The roads are good and there is no shortage of petrol stations. There are plenty of safe places to stop besides the road and explore the surroundings. Be aware, though, that it is illegal to park on the road itself and that the Guardia Civil actively check for violations (all 4 wheels need to be off the tarmac).
Discovering Huesca by bicycle is a challenge. Villages are far apart and in the lowlands, the temperatures are high and shade is scarce. In the mountains, the weather is capricious, with heat and cold, sun and rain all possible within a single day. That said, many sports cyclists visit the Pyrenees and in the lowlands the traffic is light enough for it to be safe. If you plan to visit Huesca by bicycle, you need to plan carefully in the lowlands as, unlike the Pyrenees and the *Sierras Exteriores*, there are few hotels and hostels in the Monegros (see page 220). You'd best adapt to the Spanish pace of life, with activity in the mornings and evenings and taking long lunch breaks in the local bar. The food is usually good and cheap, especially if you opt for a *menú del día*.
Travelling through Huesca on public transport is possible, but requires patience. From most larger centres (Huesca, Jaca, Sabiñánigo, Aínsa, Barbastro) there are bus services to nearly all villages in the province, but often there is only one bus a day. Consequently, speaking at least rudimentary Spanish is advisable if you are to get by. It is advisable to check bus schedules in advance via **alosa.es**.

Planning your trip

When to go

With such a variety in habitats, Huesca is of interest throughout the year, with a short dip around October and November.

In the winter time (December – February), many birds from northern regions (pigeons, thrushes, finches, Red Kites, Lapwings, etc.) winter in the Ebro basin and *Somontano*. Together with the resident eagles and vultures, warblers, sandgrouse and bustards, this makes for an attractive mix for birdwatchers. At this time iconic high altitude birds like Wallcreeper and Alpine Accentor come down to the rocky areas in the Guara to add icing on the cake. Better still, they are now much easier to see than in their remote breeding quarters. Winters are cold throughout the region (even in the Monegros) but generally with clear skies. In the early mornings, and again at dusk, the low sun vividly colours the desert mountains of the Ebro tablelands against a distant backdrop of the cold, silent and monochromatic Pyrenees.

At the end of February, the number of Cranes start to increase at Gallocanta as they later do in Sotonera. The first migrants (Black Kites, White Storks, Egyptian Vultures, Booted Eagles and Swallows) arrive in March when the Scorpion Broom, Rosemary and scores of small Daffodils of the lowlands also come into bloom. Add to this all of the winter birds and it is clear that Huesca is a magical place in March.

In April the mountain birds start to return to their breeding places and the winter visitors from further north disappear. Meanwhile, the region is flooded with birds from the south which occupy their territories and start to sing. Scores of wildflowers turn the Ebro Basin, *Somontano* and Guara into a rich bouquet which, ever changing in composition, does not disappear until the end of June.

Come May, most of the snow in the lower parts of the Pyrenees has disappeared and the spring flora is flourishing. Butterflies appear all over the lowlands and Sierra de Guara, and the last migrant birds, such as Nightjars, arrive. In June and July, the flora and butterfly fauna in the mountains is at its peak. The lowland steppes turn yellow and the big insects (Praying Mantises, Ascalaphids, Grasshoppers) emerge.

During August, the region seems to lose some of its magic. More and more tourists flood into the Pyrenees, while most flowers and butterflies are at their end. The summer birds silently assemble and start to move south.

September and October is an excellent time for long walks in the Pyrenees. Most people have left, the heat has dissipated and the Beech forests turn flamingly red (page 200). A pleasant quietude descends on the region – the season is over; both in terms of tourism and of nature.

During November, the Cranes gather in Gallocanta and small flocks of Dotterel appear in the steppes. A new winter season starts and the great cycle of nature is renewed with the arrival of birds fleeing the short northern days to spend the winter in Huesca.

Weather and temperature

Huesca does not have weather, it has weathers. It is not rare to have a rainy day in one place, but brilliant sunshine 50 km or less down the road.

Obviously, the Pyrenees have the most capricious weather type. Clouds can form within hours and what starts out as a warm and sunny day not infrequently ends with lightning and rain. This does not necessarily herald a change in weather, but merely a daily cycle as the next day may start sunny again only to be rainy later. Often, these daily showers linger in the high mountains; an incentive to stay the night lower in the valleys. In any case, pack with the possibility of rain in mind.

Rain is much less frequent in the Ebro valley. Local showers are absent and, unless a big rain front is forecast, you are likely to have a good day. Even when rain is predicted, it frequently merely stays overcast with just a few drops. However, in winter and spring the wind may surprise you and make it much colder than you'd expect. Make sure, then, to pack some warm clothes too. In valleys close to the Ebro river, thick fog may occur locally in winter and early spring, making birdwatching impossible. In this case, switch plans and go to the *Sierras Exteriores*. This fog usually stays below 700 m above which, at such times, you are sure to have a splendid day with bright sunshine.

Accommodation

If you want to explore all the landscapes of Huesca and maximise the number of ecosystems visited (and thus flora and fauna on view) you cannot avoid some travelling. We advise you to seek a pitch for your tent or to book a room in three different areas: somewhere in the High Pyrenees, the *Somontano* area (to cover the *Sierras Exteriores*) and the Ebro basin.

Accommodation in the Pyrenees: The Pyrenees form a popular tourist destination and camp sites, pensions, hotels and *casas rurales* (rural B&B's) are numerous – too many to give recommendations. It is most important to choose carefully the area in the Pyrenees you wish to visit. For this we provide some hints on page 166. Then choose whether you wish to stay in the smaller mountain villages, all of which have accommodation and some of which (e.g. Torla, Broto, Bielsa, Benasque) can be quite touristy. These villages have the advantage of being, outside the main tourist season, quiet, green and near the start of the routes we describe. On the other hand, choosing accommodation in (or near) the slightly larger towns like Jaca and Aínsa, has the advantage of being more convenient for various services and more flexible in choice of routes nearby. Being further from the mountains, these places usually have less capricious weather too.

Accommodation in the Somontano and Sierra de Guara: In and south of the *Sierras Exteriores*, there is a lot less accommodation to choose from. In this respect the general area of Alquézar, Bierge and Barbastro, where there are plenty of pensions and *casas rurales*, is the best option. There are also campsites near Alquézar. On the other side of Huesca, in the general area of Riglos, there is accommodation in Ayerbe (including campsite), Bolea and the village of Riglos itself and in the city of Huesca (including campsite).

Accommodation in the Ebro basin, Monegros and Belchite: Since finding steppe birds and enjoying the semi-desert landscape in the best possible light conditions requires visits at dusk and dawn, it is important to find accommodation nearby. It is therefore a shame that little is on offer and, what there is, is generally not of high quality. There are no camp sites and nearly all pensions and *habitaciones* (rooms) are aimed at passing truckers and travellers. For the Monegros routes, the village of Candasnos (which has two pensions which are closed on Saturday) is the most central, but the two pensions in the village of Alcolea offer a more cheerful atmosphere. There are also hotels in Sariñena. For visitors to Belchite there is a good hotel in Lécera and more reasonable ones in Fuentes de Ebro, Quinto and, a bit tacky, Belchite itself.
Accommodation in Gallocanta: Several villages around the lake have small, but attractive, hotels. We recommend *Albergue Rural Ornitológico* (**allucant.com**) in Gallocanta which scores highly by having good views of the lake, English speaking staff and information on birds.

Convenient Travel and Safety Issues

Annoyances and hazards

The greatest risks to visitors to Huesca are caused by the terrain and the climate – which are extreme. Care needs to be taken when setting off in the high mountains with their changeable weather, sudden freezing gales and dangerously deep drops. The hot lowlands with vast areas devoid of shade, requires precautions as well.
Otherwise the area poses little risk. There are few poisonous animals and those that are present (Asp Viper and Spanish Scorpion) are difficult to find, hence records of bites and stings are rare. Theft and crime in the region are low and, although one always needs to lock up, the chance of theft from cars is low.

Safety in the mountains

High mountains can be dangerous. In the Pyrenees of Huesca, about twenty people die each year. They were not prepared or they took too many risks. Don't become one of them by taking sensible precautions.
If you plan to go hiking, be aware that the weather can be changeable – a warm and sunny day can quickly turn cold, windy and rainy. Wear good quality walking boots and bring water and wind proof clothing. The best clothing is layered: a light cotton under layer, something warm to go over it, and something water and wind proof to seal it. This way, you can peel off, when the weather is warm.
Lightning is another potential danger. Cool and wet air from the French side clashes with dry and warm winds from the Spanish valleys, resulting in summer in regular short and heavy thunder storms. When a thunder storm is building up, make sure to move down into more sheltered areas.
The most frequent injuries are sprains resulting from a fall or a slide. Be aware of loose and wet (slippery) stones and avoid steep descents with loose rock. Such trails

are better taken as you ascend. Remember too, and this can be hard, not to get so carried away with the wildlife that you miss your footing or fail to take account of the terrain. In the summer months, most trails in the Pyrenees are fairly busy so people will be at hand if you need assistance. But if you are out in spring or autumn (or on little travelled tracks), tell the hotel reception of your plans. Take a mobile phone with you, in case you need assistance (be aware though, that the mountains may block the signal). The alarm number is 112 (SOS Aragón). All this being said, most trails pose little danger. None of the routes described in this book require mountaineering skills. Like all Crossbill Guides, the indication of difficulty is applicable to people in a sound physical condition, but without any extra training. The times indicated assume generous stops to observe the wildlife. After all you are here to see nature, not to break a speed record.

Safety in the steppes

The steppes can be an inhospitable place. In winter, and even in spring, it can be windy and surprisingly cold. In summer the heat and the sun are relentless so it is always important to be able to retreat to the shelter of towns or villages. Hence, travel by car and bring a good map, plenty of water and a mobile phone, in case of an emergency. Short walks can be taken into the steppes at any time of the day, but plan for longer trips in the morning or evening. Take precaution against the sun (hat, sunglasses, sun lotion). Be careful when driving along tracks. The surface may be too rough for a normal car. After periods of rain, parts of the track may be washed away or turned into axel-sucking traps. Even when the tracks are in perfect condition, be aware that they may entice you into a confusing labyrinth in which it is easy to get lost.

Responsible tourism

'*Take nothing but your photo, leave nothing but your footprint*', is the well-known phrase that summarises the idea of responsible tourism. It goes without saying that, as a visitor of a nature reserve, you have a responsibility to leave your surroundings and everything in it undisturbed. But maybe it is less than obvious what is, and isn't, damaging in the Pyrenees and steppes of Huesca. So here is what you should be especially aware of when visiting this area.

Don't go out searching for bird nests and sensitive bird species like Capercallie. Such a search automatically implies disturbance. In the steppes, birds are easily disturbed, so keep your distance (particularly photographers!) and, where possible, use your car as a hide. Some areas are closed for hunters or climbers during the breeding period. Obviously, this prohibition applies to birdwatchers as well. Catch your butterflies only on camera. In Aragón, carrying a butterfly net without a permit is not allowed. The fine is the same as that for walking around with an unlicensed rifle!

The local population depends on its nature and vice versa. When ecotourism supports the local economy, inhabitants will benefit. What appeared to be useless wilderness, becomes a source of income. Thus, buy local produce, stay in the small locally run hotels, have your meals in local restaurants and buy in local shops instead of in the big supermarkets. In doing so, you show the people that it is their land and its nature that you come for. The more binoculars people see and the more excited stories they hear about their land, the better they will value and preserve it.

Observation tips

Getting the most out of your visit

To get most out of your visit to Huesca, travel from north-south or south-north, rather than east to west. The greatest differences in landscape, climate, geology, flora and fauna are found along a north-south axis. The three main regions – that of the Pyrenees, the *Sierras Exteriores* and the dry lowlands – are orientated north-south.
In the Pyrenees, you'll want to decide in which valley(s) to spend your time. See page 166 for an overview of the differences between the Pyrenean valleys.
Choosing times of day: If butterflies are your main target, then get out into the field around 10 AM and return at the end of the afternoon as this regime coincides with their periods of greatest activity. For photographers the earlier part of the day, when the insects are less active, can be most productive. However, the other times of the day can bring surprises so vary your routine from time to time to get maximum benefit from your explorations.
Dawn best to see steppe birds and, in spring, it is the time in which most birds sing. Nocturnal mammals (Foxes, Wild Cat) are still active. For mammals, drive slowly along the minor roads, with headlights on full beam, to see what turns up. Routes 1, 3, 4, 5 and 11 are rewarding.
First 1-2 hours of light still excellent for birds. Snakes and lizards sun themselves on rocks and tarmac.
4-5 hours after sunrise still good for reptiles. Raptors and Alpine Swifts begin to stir and are often still low and easily seen.
Mid-morning-Afternoon raptor activity is at its peak. Butterflies and dragonflies are active. All wildflowers have opened.
Last hours before sunset Birds sing again. Nocturnal snakes and lizards warm themselves on rocks and tarmac.
Dusk Owls and nightjars become active. On moist evenings, amphibians are visible on the roads. Nocturnal mammals become active.

(Bird)watching the steppes

Even though they are open and there is little to block your view, finding the birds in the steppe is a challenging undertaking. For maximum success, especially in summer, it is best to be out and about at sunrise, and later again just before sunset. Birds are most active at this time of the day, but also, by late in the morning, the heat haze makes observations more difficult. Added advantage of a dusk or dawn visit is the beautiful light over the steppes.
The best way to find birds is to drive slowly along the small steppe roads.

In spring, roll down your windows to hear the bird sounds (this is the way to find Little Bustard and both sandgrouse). To help you recognise the calls load them onto your mobile phone/i-pod for instant reference in the field. Stop at good vantage points (hill tops et cetera) and take your time to scan the area with your binoculars to find birds on the ground. A telescope makes birdwatching in the steppes much more interesting.

Another ingredient for success is to recognise the, sometimes subtle, differences in steppe habitat. Flat, dry arable land, particularly on plateaux, are the areas to look for sandgrouse. You may find Short-toed Lark here too, but Lesser Short-toed Lark is exclusive to saline steppes and Dupont's you'll find only in steppes with well-spaced bushes. Deserted buildings are sometimes occupied by Lesser Kestrel, Little Owl or Red-billed Chough. Make sure to explore each of these types of steppe – our suggested routes take you through all of them. See the bird list on the following page to check the requirements of the individual steppe birds and see page 22 for a more thorough description of the different steppe types.

Birds are easily chased away by movement. It is best not to leave your car, but if you do, stay low and next to the car to prevent the birds from detecting you. If you want to explore the steppes on foot to search for wildflowers, butterflies and reptiles, you do best to choose a spot at the edge of the level steppes and the slopes. These areas are often the richest in plants, butterflies and reptiles.

Vulture feeding stations

There are few things more spectacular than watching a group of vultures devour a carcass up close. The gathering of these immense birds, their noisy squabbles for access to the food, the cackling and screaming, the clouds of dust—it's all as raw as it is impressive.

Vultures are generally wary when on the ground, but at certain feeding stations, they are accustomed to people, allowing you to get almost literally within arm's reach. These moments are magical—not just for birdwatchers and photographers, but for anyone. Fortunately, there are several places in the Pyrenees where you can witness this extraordinary spectacle.

Why are vultures being fed? Although vultures are a common sight in the Spanish Pyrenees and the Pre-Pyrenees (Prepirineos), their numbers are actually in decline. There are two main reasons for this. The first is that the animals they once depended on—mainly sheep—have largely vanished from the mountains (see page 49). Cows and other wildlife remain, but overall, less food is available.

Second, the food is less accessible. Traditionally, dead animals were either left in the countryside or brought to a central spot outside the village and left for the vultures. These places, known as muladares, don't align with EU hygiene regulations and are now restricted. Today, a fraction of the remains from modern meat production (most of it is disposed of by specialist companies) are transported deeper into the mountains and left out as supplementary food for vultures that otherwise rely on natural deaths in the wild.

This practice is subject to debate, but here we focus on what it offers to visitors.

It's important to remember that the primary goal of laying out carrion is to support the vultures—not to attract tourists. In some feeding sites, visitors are welcomed and there is sometimes a short talk about the vultures (usually in Spanish). The feeding sites and schedules are not widely publicized, nor are the muladares in easily accessible locations. Typically, you'll need to walk for about an hour to reach the site. Organization varies significantly: in the National Park, the government is in charge, whereas in the Sierra de Guara, local birding communities take the lead. Times and dates are usually shared through online communities or local websites. All of this, of course, adds to the sense of adventure and wonder.
At the time of writing, four active feeding sites can be visited:
1. **Near Aínsa** – The Fundación para la Conservación del Quebrantahuesos (Foundation for Lammergeier Conservation) feeds vultures twice a week. This is the most commercial of the feeding stations, but it's excellent for photographers. You need to book in advance (cost: €50) at **quebrantahuesos.org/#reservas** or at the Bird Center and Museum in the citadel of Aínsa.
2. **Near Escuaín** – Higher in the Pyrenees, there's a feeding station a few kilometers outside the village of Escuaín. Feeding takes place on Tuesdays and Fridays, and in summer only on Fridays, at 10:30. Attendance is free. The birds are a bit further away here. This spot is part of route 20 in this book.
3. **Sierra de Guara, near Santa Eulalia de la Peña** – The Grupo Ornitológico Oscense, an active birding group in Huesca, runs a muladar where vultures are fed once every two weeks, usually on Sundays. The site is an hour's uphill walk from Santa Eulalia de la Peña. Entry is free; see avesdehuesca.com/actividades-goo/ for directions. This is an excellent location for photography.
4. **From Santa Cilia de Guara** – The Fondo de Amigos del Buitre organizes feedings at a site a 45-minute walk from the village. This is also a remarkable event, though a bit less predictable in terms of organization, as it is run by a small group. If you want to join, contact Manuel Aguilera (in Spanish) at **info@fondoamigosdelbuitre.**org or +34 665 87 36 55.

At all of these sites, the Griffon Vulture is by far the most common species. There are usually hundreds of them, often circling for hours before the feeding. Other species—such as Lammergeier, Egyptian and Black Vultures—may also make an appearance, along with Ravens, Red and Black Kites and occasionally Golden Eagles. However, they typically only descend once the people have left. Hours after feeding, the rarer species may arrive. Of these, the Black Vulture is the rarest, but sightings are increasing thanks to reintroduction programs in other parts of the Pyrenees.

Recommended reading

Apart from the usual guidebooks and field guides, we recommend the following maps, books and websites.
Maps: Both Editorial Pirineo (**editorialpirineo.com**) and Editorial Alpina (**editorialalpina.com**) have published detailed hiking maps of the Pyrenean mountains which can be ordered online or bought in many small shops and camp sites in

the Pyrenees. For the southern areas, the Michelin road maps for Huesca are good. They show all the minor roads.

Flora: There are two excellent publications that cover the Pyrenean flora down to the Mediterranean *Sierras Exteriores*. The first is the French *La Grande Flore Illustrée des Pyrenées* by Marc Saule (ISBN 2-7459-0637-2 and ISBN 2-84182-185-4). It covers the entire Pyrenean flora, with key in French, with black-and-white line drawings. The two-volume *Flora del Pirineo Aragonés* by Villar, Sesé and Ferrández is the second (ISBN 84-89862-03-6 of the two volumes; vol I: ISBN 84-89862-04-4 and vol II: ISBN 84-8127-119-5). It has short descriptions, but includes distribution maps in Huesca, and has more lowland species. It has the same black-and-white line drawings as the *Grande Flore Illustrée*. The *Guía de la flora de la depresión del Ebro* by Javier Puente Cabeza (ISBN 84-89862-44-3) covers the flora of the arid Ebro depression (Monegros and surroundings). Although it does not have the quality of the aforementioned guides, this full colour photo guide to the most typical wildflowers of the lowlands is a very useful addition to the aforementioned books. An excellent botanical online atlas can be found at **ipe.csic.es/floragon**.

Mammals: the Spanish atlas on mammals, *Atlas y libro rojo de los mamíferos terestres de España* by Palomo L.J. (2007, ISBN 9788480147118) is the best general source for information on mammals in Huesca. There are two specific books from the hand of Kees Woutersen (one of the authors of this Crossbill Guide): *Bats of the High Aragón* (Spanish/English, ISBN: 9788460723073) and *Guía de los mamíferos, anfibios y reptiles del Pirineo* (ISBN: 9788487997013). The Spanish mammal society is *Sociedad Española para la Conservación y Estudio de los Mamíferos* (**secem.es**).

Birds: Information on breeding birds can be found in the *Aves de Aragón. Atlas de especies nidificantes* (2000, ISBN: 9788477537250), elaborated by the regional Government of Aragón. The *Atlas of the birds of Huesca* (1998, Spanish/English, ISBN: 9788460574224) by Kees Woutersen and Maarten Platteeuw covers the 12 month of the year. *Parque Nacional de Ordesa and Monte Perdido. Atlas of the birds* by Kees Woutersen and Manolo Grasa (2002, Spanish/English, ISBN: 9788460754329) gives more specific information. *ROCIN – Anuario Ornitológico de Aragón* (1999-2003 and 2004-2007) from regional SEO/BirdLife published observations on rare birds and some articles. All this can be ordered on **logi-libros.com**. Recent bird observations can be found on **avesdehuesca.es.** The Spanish BirdLife partner is *SEO* (**seo.org**).

Insects: The *Asociación Entomológica Aragonesa* (SEA, **sea-entomologia.org**) has published several thousands of articles and notes about invertebrates. A general book/atlas on butterflies, including some moths, is *Las Mariposas en Aragón* (1990, ISBN 84-7753-129-3) by Victor M. Redondo Veintemillas. The Spanish booklet *Las Libélulas del Altoaragón* by Carlos Andrés Vasco Ortiz (ISBN 84-8127-015-6) gives a good overview of the dragonfly and damselfly fauna of Huesca. The Spanish butterfly organisation is *Zerynthia Asociación* (**asociacion-zerynthia.org**)

BIRD LIST

The numbers between the brackets (...) refer to the routes from page 115 onwards.

Geese and ducks Mostly in winter and up to early spring, there are Mallard, Shoveler, Gadwall, Teal, Tufted Duck, Pochard and Pintail (1, 3, 5, 6). A few ducks breed, including Mallard, Shelduck (3) and Red-crested Pochard (1, 3, 6).

Partridges and Grouse Red-legged Partridge is common throughout the lowlands and the mountain valleys. An endemic subspecies of Grey Partridge breeds in tall-grassed alpine meadows (13, 14, 16). Quail is a scarce breeding bird in areas with cereal plots (1, 3, 4, 5, 11) and again more frequently in alpine meadows (13, 14, 16). There is a relict population of Capercaillie in the general Benasque area, which is highly threatened. For Ptarmigan, one needs to go on the highest areas of the Pyrenees. Your best chance is when climbing up from Llauset (21).

Grebes Great Crested is common but Little Grebe fairly rare on reservoirs with vegetated shores (1, 3, 5, 6). Black-necked Grebe frequents Candasnos lake (3).

Cormorants, herons and egrets Great Cormorant is frequent on large reservoirs in winter. Grey Heron is the most common heron and is widespread in the area. Little Egret breeds in colonies along the Ebro (B on page 137). Great White Egret does not (yet) breed, but is fairly widespread in the lowlands in winter (1, 3, 5, 6), Little Bittern has become rare with only a handful of observations in summer. Sariñena (5) is the stronghold of Great Bittern. Purple Heron is common at the Ebro (B on page 137) and occurs at Sariñena (3), Sotonera (6) and El Pas (C on page 138). Night Heron breeds in the Galachos del Ebro – site B on page 137. Cattle Egret occurs locally around herds (e.g. south of Huesca – 5 and El Pas, page 138).

Storks White Stork breeds in good numbers in several towns and villages along rivers in the Monegros (4) and in the *Somontano*. Villages and towns with many White Storks are Monzón, Alcolea de Cinca, Sena and Lanaja. Black Stork migrates in low numbers.

Vultures Vultures are the most conspicuous birds of the region. The Griffon Vulture is the most frequent bird and there are excellent viewpoints on routes 9, 10 and 12. Egyptian Vultures, unlike Griffons, are not colonial but are frequent, though declining, throughout the Ebro valley (routes 4, 9, 10). Lammergeier is more difficult to find, but nevertheless fairly common in the Guara and high Pyrenees. The best routes are 8, 9, 11, 13, 15, 16, 18 and the viewpoint at Santa Cilia (D on page 162) is very good as is Revilla (C on page 162). The best way to see and photograph vultures from up close is by witnessing a vulture feeding (D on page 162). Since Black Vulture is introduced in Catalonia, it is sometimes seen in the *Sierras Exteriores* and High Pyrenees.

Eagles Golden Eagle is the most common eagle, frequenting (though never common) the whole region. Best areas are the Monegros (3, 8, 9, 15, 16) and Sierra de Alcubierre (A on page 137) and the Ordesa area (15-18). Short-toed Eagle is widespread, but never numerous, in the lowlands and Guara (1-11), particularly in the *Somontano* (A on page 161). It also occurs in the high mountains (e.g. 15, 17). Booted Eagle is less common, but on the increase. It breeds in the Sierras of Alcubierre and Guara (A on page 137 and A on page 161) and there is a population in La Canal de Berdún near Jaca (12, 13). Bonelli's Eagle has become very rare, but routes 3 and particularly 7 offer a good chance of success.

Other birds of prey The Osprey is frequent on migration (5, 6 and D on page 138). Marsh Harrier is frequent on 1, 3, 5, with a large winter roost near Huesca (5) and at Sariñena lake (5). Montagu's Harrier is an uncommon breeding bird of arid fields (best 4). Red Kite is a common breeding bird in the Depresión, especially around Jaca (12, 13) and fairly common in the Somontano, especially in the west (e.g. 5, 6, 10 and D on page 138). There are big winter roosts in the gallery forests (e.g. Flúmen river – 5). Black Kite is very common in spring and summer, particularly south of the Guara (1-11). Buzzard, Sparrowhawk, Goshawk and Honey Buzzard are present in their preferred habitat, mostly in the mountains.

Falcons and kestrels Lesser Kestrel is a local breeding bird of the steppes (3, 4). After breeding, it visits Sotonera (6). Common Kestrel is a widespread, uncommon breeding bird of the lowlands and cliffs in the mountains. Peregrine is widespread and occurs in good numbers, especially in the Guara and in lesser numbers in the high Pyrenees (7, 8, 9, 10, 11). Hobby is a rare breeding bird of riverine forests (5).

Rails, crakes and gallinules Water Rail breeds at Sariñena (5), as Purple Gallinule has done. Coot and Moorhen are present in wetlands (1, 3, 5, 6).

Common Cranes and Bustards The best sites for Common Crane are Laguna de Gallocanta (1 – all winter, with peaks in November and February) and Sotonera (6 – low winter numbers, peak February-March). Several thousands winter in the rice paddies in the south of Huesca province. Both Little and Great Bustard are rare, but with some luck, both may be seen on route 3. Little Bustard also occurs on 1, 2 and 4, but is rare.

Waders, Stone Curlew and Collared Pratincole Little Ringed Plover is a common breeding bird on gravel banks in the large rivers and also occurs near channels in the steppes. Kentish Plover breeds in Gallocanta – 1 and La Playa – 3). Black-winged Stilt breeds in saline areas (1) and, uncommon, in rice paddies in the Monegros (e.g. 5). Dotterel is a rare bird on passage – best chances on 2 and 3. Stone Curlew is widespread but generally uncommon throughout the lowlands (best 1, 2, 3, 4). Other waders may be seen on passage, most likely in wetlands (best 1, also 4, 6).

Gulls and terns Yellow-legged Gull is an uncommon breeding bird along the Ebro and a frequent winter visitor. Black-headed Gull breeds at Gallocanta, sometimes near Sariñena and in the Cinca region and is a more abundant winter visitor. Gull-billed Tern breeds at Gallocanta 1. Black and Whiskered Tern is seen on wetlands during migration (e.g. 3).

Sandgrouse The Monegros are one of the best places to find sandgrouse in Europe. Both Black-bellied and Pin-tailed Sandgrouse breed in good numbers at 2, 3 and 4, but you need to be out in the field early to find them (see page 225).

Pigeons and doves Feral pigeons are widespread, but fairly 'pure' wild Rock Dove breed at Vadiello (9). Wood Pigeon and Collared Dove are common in their preferred habitat, though not frequent in the mountains. Stock Dove is a bird of the lower Ebro basin and Turtle Dove is especially abundant in riverine forest, breeding also in holm oak and Aleppo pine forest (site A on page 137 and sites A on page 161 and F on page 163).

Cuckoos Cuckoo is common throughout. Great Spotted Cuckoo breeds locally in open pine woods in the lowlands (e.g. 5 and site A on page 137). April and May are the best months to find this secretive bird.

Owls Barn Owl is frequent in villages. Tawny and Long-eared Owls are hard to spot, but frequently heard. Scops Owl is also widespread and frequent, but more often heard than seen. It breeds even in the city park of Huesca. Eagle Owl is fairly common on rock ledges in the mountain ranges of the Guara and further south. Piracés (5) is one of the better spots to hear it. Little Owl is surprisingly uncommon (3 is best). Tengmalm's Owl breeds high in the mountains. The most reliable site is at the beginning of the Pineta valley (18). Take a track left just after the Pineta reservoir, continue in the direction *la Estibeta* and listen for its call in the pine forest.

Nightjars Nightjar prefers open woodland – mostly pine, less often in holm oak wood, where it can be quite common (e.g. 5, 6, 11, 12, A on page 137). Red-necked Nightjar breeds in the southeastern corner of the Huesca province in Juniper scrub and open steppe vegetation with at least some trees (4, 5, A on page 137).

Swifts Common Swift is widespread. Pallid Swift has a small population in the city centre of Zaragoza. Alpine Swift breeds in the Guara and high Pyrenees (e.g. 8, 9, 10, 15, 16) and near Alcolea (4). They are easiest to see during the morning and evening as, in the middle of the day, they often fly very high.

Bee-eater, Roller and Hoopoe Hoopoe is widespread throughout the *Somontano* and Ebro valley (e.g. 2, 3, 4, 5, A on page 181). Bee-eater is very common in some parts of the lowlands (best 5, but also 3, 4, A on page 161 and A on page 181). There is a good, but localised population of Roller in the south-east of our area (4, El Pas, page 138).

Woodpeckers Great Spotted Woodpecker is common and widespread. Iberian Green Woodpecker is fairly rare and Wryneck fairly common, mostly along rivers, throughout the area e.g. (5, B on page 137, D on page 138 and A on page 181),. Lesser Spotted Woodpecker is rare bird of mature riverine forests (e.g. along the Ebro). Black Woodpecker is widespread in old Scots pine and beech forests (12, 13, 14, 15, 16). The very rare (under 100 pairs in Spain) White-backed Woodpecker occurs in old Beech forests just west (Selva de Irati; Navarra) and north (forest of Somport in France) and has been reported in the past in the Selva de Oza (13) and Ansó (site B on page 181).

Larks see also box on page 25. Skylark breeds in alpine meadows (14, 18, 21, site B on page 202) and winters in the Ebro basin. Woodlark is fairly frequent in open woodland (11, 14, 20, site A on page 161 and site A on page 137). Crested Lark occurs along roads in the *Somontano* and Ebro basin, while Thekla Lark is frequent in bushy steppes (2, 3, 4, 5). Calandra Lark is common in grain fields in the steppes (1-6), and Short-toed Lark is found on ploughed fields and grassy steppes (1-5). Look for Lesser Short-toed Lark in salt pans (2, 3) and Dupont's Lark in flat bushy steppes (1, 2).

Swallows and martins Barn Swallow and House Martin are common throughout. Red-rumped Swallow is a scarce breeding bird. Crag Martin is common near cliffs in the mountains (e.g. 5, 8, 9, 10, 13, 15, 16, 17, 20, 21).

Pipits and wagtails Tawny Pipit is a scarce breeding bird (1, 2, 3). Meadow Pipit a common winter bird in the lowlands. Water Pipit breeds in alpine pastures (13, 14, 15, 18, 21, site B on page 202) and winters in the Ebro basin. Few White Wagtails breed, but it is very abundant in the lowlands during winter. Grey Wagtail occurs along streams in the mountains (7, 13, 15, 17, 18, 20), while Yellow Wagtail is mostly seen on migration.

Dipper and accentors Dipper breeds in mountain streams (13, 14, 15, 17, 19). Dunnock breeds in open pine forests, above 1,000 metres (e.g. 11, 13, 14, 18, 19, 20). Alpine Accentor breeds high up in alpine meadows (21, B on page 202 and B on page 215). In winter it descends and is frequently seen at rocky places (9, 10, 11, 12, El Portalet – 14).

Thrushes, chats, wheatears, redstarts and allies Song Thrush breeds in beech and mixed mountain woodlands (e.g. 13, 15, 18), being a common winter visitor in the south. Mistle Thrush is a fairly common resident of mountain pine woods (e.g. 11, 12, 13, 14, 19, 20). Ring Ouzel is often difficult to find, but breeds all over the high mountain pinewoods just under the treeline (e.g. 13, 14, 15, 16, 18, 19, site C on page 182 an D on page 203). Blackbird is common in its usual habitat, Fieldfare and Redwing are irregular winter visitors. At higher altitudes Robins are common breeding birds, mainly wintering in lower places. Nightingale is very common in wet areas mostly in the lowlands. Blue Rock Thrush is most frequent in rocky areas in the Guara (7, 8, 9, 10) and a resident. Common Rock Thrush breeds mostly higher up in the mountains, in rocky terrain around the tree line (13, 14, 15, 18, 20, 21 and sites C on page 182 and B on page 202). Stonechat breeds in low numbers and is abundant in the Ebro basin in winter. Whinchat can be found during migration and is a rare breeding bird of alpine meadows (e.g. 14). Northern Wheatear is frequent in stony areas above and around the treeline (e.g. 13, 14, 15, 18, 19, 21, B on page 202) and an uncommon breeding bird in the steppe (e.g. 3 – common at 1). Black-eared Wheatear is fairly common in stony steppes (e.g. 3, 4, site A on page 137). Black Wheatear is typical of dry, sandstone cliffs and rocky terrain on the south slopes of the Guara. It is in decline, but still fairly easily found at 3, 4, 5 and 10. Black Redstart is common in villages and above the treeline. Few Common Redstarts breed, but they are seen on migration.

'Sylvia' warblers Sardinian and Dartford Warbler are common birds of Mediterranean scrubland (1, 3 to 11). Subalpine Warbler is frequent in open Holm Oak forest with scrub (e.g. 6, 7, 8, 9, site A on page 161). Orphean Warbler is difficult to find, but locally common in dry areas with scattered trees, like Aleppo Pines, Spanish Junipers and Holm Oak (8, site A on page 137). Spectacled Warbler is uncommon in bushy steppes (2, 3, 4, 5). Blackcap is widespread in any type of woody vegetation in the mountains and along rivers in the lowlands. Garden Warbler has a preference for areas of rose bush in the mountains (e.g. 12, 14, 16, 18).

'Brown' warblers Zitting Cisticola (Fan-tailed Warbler) occurs in damp meadows along rivers in the lowlands (5, 6, sites B, C, D on pages 137-138). Cetti's Warbler is, like Nightingale, common in bushes near streams (3, 4, 5, 6, 8, 11). Melodious Warbler too, occurs in bushes along rivers (4, 5, sites A on pages 161 and 181 and D on 138). Chiffchaff is an abundant winter visitor and a breeding bird of mountain forests. The precise status of Iberian Chiffchaff, a 'split' from the commoner bird, remains to be clarified. It is best distinguished vocally, but 'mixed singers' exist to the north of its range. Willow Warbler is seen only on migration. Bonelli's Warbler is a common breeding bird in pine and holm oak woods. Great Reed Warbler breeds in marshlands and isolated reedbeds (4, 5, 6, sites B and C on pages 137-138). Reed Warbler is less common in similar terrain.

Goldcrest, Firecrest and Wren Firecrest is a common breeding bird of coniferous forests throughout, except at high altitudes. Goldcrest breeds in high altitude Scots and Pyrenean pine forests (15, 19). Wren breeds in well vegetated areas, most commonly in the mountains.

Flycatchers Spotted Flycatcher is an uncommon breeding bird in the mountains and the *Somontano*. Pied Flycatcher is a frequent migrant and most easily seen in small woodlands and bushes in the more barren lowlands (e.g. 2, 5).

Tits Great, Blue and Long-tailed Tits are frequent throughout. Coal and Crested Tits are common in any coniferous woodland in the mountains. Marsh Tit breeds in high altitude beech woods and frequently feeds in bushes along mountain rivers and in meadows in the mountains (13, 14, 15, 16, 18, 19). Penduline Tit breeds along the Ebro, Cinca and marshland with reeds and willows (5, sites B and D on pages 137-138). Bearded Tit breeds in the extensive reedbeds of Sariñena (5).

Nuthatch and creepers Nuthatch is surprisingly rare and occurs only in the older pine, beech and mixed forests of the high Pyrenees (12, 13, 15, 18). Short-toed Treecreeper is fairly common throughout (partially) wooded areas, while Eurasian Treecreeper is a fairly rare breeding bird of high altitude coniferous forests (15, 19). Wallcreeper breeds on high altitude, difficult-to-accesss south-facing rock cliffs (best 13) and is most easily found in winter when it descends to lower altitudes, particularly the south-facing Guara (especially 8, 9, 10).

Shrikes Red-backed Shrike is a typical breeding bird of grazed pastures with many rose bushes in the mountains (10, 11, 13, 14, 16, 17, 18, 20). Woodchat Shrike takes over in the *Depresión, Somontano* and Ebro basin, where it is fairly common in areas with open Holm Oak forest (3, 5, 6, 8, 9, particularly sites A on pages 137 and 161). Iberian Grey Shrike is scarce and declining, but occurs throughout much of the Ebro Basin and *Somontano* (e.g. 3, 4, 21, sites A on pages 137 and 161). Note that, despite what some older books may indicate, both Lesser Grey Shrike and (Northern) Great Grey Shrike are not present. The first went extinct many years ago and the second was probably never here.

Crows and allies Jackdaws, Jays, Crows and Magpies occur in their preferred habitat, although both Jackdaw and Carrion Crow are not very frequent. Raven is common throughout, and Red-billed Chough has colonies in many places (e.g. 4, 7, 8, 9, 10, 12, 13, 14, 15, 16). Alpine Chough breeds at high altitudes (e.g. 16, 19, 21, site B on page 202).

Starlings Spotless Starling is common in the Ebro valley and lower valleys. In winter it is joined by varying numbers of Common Starling. Golden Oriole is frequent in riverine woodlands and denser lowland forests (e.g. 3, 5, 8, 9, 11, 12, 13, 14, 20).

Sparrows House Sparrow is common. Rock Sparrow is fairly common, though elusive at times, in rocky areas, often near water (e.g. 1, 5, 10, site A on page 181 and on the citadel in Jaca). Tree Sparrow is locally common.

Finches and allies Chaffinch, Greenfinch, Goldfinch, Serin and Linnet are all common or fairly common in their preferred habitat. The latter is particularly frequent in rocky alpine meadows. Hawfinch is mainly a winter bird. Bullfinch, here at the extreme edge of its range, is quite rare in mixed woodland, coming down in winter and Crossbill can turn up in any coniferous forest. Citril Finch breeds in varying numbers in open pine woods just below the treeline (e.g. 12, 13, 14, 15, 16, 18, 19, site C on page 182 and D on page 203). Snowfinch breeds in rocky alpine meadows above 2,000 metres (21) and descends in winter to mountain passes and ski resorts where it is easier to find (e.g. 14, B on page 215).

Buntings Corn Bunting is very common in the lowlands and even in some agricultural land in the mountains (e.g. 13, 14, 16, 20). Rock Bunting is fairly common on rocky slopes in both the Pyrenees and the *Sierras Exteriores* (e.g. 8, 9, 10, 11, 13, 14, 16, 18, 19, 20, 21). Cirl Bunting is frequent in open woodland (e.g. 5, 6, 7, 9, 12, 20, site A on page 161). Reed Bunting is mainly a winter bird. Yellowhammer occurs, together with the much rarer Ortolan Bunting, in alpine meadows with rose bushes, where cattle grazes (e.g. 13, 14, 16, 18).

SPECIES LIST & TRANSLATION

The following list comprises all species mentioned in this guidebook and gives their scientific, German and Dutch names. It is not a complete checklist of the species of Huesca. Some names have an asterisk (*) behind them, indicating an unofficial name. See page 7 for more details.

PLANTS

English	Scientific	German	Dutch
Adenostyles	*Adenostyles alliariae*	Grauer Alpendost	Grauwe klierstijl
Aizoon, Spanish	*Aizoon hispanicum*	Spanisches Eiskraut	Spaans ijskruid
Alder, Green	*Alnus viridis*	Grün-Erle	Groene els
Alison, Mountain	*Alyssum montanum*	Berg-Steinkraut	Bergschildzaad
Alpenrose	*Rhododendron ferrugineum*	Rostblättrige Alpenrose	Roestbladig alpenroosje
Anemone, Narcissus-flowered	*Anemone narcissiflora*	Narzissen-Windröschen	Narcisanemoon
Anemone, Yellow	*Anemone ranunculoides*	Gelbes Windröschen	Gele anemoon
Aphyllanthes, Blue	*Aphyllanthes monspeliensis*	Blaue Binsenlilie*	Blauwe bieslelie
Arnica	*Arnica montana*	Arnika	Valkruid
Asphodel, Hollow-stemmed	*Asphodelus fistulosus*	Röhriger Affodill	Holle affodil*
Asphodel, Tofield's	*Tofieldia calyculata*	Gewöhnliche Simsenlilie	Gewone bieslelie
Asphodel, White	*Asphodelus albus*	Weisser Affodill	Witte affodil
Aster, Alpine	*Aster alpinus*	Alpen-Aster	Alpenaster
Avens, Mountain	*Dryas octopetala*	Silberwurz	Achtster
Balm, Bastard	*Melittis melissophyllum*	Immenblad	Bijenblad
Baneberry	*Actaea spicata*	Christophskraut	Christoffelkruid
Bartsia, Alpine	*Bartsia alpina*	Alpenhelm	Alpenhelm
Bearberry	*Arctostaphylos uva-ursi*	Echte Bärentraube	Berendruif
Bedstraw, Round-leaved	*Galium rotundifolium*	Rundblättriges Labkraut	Rondbladig walstro*
Beech	*Fagus sylvatica*	Buche	Beuk
Bellflower, Celandine*	*Campanula ficarioides*	Scharbockähnliche Glockenblume*	Speenkruidklokje*
Bellflower, Clustered	*Campanula glomerata*	Geknäuelte Glockenblume	Kluwenklokje
Bellflower, Peach-leaved	*Campanula persicifolia*	Pfirschblättrige Glockenblume	Prachtklokje
Bellflower, Pyrenean	*Campanula speciosa*	Pyrenäen-Glockenblume	Pyreneeën klokje
Bellflower, Scheuchzer's	*Campanula scheuchzeri*	Scheuchzers Glockenblume	Scheuchzers klokje*
Bellflower, Spreading	*Campanula patula*	Wiesen-Glockenblume	Weideklokje
Betony, Yellow	*Stachys alopecuros*	Gelber Betonie	Gele betonie
Bilberry	*Vaccinium myrtillus*	Blaubeere	Blauwe bosbes
Bilberry, Bog	*Vaccinium uliginosum*	Rauschbeere	Rijsbes

Bindweed, Pygmy	*Convolvulus lineatus*	Gestrichelte Winde	Calandsklokje
Bindweed, Southern	*Convolvulus cantabrica*	Kantabrische Winde	Kantabrische winde
Bindweed, Woolly	*Convolvulus lanuginosus*	Kurzwollige Winde	Wollige winde*
Bird's-nest, Violet	*Limodorum abortivum*	Violetter Dingel	Paarse aspergeorchis
Bird's-nest, Yellow	*Monotropa hypopitys*	Fichtenspargel	Stofzaad
Black Bog-rush	*Schoenus nigricans*	Schwarzes Kopfried	Knopbies
Bladder-fern, Brittle	*Cystopteris fragilis*	Zerbrechlicher Blasenfarn	Blaasvaren
Bluebell, Brown	*Dipcadi serotinum*	Schweifblatt	Bruine hyacint*
Blue-sowthistle, Hairless	*Cicerbita plumieri*	Französischer Milchlattich	Franse bergsla*
Bogbean	*Menyanthes trifoliata*	Fieberklee	Waterdrieblad
Bog-rush, Black	*Schoenus nigricans*	Schwarzes Kopfried	Knopbies
Boleum	*Boleum asperum*	Boleum*	Boleum*
Box	*Buxus sempervirens*	Buchsbaum	Buxus
Broom, Scorpion	*Genista scorpius*	Skorpion-Ginster	Schorpioenbrem*
Broom, Silver-lined*	*Argyrolobium zanonii*	Silberginster	Zilverbrem*
Broom, Yellow Hedgehog*	*Echinospartum horridum*	Schreklige Igelginster*	Stekende egelbrem*
Broomrape, Rosemary	*Orobanche latisquama*	Breitschuppige Sommerwurz	Rozemarijn-bremraap*
Broomrape, Sand	*Orobanche arenaria*	Sand-Sommerwurz	Zandbremraap*
Buckthorn, Dwarf	*Rhamnus pumila*	Zwerg-Kreuzdorn	Dwergwegedoorn
Buttercup, Aconite-leaved	*Ranunculus aconitifolius*	Eisenhutblättriger Hahnenfuss	Monnikskapranonkel
Buttercup, Clasping*	*Ranunculus amplexicaulis*	Weisser Hahnenfuss	Stengelomvattende boterbloem
Buttercup, Gouan's	*Ranunculus gouani*	Gouan Hahnenfuss*	Gouan boterbloem*
Buttercup, Grass-leaved	*Ranunculus gramineus*	Grasblättriger Hahnenfuss	Grasbladige boterbloem*
Buttercup, Parnassus-leaved	*Ranunculus parnassifolius*	Herzblättriger Hahnenfuss	Parnassiaboterbloem*
Buttercup, Pyrenean	*Ranunculus pyrenaeus*	Pyrenäen-Hahnenfuss	Pyreneese boterbloem
Buttercup, Thore's	*Ranunculus thora*	Schildblatt-Hahnenfuss	Schildboterbloem*
Butterwort, Alpine	*Pinguicula alpina*	Alpen-Fettkraut	Alpenvetblad
Butterwort, Common	*Pinguicula vulgaris*	Gewöhnliches Fettkraut	Gewoon vetblad
Butterwort, Large-flowered	*Pinguicula grandiflora*	Grossblütiges Fettkraut	Grootbloemig vetblad
Butterwort, Long-leaved	*Pinguicula longifolia*	Langblättriges Fettkraut	Langbladig vetblad
Calamint, Alpine	*Acinos alpinus*	Alpen-Steinquendel	Alpensteentijm
Camphor, Wild *	*Camphorosma monspeliaca*	Montpellier-Kampferkraut	Montpellierkamfer*
Campion, Moss	*Silene acaulis*	Stengelloses Leimkraut	Stengelloze silene
Catananche, Blue	*Catananche caerulea*	Blaue Rasselblume	Blauwe strobloem
Catchfly, Saxifrage*	*Silene saxifraga*	Steinbrech-Leimkraut	Steenbreeksilene
Cephalaria, White	*Cephalaria leucantha*	Weisser Schuppenkopf	Witte schijnbeemdkroon*
Cinquefoil, Lady's-mantle-leaved	*Potentilla alchemilloides*	Weisses Pyrenäen-Fingerkraut	Vrouwenmantelganzerik*
Cinquefoil, Lax	*Potentilla caulescens*	Stängel-Fingerkraut	Steenganzerik*
Cinquefoil, Snowy*	*Potentilla nivalis*	Schnee-Fingerkraut	Sneeuwganzerik*
Cistus, Laurel-leaved	*Cistus laurifolius*	Lorbeerblättrige Zistrose	Laurierbladig zonneroosje*

Cistus, Rosemary-leaved*	*Cistus clusii*	Clusius-Zistrose	Rozemarijnbladig zonneroosje*
Cistus, Sage-leaved	*Cistus salvifolius*	Salbeiblättriges Zistrose	Saliebladig zonneroosje
Clover, Alpine	*Trifolium alpinum*	Alpen-Klee	Alpenklaver
Columbine, Common	*Aquilegia vulgaris*	Gewöhnliche Akelei	Wilde akelei
Columbine, Pyrenean	*Aquilegia pyrenaica*	Pyrenäenakelei	Pyreneese akelei
Columbine, Sticky*	*Aquilegia viscosa*	Klebrige Akelei	Kleverige akelei*
Coralroot, Pinnate	*Cardamine pentaphyllos*	Finger-Zahnwurz	Vijfbladig tandkruid*
Coris	*Coris monspeliensis*	Stachelträubchen	Blauwe coris*
Cottongrass	*Eriophorum sp.*	Wollgras	Wollegras
Crane's-bill, Ashy	*Geranium cinereum*	Grauer Storchschnabel	Grauwe ooievaarsbek
Crane's-bill, Bloody	*Geranium sanguineum*	Blutroter Storchschnabel	Bloedooievaarsbek
Crane's-bill, Wood	*Geranium sylvaticum*	Wald-Storchschnabel	Bosooievaarsbek
Cressa	*Cressa cretica*	Cressa*	Cressa*
Crowfoot, Glacier	*Ranunculus glacialis*	Gletscher-Hahnenfuss	Gletsjerranonkel
Daffodil, Wild	*Narcissus pseudonarcissus*	Gelbe Narzisse	Wilde narcis
Dragon Mouth, Pyrenean	*Horminum pyrenaicum*	Pyrenäen-Drachenmaul	Pyreneese drakenmuil
Edelweiss	*Leontopodium alpinum*	Edelweiss	Edelweiss
Elder, Red-berried	*Sambucus racemosa*	Trauben-Holunder	Trosvlier
Elm	*Ulmus sp.*	Ulme	Iep
Eryngo, Field	*Eryngium campestre*	Feld-Mannstreu	Echte kruisdistel
Eryngo, Pyrenean	*Eryngium bourgatii*	Spanischer-Mannstreu	Pyreneese kruisdistel
Esparto	*Lygeum spartum*	Espartogras	Espartogras
Fern, Beech	*Phegopteris connectilis*	Gewöhnlicher Buchenfarn	Smalle beukvaren
Fern, Limestone	*Gymnocarpium robertianum*	Ruprechtsfarn	Rechte driehoeksvaren
Fern, Maidenhair	*Adiantum capillus-veneris*	Venushaarfarn	Venushaar
Fern, Parsley	*Cryptogramma crispa*	Krauser Rollfarn	Gekroesde rolvaren
Figwort, Alpine	*Scrophularia alpestris*	Alpine Braunwurz	Alpenhelmkruid*
Figwort, Pyrenean	*Scrophularia pyrenaica*	Pyrenäen-Braunwurz	Pyrenees helmkruid
Fir, Silver	*Abies alba*	Weisstanne	Gewone zilverspar
Flax, Alpine	*Linum alpinum*	Alpen-Lein	Alpenvlas*
Flax, Beautiful	*Linum narbonense*	Französischer Lein	Frans vlas
Flax, Bellflower*	*Linum campanulatum*	Glocken-Lein	Klokjesvlas*
Flax, Sticky	*Linum viscosum*	Klebriger Lein	Kleverig vlas
Flax, Upright Yellow	*Linum strictum*	Steifer Lein	Stijf vlas
Flax, White	*Linum suffruticosum*	Strauchiger Lein	Wit vlas*
Foxglove, Fairy	*Erinus alpinus*	Steinbalsam	Alpenbalsem
Foxglove, Yellow	*Digitalis lutea*	Kleinblütiger Fingerhut	Geel vingerhoedskruid
Frankenia, Thyme-leaved*	*Frankenia thymifolia*	Thymian-Blättriger Frankenie*	Tijmbladige zeehei*
Frankenia, White*	*Frankenia pulverulenta*	Seeheide	Witte zeehei*
Fritillary, Spanish	*Fritillaria lusitanica*	Portugiesische Schachblume	Iberische kievitsbloem
Fritillary, Pyrenean	*Fritillaria pyrenaica*	Pyrenäen-Schachblume	Pyreneeën kievitsbloem*
Garlic, Rosy	*Allium roseum*	Rosen-Lauch	Roze look
Garlic, Yellow	*Allium moly*	Goldlauch	Goudlook
Gentian, Alpine	*Gentiana alpina*	Alpen-Enzian	Zuidelijke gentiaan
Gentian, Burser's	*Gentiana burseri*	Pyrenäen Tüpfel-Enzian*	Pyreneese stippelgentiaan*

Gentian, Cross-leaved	*Gentiana cruciata*	Kreuz-Enzian	Kruisbladgentiaan
Gentian, Field	*Gentianella campestris*	Feld-Enzian	Veldgentiaan
Gentian, Great Yellow	*Gentiana lutea*	Gelber Enzian	Gele gentiaan
Gentian, Snow	*Gentiana nivalis*	Schnee-Enzian	Sneeuwgentiaan
Gentian, Spring	*Gentiana verna*	Frühlings-Enzian	Voorjaarsgentiaan
Gentian, Trumpet	*Gentiana acaulis*	Kochs Enzian	Stengelloze gentiaan
Germander, Cudweed*	*Teucrium gnaphalodes*	Ruhrkraut-Gamander*	Droogbloemgamander*
Germander, Pyrenean	*Teucrium pyrenaicum*	Pyrenäen-Gamander	Pyreneese gamander
Germander, Wall	*Teucrium chamaedrys*	Echter Gamander	Echte gamander
Glasswort, Relict*	*Microcnemum coralloides*	Türkischer Queller*	Turkse zeekraal*
Globeflower	*Trollius europaeus*	Trollblume	Trollius
Globularia, Common	*Globularia vulgaris*	Gemeine Kugelblume	Gewone kogelbloem
Globularia, Creeping	*Globularia repens*	Kriechende Kugelblume	Kruipende kogelbloem*
Globularia, Graceful*	*Globularia gracilis*	Zierliche Kugelblume*	Sierlijke kogelbloem*
Globularia, Heart-leaved	*Globularia cordifolia*	Herzblättrige Kugelblume	Hartbladige kogelbloem
Globularia, Leafless-stemmed	*Globularia nudicaulis*	Nacktstängelige Kugelblume	Naaktstengelige kogelbloem
Globularia, Shrubby	*Globularia alypum*	Strauchkugelblume	Struikkogelbloem*
Goldendrop, Bubani's	*Onosma bubanii*	Pyrenäen-Lotwurz	Pyreneese gouddruppel
Goldenrod	*Solidago virgaurea*	Gewöhnliche Goldrute	Echte guldenroede
Grass-of-Parnassus	*Parnassia palustris*	Sumpf-Herzblatt	Parnassiaboterbloem*
Grass, False Esparto	*Lygeum spartum*	Espartogras	Vals espartogras*
Gromwell, Golden Dwarf*	*Neatostema apulum*	Apulischer Steinsame	Geel parelzaad
Gromwell, Shrubby	*Lithodora fruticosa*	Strauch-Steinsame*	Struikparelzaad*
Gypsophila, Spanish	*Gypsophila struthium hispanica*	Spanisches Gipskraut*	Spaans gipskruid*
Halopeplis	*Halopeplis amplexicaulis*	Halopeplis*	Halopeplis*
Hart's-tongue	*Asplenium scolopendrium*	Hirschzunge	Tongvaren
Hawk's-beard, Pygmy	*Crepis pygmaea*	Zwerg-Pippau	Dwergstreepzaad*
Hawkweed, Gypsum*	*Launaea pumila*	Gips-Habichtskraut*	Gipshavikskruid*
Hazel	*Corylus avellana*	Haselstrauch	Hazelaar
Heather	*Calluna vulgaris*	Heidekraut	Struikhei
Helleborine, Broad-leaved	*Epipactis helleborine*	Breitblättrige Stendelwürz	Brede wespenorchis
Helleborine, Dark-red	*Epipactis atrorubens*	Braunrote Stendelwürz	Bruinrode wespenorchis
Helleborine, False	*Veratrum album*	Weisser Germer	Witte nieswortel
Helleborine, Marsh	*Epipactis palustris*	Echte Sumpfwurz	Moeraswespenorchis
Helleborine, Narrow-leaved	*Cephalanthera longifolia*	Schwertblättriges Waldvögelein	Wit bosvogeltje
Helleborine, Red	*Cephalanthera rubra*	Rotes Waldvögelein	Rood bosvogeltje
Helleborine, Small-leaved	*Epipactis microphylla*	Kleinblättrige Stendelwurz	Kleinbladige wespenorchis
Helleborine, White	*Cephalanthera damasonium*	Weisses Waldvöglein	Bleek bosvogeltje
Herb-paris	*Paris quadrifolia*	Einbeere	Eenbes
Honeysuckle, Alpine	*Lonicera alpigena*	Alpen-Heckenkirsche	Alpenkamperfoelie
Honeysuckle, Etruscan	*Lonicera etrusca*	Toskanischen Geissblatt	Toscaanse kamperfoelie*
Honeysuckle, Pyrenean	*Lonicera pyrenaica*	Pyrenäen-Heckenkirsche	Pyreneese kamperfoelie

Hyacinth, Pyrenean	*Brimeura amethystina*	Amethyst-Wildhyazinthe	Pyreneese hyacint
Hypecoum	*Hypecoum imberbe*	Hypecoum*	Hypecoum*
Iris, Pyrenean	*Iris latifolia*	Pyrenäen-Schwertlilie	Pyreneese lis*
Ironwort, Hyssop-leaved*	*Sideritis hyssopifolia*	Ysopblättriges Gliedkraut	Hyssopbladig ijzerkruid*
Ironwort, Hairy	*Sideritis hirsuta*	Behaartes Gliedkraut	Behaard ijzerkruid*
Jerusalem-sage, Iberian	*Phlomis lychnitis*	Filziges Brandkraut	Viltbrandkruid*
Jerusalem-sage, Iranian	*Phlomis herba-venti*	Wind-Brandkraut	Iraans brandkruid*
Joint-pine, Large*	*Ephedra major*	Grosse Meerträubel	Grote zeedruif*
Jonquil, Rush-leaved	*Narcissus assoanus*	Binsenblättriges Narzisse*	Rusbladige narcis*
Juniper, Phoenician	*Juniperus phoenicea*	Phönizischer Wacholder	Phoenicische jeneverbes
Juniper, Spanish	*Juniperus thurifera*	Spanischer Wacholder	Spaanse jeneverbes
Lady's-slipper	*Cypripedium calceolus*	Frauenschuh	Vrouwenschoentje
Lady's-tresses, Creeping	*Goodyera repens*	Netzblatt	Dennenorchis
Laurustinus	*Viburnum tinus*	Immergrüner Schneeball	Altijdgroene sneeuwbal
Lavender, Common	*Lavandula angustifolia*	Schmalblättriger Lavendel	Echte lavendel
Leek, Alpine	*Allium victorialis*	Allermannsharnisch	Alpenlook
Leek, Round-headed	*Allium sphaerocephalon*	Kugel-Lauch	Kogellook
Lettuce, Purple	*Prenanthes purpurea*	Hasenlattich	Hazensla
Leuzea	*Leuzea conifera*	Kegel-Flockenblume*	Kegelcentaurie*
Lily, Martagon	*Lilium martagon*	Türkenbund-Lilie	Turkse lelie
Lily, Pyrenean	*Lilium pyrenaicum*	Pyrenäen-Lilie	Pyreneese lelie
Lily-of-the-Valley	*Convallaria majalis*	Maiglöckchen	Lelietje-van-dalen
Linden	*Tilia sp.*	Linde	Linde
Liverleaf	*Hepatica nobilis*	Leberblümchen	Leverbloempje
Lousewort, Leafy	*Pedicularis foliosa*	Durchblättertes Läusekraut	Pluimkartelblad
Lousewort, Purple-beaked	*Pedicularis mixta*	Purperlippig Läusekraut*	Purperlipkartelblad*
Lousewort, Pyrenean	*Pedicularis pyrenaica*	Pyrenäen-Läusekraut	Pyrenees kartelblad
Mallow, Sea	*Lavatera maritima*	Meer-Strauchpappel	Zee-struikmalva*
Maple	*Acer sp.*	Ahorn	Esdoorn
Marjoram, Wild	*Origanum vulgare*	Echter Dost	Wilde marjolein
Masterwort, Great	*Astrantia major*	Grosse Sterndolde	Groot sterrenscherm
Masterwort, Lesser	*Astrantia minor*	Kleine Sterndolde	Klein sterrenscherm
Meadow-rue, Large-flowered*	*Thalictrum tuberosum*	Grossblütige Wiesenraute*	Grootbloemige ruit*
Milk-vetch, Foxtail*	*Astragalus alopecuroides*	Fuchsschwanz-Tragant	Vossenstaarttragant*
Milk-vetch, Grey*	*Astragalus incanus*	Grauer Tragant	Grijze tragant*
Milk-vetch, Mountain	*Astragalus sempervirens*	Dorniger Tragant	Immergroene tragant
Milkvetch, Samnitic	*Oxytropis neglecta*	Insubrischer Spitzkiel	Pyreneese spitskiel
Monk's-hood	*Aconitum napellus*	Blauer Eisenhut	Blauwe monnikskap
Moonwort	*Botrychium lunaria*	Mondraute	Gelobde maanvaren
Moricandia, Large*	*Moricandia moricandioides*	Grosse Moricandie*	Grote moricandia*
Needlegrass, Lagasca's	*Stipa lagascae*	Lagasca's Federgras*	Lagasca's vedergras*
Needlegrass, Small-flowered*	*Stipa parviflora*	Kleinblütiges Federgras*	Kleinbloemig vedergras*

Oak, Holm	*Quercus ilex*	Stein-Eiche	Steeneik
Oak, Kermes	*Quercus coccifera*	Kermes-Eiche	Hulsteik
Oak, Portuguese	*Quercus faginea*	Portugiesische Eiche	Portugese eik
Orache, Shrubby	*Atriplex halimus*	Strauch-Melde	Struikmelde
Orchid, Bee	*Ophrys apifera*	Bienen-Ragwurz	Bijenorchis
Orchid, Bird's-nest	*Neottia nidus-avis*	Nestwurz	Vogelnestje
Orchid, Broad-leaved Marsh	*Dactylorhiza majalis*	Breitblättriges Knabenkraut	Brede orchis
Orchid, Burnt	*Neotinea ustulata*	Brand-Knabenkraut	Aangebrande orchis
Orchid, Common Spotted	*Dactylorhiza fuchsii*	Fuchs' Knabenkraut	Bosorchis
Orchid, Dull Bee	*Ophrys fusca*	Braune Ragwurz	Bruine orchis
Orchid, Early Spider	*Ophrys atrata*	Schwarze Ragwurz	Zwarte spinnenorchis
Orchid, Early-purple	*Orchis mascula*	Mannliches Knabenkraut	Mannetjesorchis
Orchid, Elder-flowered	*Dactylorhiza sambucina*	Holunder-Knabenkraut	Vlierorchis
Orchid, Fly	*Ophrys insectifera*	Fliegen-Ragwurz	Vliegenorchis
Orchid, Fragrant	*Gymnadenia conopsea*	Mücken-Händelwurz	Grote muggenorchis
Orchid, Fragrant Bug	*Anacamptis fragrans*	Wohlriechendes Wanzenknabenkraut	Welriekende wantsenorchis*
Orchid, Frog	*Dactylorhiza viride*	Hohlzunge	Groene nachtorchis
Orchid, Greater Butterfly	*Platanthera chlorantha*	Berg-Waldhyazinthe	Bergnachtorchis
Orchid, Green-winged	*Anacamptis morio*	Kleines Knabenkraut	Harlekijn
Orchid, Heath Spotted	*Dactylorhiza maculata*	Geflecktes Knabenkraut	Gevlekte orchis
Orchid, Lady	*Orchis purpurea*	Purpur-Knabenkraut	Purperorchis
Orchid, Lange's	*Orchis langei*	Spanisches Knabenkraut	iJle mannetjesorchis
Orchid, Lesser Butterfly	*Platanthera bifolia*	Weisse Waldhyazinthe	Welriekende nachtorchis
Orchid, Mirror	*Ophrys speculum*	Spiegel-Ragwurz	Spiegelorchis
Orchid, Pale	*Orchis pallens*	Blasses Knabenkraut	Bleke orchis
Orchid, Pyramidal	*Anacamptis pyramidalis*	Hundswurz	Hondskruid
Orchid, Robust Marsh	*Dactylorhiza elata*	Hohes Knabenkraut	Grote rietorchis
Orchid, Southern Marsh	*Dactylorhiza praetermissa*	Übersehenes Knabenkraut	Rietorchis
Orchid, Vanilla	*Gymnadenia austriaca & G. gabasiana*	Kohlröschen	Vanilleorchis
Orchid, Woodcock	*Ophrys scolopax*	Schnepfen-Ragwurz	Snippenorchis
Orchid, Yellow-fringed Fly	*ophrys subinsectifera*	Kleinblütige Fliegen-Ragwurz	Pyreneese vliegenorchis*
Pansy, Horned	*Viola cornuta*	Pyrenäen-Stiefmütterchen	Hoornviooltje
Pasqueflower, Alpine	*Pulsatilla alpina*	Alpen-Kuhschelle	Alpenanemoon
Pea, Black	*Lathyrus niger*	Schwarzwerdende Platterbse	Zwarte lathyrus
Peganum	*Peganum harmala*	Steppenraute	Stepperuit
Pepperwort, Gypsum*	*Lepidium subulatum*	Gips-Kresse*	Gipskruidkers*
Petrocoptis	*Petrocoptis sp.*	Kalk-Nelke*	Kalk-anjer*
Pheasant's-eye, Pyrenean	*Adonis pyrenaica*	Pyrenäen-Adonisröschen	Pyreneeënadonis*
Pheasant's-eye, Toothed*	*Adonis dentata*	Gezähnte Adonisröschen	Getande adonis*
Pheasant's-eye, Small-seeded*	*Adonis microcarpa*	Kleinfrüchtiges Adonisröschen	Kleine adonis*
Pine, Aleppo	*Pinus halepensis*	Allepo-Kiefer	Aleppo den
Pine, Austrian	*Pinus nigra*	Schwarzkiefer	Zwarte den
Pine, Dwarf	*Pinus (mugo) mugo*	Latsche	Bergden

Pine, Pyrenean	*Pinus (mugo) uncinata*	Haken-Kiefer	Grote bergden*
Pine, Scots	*Pinus sylvestris*	Waldkiefer	Grove den
Platycapnos	*Platycapnos spicatus*	Ähriger Breitsporn	Platycapnos*
Poplar, White	*Populus alba*	Silber-Pappel	Witte abeel
Poppy, Cambrian	*Meconopsis cambrica*	Gelber Scheinmohn	Schijnpapaver
Primrose, Bird's-eye	*Primula farinosa*	Mehlige Schlüsselblume	Melige sleutelbloem
Primrose, Entire-leaved	*Primula integrifolia*	Ganzblättrige Primel	Gaafrandige sleutelbloem
Ragwort, Pheasant's-eye-leaved*	*Senecio adonidifolius*	Polster-Greiskraut	Adoniskruiskruid*
Ramonda	*Ramonda myconi*	Pyrenäen-Felsenteller	Ramonda*
Rampion, Charmeil's*	*Phyteuma charmelii*	Charmeils Rapunzel	Charmeils rapunzel*
Rampion, Pyrenean	*Phyteuma pyrenaicum*	Pyrenäen-Teufelskralle	Pyreneeënrapunzel
Rampion, Round-headed	*Phyteuma orbiculare*	Kugelige Teufelskralle	Bolrapunzel
Restharrow, Round-leaved	*Ononis rotundifolia*	Rundblättrige Hauhechel	Rondbladig stalkruid
Restharrow, Three-toothed*	*Ononis tridentata*	Dreizähnige Hauhechel*	Drietandig stalkruid*
Rock-jasmine, Lagger's	*Androsace laggeri*	Laggers Mannsschild*	Laggers mansschild*
Rock-jasmine, Pink	*Androsace carnea*	Fleischroter Mannsschild	Vleeskleurig mansschild
Rock-jasmine, Pyrenean	*Androsace pyrenaica*	Pyrenäen-Mannsschild	Pyrenees mansschild
Rock-jasmine, Woolly	*Androsace villosa*	Zottiger mannsschild	Zilverwit mansschild
Rockrose, Pale-leaved*	*Helianthemum squamatum*	Bleich-Blättriges Sonnenröschen*	Bleekbladig zonneroosje*
Rockrose, Small-leaved*	*Helianthemum marifolium*	Schmall-Blättriges Sonnenröschen*	Smalbladig zonneroosje*
Rockrose, White	*Helianthemum apenninum*	Weisses Sonnenröschen	Wit zonneroosje
Rosemary	*Rosmarinus officinalis*	Rosmarin	Rozemarijn
Rue, Narrow-leaved	*Ruta angustifolia*	Schmalblättrige Raute	Smalbladige wijnruit*
Sage, Lavender-leaved	*Salvia lavandulifolia*	Lavendelblättriger Salbei	Spaanse salie
Saltmarsh-grass, Spiny*	*Puccinellia pungens*	Stechender Salzschwaden*	Stekend kweldergras*
Saltwort, Mediterranean	*Salsola vermiculata*	Mediterranes Salzkraut	Behaard loogkruid*
Sandwort, Pink	*Arenaria purpurascens*	Purper-Sandkraut	Roze zandmuur*
Sanicle	*Sanicula europaea*	Sanikel	Heelkruid
Sarcocapnos	*Sarcocapnos enneaphylla*	Neunblättriger Dicksporn	Pyreneese helmbloem*
Saw-wort, Giant*	*Rhaponticum centauroides*	Flockenblume-Bergscharte*	Schubbig zaagblad
Saxifrage, Blue	*Saxifraga caesia*	Blaugrüner Steinbrech	Wratjessteenbreek*
Saxifrage, Fragile	*Saxifraga fragilis*	Bruch-Steinbrech*	Breeksteenbreek*
Saxifrage, Hariot's	*Saxifraga hariotii*	Hariots-Steinbrech*	Hariot's steenbreek*
Saxifrage, Irati's*	*Saxifraga pubescens iratiana*	Iratis-Steinbrech*	Irati's steenbreek*
Saxifrage, Livelong	*Saxifraga paniculata*	Trauben-Steinbrech	Trossteenbreek
Saxifrage, Long-leaved	*Saxifraga longifolia*	Königs-Steinbrech	Langbladige steenbreek
Saxifrage, Mossy	*Saxifraga bryoides*	Moos-Steinbrech	Gestippelde mossteenbreek*
Saxifrage, Neglected	*Saxifraga praetermissa*	Vernachlässigter Steinbrech	Vergeten steenbreek*
Saxifrage, Purple	*Saxifraga oppositifolia*	Gegenblättriger Steinbrech	Zuiltjessteenbreek

Saxifrage, Rock-jasmine*	*Saxifraga androsacea*	Mannsschild-Steinbrech	Mansschild steenbreek
Saxifrage, Starry	*Saxifraga stellaris*	Stern-Steinbrech	Stersteenbreek
Saxifrage, Water	*Saxifraga aquatica*	Wasser-Steinbrech	Watersteenbreek
Saxifrage, White Musky	*Saxifraga exarata moschata*	Moschus-Steinbrech	Muskussteenbreek
Saxifrage, Pyrenean	*Saxifraga umbrosa*	Schatten-Steinbrech	Schildersverdriet
Saxifrage, Yellow	*Saxifraga aizoides*	Fetthennen-Steinbrech	Gele bergsteenbreek
Saxifrage, Yellow Mountain	*Saxifraga aretioides*	Gelbe Pyrenäen-Steinbrech*	Gele pyreneeënsteenbreek*
Scabious, Starry*	*Scabiosa stellata*	Sternskabiose	Sterduifkruid*
Scorpion-vetch, Dwarf	*Coronilla minima*	Kleine Kronwicke	Klein kroonkruid
Scurvy-grass, Aragon	*Cochlearia aragonensis*	Aragon Löffelkraut*	Aragon-lepelblad*
Seablite, Shrubby	*Suaeda vera*	Strauch-Sode*	Struikschorrenkruid*
Sea-lavender	*Limonium sp.*	Strandflieder	Lamsoor
Sedge, Yellow	*Carex flava*	Gelb-Segge	Gele zegge
Shield-fern, Soft	*Polystichum setiferum*	Borstiger Schildfarn	Zachte naaldvaren
Sibbaldia	*Sibbaldia procumbens*	Alpen-Gelbling	Sibbaldia*
Snapdragon	*Antirrhinum majus*	Garten-Löwenmaul	Grote leeuwenbek
Snapdragon, Evergreen	*Antirrhinum sempervirens*	Pyrenäen-Löwenmaul	Immergroene leeuwenbek
Snapdragon, Woolly	*Antirrhinum molle*	Wolliger Löwenmaul*	Zachte leeuwenbek
Snowbell, Alpine	*Soldanella alpina*	Gewöhnliches Alpenglöckchen	Alpenkwastjesbloem
Soapwort, Tufted	*Saponaria caespitosa*	Pyrenäen-Seifenkraut	Zodevormend zeepkruid
Solomons-seal, Whorled	*Polygonatum verticillatum*	Quirlblättrige Weisswurz	Kranssalomonszegel
Speedwell, Pona's*	*Veronica ponae*	Pyrenäen-Nesselblättriger Ehrenpreis*	Pyreneese netelereprijs*
Speedwell, Wood	*Veronica montana*	Berg-Ehrenpreis	Bosereprijs
Spleenwort, Black	*Asplenium adiantum-nigrum*	Schwarze Streifenfarn	Zwartsteel
Spleenwort, Green	*Asplenium viride*	Grüner Streifenfarn	Groensteel
Spleenwort, Maidenhair	*Asplenium trichomanes*	Braunstieliger Streifenfarn	Steenbreekvaren
Spleenwort, Smooth	*Asplenium fontanum*	Jura-Streifenfarn	Genaalde streepvaren
Spurge, Irish	*Euphorbia hyberna*	Irische Wolfsmilch	Ierse wolfsmelk
Spurge, Serrate	*Euphorbia serrata*	Sägeblatt-Wolfsmilch	Gezaagde wolfsmelk*
Squill, Pyrenean	*Scilla lilio-hyacinthus*	Pyrenäen-Blaustern	Pyreneese sterhyacint
Squill, Spring	*Scilla verna*	Frühlings-Blaustern	Lente-sterhyacint
St. John's-wort, Burser's	*Hypericum richeri burseri*	Bursers Johanniskraut	Burser's hertshooi*
St. John's-wort, Slender	*Hypericum pulchrum*	Schönes Johanniskraut	Fraai hertshooi
Sternbergia, Slender	*Sternbergia colchiciflora*	Schmallblättrige Goldbecher*	Smalbladige goudkrokus*
Stock, Sad	*Matthiola fruticulosa*	Kleine Levkoje	Struikviolier
Stonecrop, Thick-leaved	*Sedum dasyphyllum*	Buckliger Mauerpfeffer	Dik vetkruid
Stork's-bill, Pyrenean*	*Erodium glandulosum*	Pyrenäen-Reiherschnabel*	Pyreneese reigersbek*
Streptopus	*Streptopus amplexifolius*	Stängelumfassender Knotenfuss	Streptopus
Tamarisk, African	*Tamarix africanus*	Afrikanische Tamariske	Afrikaanse tamarisk

Tea, Rock	*Jasonia glutinosa*	Felsentee	Rotsthee*
Thistle, Ruthenian Globe	*Echinops ritro*	Ruthenische Kugeldistel	Rutheense kogeldistel*
Thymelea, Purgative*	*Thymelaea tinctoria*	Färber-Vogelkopf*	Verfvogelkop*
Toadflax, Alpine	*Linaria alpina*	Alpen-Leinkraut	Alpenleeuwenbek
Toadflax, Malling	*Chaenorhinum origanifolium*	Origanblättriges Zwergleinkraut	Marjoleinbekje
Toadflax, Prostrate	*Linaria supina*	Niederliegendes Leinkraut	Liggende leeuwenbek
Tree, Strawberry	*Arbutus unedo*	Erdbeerbaum	Aardbeiboom
Tree, Wayfaring	*Viburnum lantana*	Wolliger Schneeball	Wollige sneeuwbal
Tulip, Wild	*Tulipa australis*	Südliche Tulpe	Zuidelijke tulp
Twayblade, Common	*Neottia ovata*	Grosses Zweiblatt	Grote keverorchis
Valerian, Globularia-leaved*	*Valeriana apula*	Kugelblumblättriger Baldrian*	Kogelbloemvaleriaan*
Valerian, Long-flowered*	*Valeriana longiflora*	Langblütiger Baldrian	Langbloemige valeriaan
Valerian, Pyrenean	*Valeriana pyrenaica*	Pyrenäen-Baldrian	Pyreneese valeriaan
Valerian, Tuberous	*Valeriana tuberosa*	Knolliger Baldrian	Knolvaleriaan*
Vetch, False	*Astragalus monspessulanus*	Französischer Tragant	Montpellier hokjespeul
Vetch, Pyrenean	*Vicia pyrenaica*	Pyrenäen-Wicke	Pyreneese wikke
Violet, Yellow Mountain	*Viola biflora*	Zweiblütiges Veilchen	Tweebloemig viooltje
Vitaliana	*Androsace vitaliana*	Goldprimel	Goudmansschild*
Whitlowgrass, Pyrenean	*Petrocallis pyrenaica*	Steinschmückel	Pyreneese kalksteenkers
Willow, Pyrenean	*Salix pyrenaica*	Pyrenäen-Weide	Pyreneese wilg
Winterfat, Pamirian	*Krascheninnikovia ceratoides*	Europäische Hornmelde	Europese hoornmelde*
Wintergreen, Common	*Pyrola minor*	Kleines Wintergrün	Klein wintergroen
Wintergreen, Green	*Pyrola chlorantha*	Grünblütiges Wintergrün	Groen wintergroen
Wintergreen, One-flowered	*Moneses uniflora*	Moosauge	Eenbloemig wintergroen
Wintergreen, Serrated	*Orthilia secunda*	Nickendes Wintergrün	Eenzijdig wintergroen
Wolfsbane	*Aconitum vulparia*	Gelber Eisenhut	Gele monnikskap
Wormwood, White*	*Artemisia herba-alba*	Weisser Wermut	Witte bijvoet*
Woundwort, Yellow	*Stachys recta*	Aufrechte Ziest	Bergandoorn
Yam, Pyrenean	*Borderea pyrenaica*	Pyrenäen-Yam*	Pyreneese yam*

MAMMALS

English	**Scientific**	**German**	**Dutch**
Badger	*Meles meles*	Dachs	Das
Barbastelle	*Barbastella barbastellus*	Mopsfledermaus	Mopsvleermuis
Bat, Alpine Long-eared	*Plecotus macrobullaris*	Alpen-Langohr	Alpengrootoorvleermuis
Bat, Daubenton's	*Myotis daubentonii*	Wasserfledermaus	Watervleermuis
Bat, European Free-tailed	*Tadarida teniotis*	Bulldoggfledermaus	Bulvleermuis
Bat, Greater Horseshoe	*Rhinolophus ferrumequinum*	Grosse Hufeisennase	Grote hoefijzerneus
Bat, Leisler's	*Nyctalus leisleri*	Kleiner Abendsegler	Bosvleermuis
Bat, Lesser Horseshoe	*Rhinolophus hipposideros*	Kleine Hufeisennase	Kleine hoefijzerneus
Bat, Lesser Mouse-eared	*Myotis oxygnatus*	Kleines Mausohr	Kleine vale vleermuis

Bat, Natterer's	*Myotis nattereri*	Fransenfledermaus	Franjestaart
Bat, Schreibers	*Miniopterus schreibersii*	Langflügelfledermaus	Schreibers Vleermuis
Bear, Brown	*Ursus arctos*	Braunbär	Bruine beer
Boar, Wild	*Sus scrofa*	Wildschwein	Wild zwijn
Cat, Wild	*Felis silvestris*	Wildkatze	Wilde kat
Chamois, Pyrenean	*Rupicapra pyrenaica*	Pyrenäengemse	Apennijnse gems
Deer, Red	*Cervus elaphus*	Rothirsch	Edelhert
Deer, Roe	*Capreolus capreolus*	Reh	Ree
Desman, Pyrenean	*Galemys pyrenaicus*	Pyrenäen-Desman	Pyreneese desman
Fox, Red	*Vulpes vulpes*	Rotfuchs	Vos
Genet	*Genetta genetta*	Ginsterkatze	Genetkat
Hare, European	*Lepus europaeus*	Hase	Haas
Hare, Iberian	*Lepus granatensis*	Iberische Hase	Iberische haas
Ibex, Iberian	*Capra pyrenaica hispanica*	Iberischen Steinbock	Iberische steenbok
Ibex, Pyrenean	*Capra pyrenaica pyrenaica*	Pyrenäen-Steinbock	Pyreneese steenbok
Isard	*see* Chamois, Pyrenean		
Lynx	*Lynx lynx*	Luchs	Lynx
Marmot, Alpine	*Marmota marmota*	Alpenmurmeltier	Alpenmarmot
Marten, Beech	*Martes foina*	Steinmarder	Steenmarter
Marten, Pine	*Martes martes*	Baummarder	Boommarter
Noctule, Common	*Nyctalus noctula*	Grosser Abendsegler	Rosse vleermuis
Noctule, Greater	*Nyctalus lasiopterus*	Riesenabendsegler	Grote rosse vleermuis
Otter	*Lutra lutra*	Fischotter	Otter
Pipistrelle, Common	*Pipistrellus pipistrellus*	Zwergfledermaus	Gewone dwergvleermuis
Pipistrelle, Kuhl´s	*Pipistrellus kuhlii*	Weissrandfledermaus	Kuhl's dwergvleermuis
Pipistrelle, Savi´s	*Hypsugo savii*	Alpenfledermaus	Savi's dwergvleermuis
Pipistrelle, Soprano's	*Pipistrellus pygmaeus*	Mückenfledermaus	Kleine dwergvleermuis
Wolf	*Canis lupus*	Wolf	Wolf

BIRDS

English	**Scientific**	**German**	**Dutch**
Accentor, Alpine	*Prunella collaris*	Alpenbraunelle	Alpenheggemus
Avocet	*Recurvirostra avosetta*	Säbelschnäbler	Kluut
Bee-eater	*Merops apiaster*	Bienenfresser	Bijeneter
Bittern, Great	*Botaurus stellaris*	Rohrdommel	Roerdomp
Bittern, Little	*Ixobrychus minutus*	Zwergdommel	Woudaapje
Blackbird	*Turdus merula*	Amsel	Merel
Blackcap	*Sylvia atricapilla*	Mönchsgrasmücke	Zwartkop
Bullfinch	*Pyrrhula pyrrhula*	Gimpel	Goudvink
Bunting, Cirl	*Emberiza cirlus*	Zaunammer	Cirlgors
Bunting, Corn	*Miliaria calandra*	Grauammer	Grauwe gors
Bunting, Ortolan	*Emberiza hortulana*	Ortolan	Ortolaan
Bunting, Reed	*Emberiza schoeniclus*	Rohrammer	Rietgors
Bunting, Rock	*Emberiza cia*	Zippammer	Grijze gors
Bustard, Great	*Otis tarda*	Grosstrappe	Grote trap
Bustard, Little	*Tetrax tetrax*	Zwergtrappe	Kleine trap
Buzzard	*Buteo buteo*	Mäusebussard	Buizerd
Buzzard, Honey	*Pernis apivorus*	Wespenbussard	Wespendief

Capercaillie	*Tetrao urogallus*	Auerhuhn	Auerhoen
Chaffinch	*Fringilla coelebs*	Buchfink	Vink
Chiffchaff	*Phylloscopus collybita*	Zilpzalp	Tjiftjaf
Chough, Alpine	*Pyrrhocorax graculus*	Alpendohle	Alpenkauw
Chough, Red-billed	*Pyrrhocorax pyrrhocorax*	Alpenkrähe	Alpenkraai
Cisticola, Zitting	*See Warbler, Fan-tailed*		
Coot	*Fulica atra*	Blässhuhn	Meerkoet
Cormorant, Great	*Phalacrocorax carbo*	Kormoran	Aalscholver
Crane, Common	*Grus grus*	Kranich	Kraanvogel
Crossbill	*Loxia curvirostra*	Fichtenkreuzschnabel	Kruisbek
Crow, Carrion	*Corvus corone*	Aaskrähe	Zwarte kraai
Cuckoo, Common	*Cuculus canorus*	Kuckuck	Koekoek
Cuckoo, Great Spotted	*Clamator glandarius*	Häherkuckuck	Kuifkoekoek
Curlew, Stone	*Burhinus oedicnemus*	Triel	Griel
Dipper	*Cinclus cinclus*	Wasseramsel	Waterspreeuw
Dotterel	*Charadrius morinellus*	Mornellregenpfeifer	Morinelplevier
Dove, Collared	*Streptopelia decaocto*	Türkentaube	Turkse tortel
Dove, Rock	*Columba livia*	Felsentaube	Rotsduif
Dove, Stock	*Columba oenas*	Hohltaube	Holenduif
Dove, Turtle	*Streptopelia turtur*	Turteltaube	Tortelduif
Duck, Tufted	*Aythya fuligula*	Reiherente	Kuifeend
Dunnock	*Prunella modularis*	Heckenbraunelle	Heggenmus
Eagle, Bonelli's	*Hieraaetus fasciatus*	Habichtsadler	Havikarend
Eagle, Booted	*Hieraaetus pennatus*	Zwergadler	Dwergarend
Eagle, Golden	*Aquila chrysaetos*	Steinadler	Steenarend
Eagle, Short-toed	*Circaetus gallicus*	Schlangenadler	Slangenarend
Egret, Cattle	*Bubulcus ibis*	Kuhreiher	Koereiger
Egret, Great	*Ardea alba*	Silberreiher	Grote zilverreiger
Egret, Little	*Egretta garzetta*	Seidenreiher	Kleine zilverreiger
Fieldfare	*Turdus pilaris*	Wacholderdrossel	Kramsvogel
Finch, Citril	*Serinus citrinella*	Zitronengirlitz	Citroenkanarie
Firecrest	*Regulus ignicapillus*	Sommergoldhähnchen	Vuurgoudhaantje
Flycatcher, Pied	*Ficedula hypoleuca*	Trauerschnäpper	Bonte vliegenvanger
Flycatcher, Spotted	*Muscicapa striata*	Grauschnäpper	Grauwe vliegenvanger
Gadwall	*Anas strepera*	Schnatterente	Krakeend
Gallinule, Purple	*Porphyrio porphyrio*	Purpurhuhn	Purperkoet
Goldcrest	*Regulus regulus*	Wintergoldhähnchen	Goudhaan
Goldfinch	*Carduelis carduelis*	Distelfink	Putter
Goshawk	*Accipiter gentilis*	Habicht	Havik
Grebe, Black-necked	*Podiceps nigricollis*	Schwarzhalstaucher	Geoorde fuut
Grebe, Great Crested	*Podiceps cristatus*	Haubentaucher	Fuut
Grebe, Little	*Tachybaptus ruficollis*	Zwergtaucher	Dodaars
Greenfinch	*Carduelis chloris*	Grünling	Groenling
Gull, Black-headed	*Chroicocephalus ridibundus*	Lachmöwe	Kokmeeuw
Gull, Yellow-legged	*Larus michahellis*	Weisskopfmöwe	Geelpootmeeuw
Harrier, Marsh	*Circus aeruginosus*	Rohrweihe	Bruine kiekendief
Harrier, Montagu's	*Circus pygargus*	Wiesenweihe	Grauwe kiekendief
Hawfinch	*Coccothraustes coccothraustes*	Kernbeisser	Appelvink

Heron, Grey	*Ardea cinerea*	Graureiher	Blauwe reiger
Heron, Night	*Nycticorax nycticorax*	Nachtreiher	Kwak
Heron, Purple	*Ardea purpurea*	Purpurreiher	Purperreiger
Heron, Squacco	*Ardeola ralloides*	Rallenreiher	Ralreiger
Hobby	*Falco subbuteo*	Baumfalke	Boomvalk
Hoopoe	*Upupa epops*	Wiedehopf	Hop
Jackdaw	*Corvus monedula*	Dohle	Kauw
Jay	*Garrulus glandarius*	Eichelhäher	Gaai
Kestrel, Common	*Falco tinnunculus*	Turmfalke	Torenvalk
Kestrel, Lesser	*Falco naumanni*	Rötelfalke	Kleine torenvalk
Kingfisher	*Alcedo atthis*	Eisvogel	IJsvogel
Kite, Black	*Milvus migrans*	Schwarzmilan	Zwarte wouw
Kite, Red	*Milvus milvus*	Rotmilan	Rode wouw
Lammergeier	*Gypaetus barbatus*	Bartgeier	Lammergier
Lapwing	*Vanellus vanellus*	Kiebitz	Kievit
Lark, Calandra	*Melanocorypha calandra*	Kalanderlerche	Kalanderleeuwerik
Lark, Crested	*Galerida cristata*	Haubenlerche	Kuifleeuwerik
Lark, Dupont's	*Chersophilus duponti*	Dupontlerche	Duponts leeuwerik
Lark, Lesser Short-toed	*Calandrella rufescens*	Stummellerche	Kleine kortteenleeuwerik
Lark, Short-toed	*Calandrella brachydactyla*	Kurzzehenlerche	Kortteenleeuwerik
Lark, Thekla	*Galerida theklae*	Theklalerche	Theklaleeuwerik
Linnet	*Carduelis cannabina*	Bluthänfling	Kneu
Magpie	*Pica pica*	Elster	Ekster
Mallard	*Anas platyrhynchos*	Stockente	Wilde eend
Martin, Crag	*Ptyonoprogne rupestris*	Felsenschwalbe	Rotszwaluw
Martin, House	*Delichon urbicum*	Mehlschwalbe	Huiszwaluw
Martin, Sand	*Riparia riparia*	Uferschwalbe	Oeverzwaluw
Moorhen	*Gallinula chloropus*	Teichhuhn	Waterhoen
Nightingale	*Luscinia megarhynchos*	Nachtigall	Nachtegaal
Nightjar	*Caprimulgus europaeus*	Ziegenmelker	Nachtzwaluw
Nightjar, Red-necked	*Caprimulgus ruficollis*	Rothalsziegenmelker	Moorse nachtzwaluw
Nuthatch	*Sitta europaea*	Kleiber	Boomklever
Oriole, Golden	*Oriolus oriolus*	Pirol	Wielewaal
Osprey	*Pandion haliaetus*	Fischadler	Visarend
Ouzel, Ring	*Turdus torquatus*	Ring ouzel	Beflijster
Owl, Barn	*Tyto alba*	Schleiereule	Kerkuil
Owl, Eagle	*Bubo bubo*	Uhu	Oehoe
Owl, Little	*Athene noctua*	Steinkauz	Steenuil
Owl, Long-eared	*Asio otus*	Waldohreule	Ransuil
Owl, Scops	*Otus scops*	Zwergohreule	Dwergooruil
Owl, Tawny	*Strix aluco*	Waldkauz	Bosuil
Owl, Tengmalm's	*Aegolius funereus*	Raufusskauz	Ruigpootuil
Partridge, Grey	*Perdix perdix*	Rebhuhn	Patrijs
Partridge, Red-legged	*Alectoris rufa*	Rothuhn	Rode patrijs
Peregrine	*Falco peregrinus*	Wanderfalke	Slechtvalk
Pigeon, Wood	*Columba palumbus*	Ringeltaube	Houtduif
Pintail	*Anas acuta*	Spiessente	Pijlstaart
Pipit, Meadow	*Anthus pratensis*	Wiesenpieper	Graspieper
Pipit, Tawny	*Anthus campestris*	Brachpieper	Duinpieper

Pipit, Tree	*Anthus trivialis*	Baumpieper	Boompieper
Pipit, Water	*Anthus spinoletta*	Bergpieper	Waterpieper
Plover, Kentish	*Charadrius alexandrinus*	Seeregenpfeifer	Strandplevier
Plover, Little Ringed	*Charadrius dubius*	Flussregenpfeifer	Kleine plevier
Pochard	*Aythya ferina*	Tafelente	Tafeleend
Pochard, Red-crested	*Netta rufina*	Kolbenente	Krooneend
Ptarmigan	*Lagopus mutus*	Alpenschneehuhn	Alpensneeuwhoen
Quail	*Coturnix coturnix*	Wachtel	Kwartel
Rail, Water	*Rallus aquaticus*	Wasserralle	Waterral
Raven	*Corvus corax*	Kolkrabe	Raaf
Redstart, Black	*Phoenicurus ochruros*	Hausrotschwanz	Zwarte roodstaart
Redstart, Common	*Phoenicurus phoenicurus*	Gartenrotschwanz	Gekraagde roodstaart
Redwing	*Turdus iliacus*	Rotdrossel	Koperwiek
Robin	*Erithacus rubecula*	Rotkehlchen	Roodborst
Roller	*Coracias garrulus*	Blauracke	Scharrelaar
Ruff	*Philomachus pugnax*	Kampfläufer	Kemphaan
Sandgrouse, Black-bellied	*Pterocles orientalis*	Sandflughuhn	Zwartbuikzandhoen
Sandgrouse, Pin-tailed	*Pterocles alchata*	Spiessflughuhn	Witbuikzandhoen
Serin	*Serinus serinus*	Girlitz	Europese kanarie
Shelduck	*Tadorna tadorna*	Brandgans	Bergeend
Shoveler	*Anas clypeata*	Löffelente	Slobeend
Shrike, Iberian Grey	*Lanius meridionalis*	Südlicher Raubwürger	Zuidelijke klapekster
Shrike, Red-backed	*Lanius collurio*	Neuntöter	Grauwe klauwier
Shrike, Woodchat	*Lanius senator*	Rotkopfwürger	Roodkopklauwier
Skylark	*Alauda arvensis*	Feldlerche	Veldleeuwerik
Snowfinch	*Montifringilla nivalis*	Schneesperling	Sneeuwvink
Sparrow, House	*Passer domesticus*	Haussperling	Huismus
Sparrow, Rock	*Petronia petronia*	Steinsperling	Rotsmus
Sparrow, Tree	*Passer montanus*	Feldsperling	Ringmus
Sparrowhawk	*Accipiter nisus*	Sperber	Sperwer
Starling, Common	*Sturnus vulgaris*	Star	Spreeuw
Starling, Spotless	*Sturnus unicolor*	Einfarbstar	Zwarte spreeuw
Stilt, Black-winged	*Himantopus himantopus*	Stelzenläufer	Steltkluut
Stonechat	*Saxicola torquata*	Schwarzkehlchen	Roodborsttapuit
Stork, White	*Ciconia ciconia*	Weissstorch	Ooievaar
Swallow, Barn	*Hirundo rustica*	Rauchschwalbe	Boerenzwaluw
Swallow, Red-rumped	*Hirundo daurica*	Rötelschwalbe	Roodstuitzwaluw
Swift, Alpine	*Apus melba*	Alpensegler	Alpengierzwaluw
Swift, Common	*Apus apus*	Mauersegler	Gierzwaluw
Swift, Pallid	*Apus pallidus*	Fahlsegler	Vale gierzwaluw
Teal	*Anas crecca*	Krickente	Wintertaling
Tern, Black	*Chlidonias niger*	Trauerseeschwalbe	Zwarte stern
Tern, Gull-billed	*Gelochelidon nilotica*	Lachseeschwalbe	Lachstern
Tern, Whiskered	*Chlidonias hybridus*	Weissbart-Seeschwalbe	Witwangstern
Thrush, Blue Rock	*Monticola solitarius*	Blaumerle	Blauwe rotslijster
Thrush, Common Rock	*Monticola saxatilis*	Steinrötel	Rode rotslijster
Thrush, Mistle	*Turdus viscivorus*	Misteldrossel	Grote lijster
Thrush, Song	*Turdus philomelos*	Singdrossel	Zanglijster
Tit, Bearded	*Panurus biarmicus*	Bartmeise	Baardman

Tit, Blue	*Parus caeruleus*	Blaumeise	Pimpelmees
Tit, Coal	*Periparus ater*	Tannenmeise	Zwarte mees
Tit, Crested	*Parus cristatus*	Haubenmeise	Kuifmees
Tit, Great	*Parus major*	Kohlmeise	Koolmees
Tit, Long-tailed	*Aegithalos caudatus*	Schwanzmeise	Staartmees
Tit, Marsh	*Parus palustris*	Sumpfmeise	Glanskop
Tit, Penduline	*Remiz pendulinus*	Beutelmeise	Buidelmees
Treecreeper, Eurasian	*Certhia familiaris*	Waldbaumläufer	Taigaboomkruiper
Treecreeper, Short-toed	*Certhia brachydactyla*	Gartenbaumläufer	Boomkruiper
Vulture, Bearded	*See Lammergeier*		
Vulture, Black	*Aegypius monachus*	Mönchsgeier	Monniksgier
Vulture, Egyptian	*Neophron percnopterus*	Schmutzgeier	Aasgier
Vulture, Griffon	*Gyps fulvus*	Gänsegeier	Vale gier
Wagtail, Grey	*Motacilla cinerea*	Gebirgsstelze	Grote gele kwikstaart
Wagtail, White	*Motacilla alba*	Bachstelze	Witte kwikstaart
Wagtail, Yellow	*Motacilla flava*	Schafstelze	Gele kwikstaart
Wallcreeper	*Tichodroma muraria*	Mauerläufer	Rotskruiper
Warbler, Bonelli's	*Phylloscopus bonelli*	Berglaubsänger	Bergfluiter
Warbler, Cetti's	*Cettia cetti*	Seidensänger	Cetti's zanger
Warbler, Dartford	*Sylvia undata*	Provencegrasmücke	Provençaalse grasmus
Warbler, Fan-tailed	*Cisticola juncidis*	Cistensänger	Graszanger
Warbler, Garden	*Sylvia borin*	Gartengrasmücke	Tuinfluiter
Warbler, Great Reed	*Acrocephalus arundinaceus*	Drosselrohrsänger	Grote karekiet
Warbler, Melodious	*Hippolais polyglotta*	Orpheusspötter	Orpheusspotvogel
Warbler, Orphean	*Sylvia hortensis*	Orpheusgrasmücke	Orpheusgrasmus
Warbler, Reed	*Acrocephalus scirpaceus*	Teichrohrsänger	Kleine karekiet
Warbler, Sardinian	*Sylvia melanocephala*	Samtkopf-Grasmücke	Kleine zwartkop
Warbler, Spectacled	*Sylvia conspicillata*	Brillengrasmücke	Brilgrasmus
Warbler, Subalpine	*Sylvia cantillans*	Weissbart-Grasmücke	Baardgrasmus
Warbler, Willow	*Phylloscopus trochilus*	Fitis	Fitis
Wheatear, Black	*Oenanthe leucura*	Trauersteinschmätzer	Zwarte tapuit
Wheatear, Black-eared	*Oenanthe hispanica*	Mittelmeer-Steinschmätzer	Blonde tapuit
Wheatear, Northern	*Oenanthe oenanthe*	Steinschmätzer	Tapuit
Whinchat	*Saxicola rubetra*	Braunkehlchen	Paapje
Woodlark	*Lullula arborea*	Heidelerche	Boomleeuwerik
Woodpecker, Black	*Dryocopus martius*	Schwarzspecht	Zwarte specht
Woodpecker, Great Spotted	*Dendrocopos major*	Buntspecht	Grote bonte specht
Woodpecker, Green	*Picus viridis*	Grünspecht	Groene specht
Woodpecker, Lesser Spotted	*Dendrocopos minor*	Kleinspecht	Kleine bonte specht
Woodpecker, White-backed	*Dendrocopos leucotos*	Weissrückenspecht	Witrugspecht
Wren	*Troglodytes troglodytes*	Zaunkönig	Winterkoning
Wryneck	*Jynx torquilla*	Wendehals	Draaihals
Yellowhammer	*Emberiza citrinella*	Goldammer	Geelgors

REPTILES AND AMPHIBIANS

English	Scientific	German	Dutch
Frog, Common	*See Frog, Grass*		
Frog, East Iberian Painted	*Discoglossus jeanneae*	Iberischer Scheibenzüngler	Oost-Iberische schijftongkikker
Frog, Graf's Hybrid	*Rana grafi*	Grafscher Hybridfrosch	Graf's bastaardkikker
Frog, Grass	*Rana temporaria*	Grasfrosch	Bruine kikker
Frog, Iberian Water	*Rana perezi*	Iberischer Wasserfrosch	Iberische groene kikker
Frog, Parsley	*Pelodytes punctatus*	Westlicher Schlammtaucher	Groengestipte kikker
Frog, Pyrenean	*Rana pyrenaica*	Pyrenäenfrosch	Pyreneeënbeekkikker
Frog, Stripeless Tree	*Hyla meridionalis*	Mittelmeer-Laubfrosch	Mediterrane boomkikker
Gecko, Moorish	*Tarentola mauretanica*	Maurischer Gecko	Muurgekko
Gecko, Turkish	*Hemidactylus turcicus*	Europäischer Halbfinger	Europese tjiktjak
Lizard, Iberian Wall	*Podarcis hispanica*	Spanische Mauereidechse	Spaanse muurhagedis
Lizard, Iberian Worm	*Blanus cinereus*	Maurische Netzwühle	Moorse wormhagedis
Lizard, Ocellated	*Lacerta lepida*	Perleidechse	Parelhagedis
Lizard, Pyrenean Rock	*Lacerta bonnali*	Pyrenäen-Gebirgseidechse	Pyreneeënberghagedis
Lizard, Spiny-footed	*Acanthodactylus erythrurus*	Europäischer Fransenfinger	Franjeteenhagedis
Lizard, Viviparous	*Lacerta viviparia*	Bergeidechse	Levendbarende hagedis
Lizard, Wall	*Podarcis muralis*	Mauereidechse	Muurhagedis
Lizard, Western Green	*Lacerta bilineata*	Westliche Smaragdeidechse	Westelijke smaragdhagedis
Newt, Marbled	*Triturus marmoratus*	Marmormolch	Marmersalamander
Newt, Palmate	*Triturus helveticus*	Fadenmolch	Vinpootsalamander
Newt, Pyrenean Brook	*Calotriton asper*	Pyrenäen-Gebirgsmolch	Pyreneeënbeeksalamander
Psammodromus, Large	*Psammodromus algirus*	Algirischer Sandläufer	Algerijnse zandloper
Psammodromus, Spanish	*Psammodromus hispanicus*	Spanischer Sandläufer	Spaanse zandloper
Salamander, Fire	*Salamandra salamandra*	Feuersalamander	Vuursalamander
Skink, Bedriaga's	*Chalcides bedriagai*	Iberischer Walzenskink	Iberische skink
Skink, Western Three-toed	*Chalcides striatus*	Westliche Erzschleiche	Gestreepte hazelskink
Snake, Aesculapian	*Elaphe longissima*	Äskulapnatter	Esculaapslang
Snake, False Smooth	*Macroprotodon cucullatus*	Kapuzennatter	Mutsslang
Snake, Grass	*Natrix natrix*	Ringelnatter	Ringslang
Snake, Horseshoe Whip	*Coluber hippocrepis*	Hufeisennatter	Hoefijzerslang
Snake, Ladder	*Elaphe scalaris*	Treppennatter	Trapslang
Snake, Montpellier	*Malpolon monspessulanus*	Eidechsennatter	Hagedisslang
Snake, Smooth	*Coronella austriaca*	Schlingnatter	Gladde slang
Snake, Southern Smooth	*Coronella girondica*	Girondische Glattnatter	Girondische gladde slang
Snake, Viperine	*Natrix maura*	Vipernatter	Adderringslang
Snake, Western Whip	*Coluber viridiflavus*	Gelbgrüne Zornnatter	Geelgroene toornslang
Spadefoot, Western	*Pelobates cultripes*	Messerfuss	Iberische knoflookpad
Terrapin, European Pond	*Emys orbicularis*	Europäische Sumpfschildkröte	Europese moerasschildpad
Terrapin, Spanish	*Mauremys leprosa*	Spanische Wasserschildkröte	Moorse beekschildpad

Toad, Spiny	*Bufo spinosa*	Mittelmeer-Erdkröte*	Mediterrane pad*
Toad, Midwife	*Alytes obstetricans*	Geburtshelferkröte	Vroedmeesterpad
Toad, Natterjack	*Bufo calamita*	Kreuzkröte	Rugstreeppad
Viper, Asp	*Vipera aspis*	Aspisviper	Aspisadder
Viper, Lataste's	*Vipera latasti*	Stülpnasenotter	Wipneusadder
Worm, Slow	*Anguis fragilis*	Blindschleiche	Hazelworm

INVERTEBRATES

English	**Scientific**	**German**	**Dutch**
Admiral, Red	*Vanessa atalanta*	Admiral	Atalanta
Admiral, Southern White	*Limenitis reducta*	Blauschwarzer Eisvogel	Blauwe ijsvogelvlinder
Admiral, White	*Limenitis camilla*	Kleiner Eisvogel	Kleine ijsvogelvlinder
Apollo	*Parnassius apollo*	Apollofalter	Apollovlinder
Apollo, Clouded	*Parnassius mnemosyne*	Schwarze Apollo	Zwarte apollovlinder
Argus, Geranium	*Aricia eumedon*	Storchschnabel-Bläuling	Zwart blauwtje
Argus, Mountain	*Aricia artaxerxes*	Grosser Sonnenröschen-Bläuling	Vals bruin blauwtje
Argus, Spanish	*Aricia morronensis*	Spanischer Kleiner Sonnenröschen-Bläuling	Spaans bruin blauwtje
Ascalaphid, Yellow-veined*	*Libelloides longicornis*	Langfühleriger Schmetterlingshaft	Langsprietvlinderhaft*
Beauty, Camberwell	*Nymphalis antiopa*	Trauermantel	Rouwmantel
Beetle, Stag	*Lucanus cervus*	Hirschkäfer	Vliegend hert
Beetle, Weaver	*Lamia textor*	Schwarzer Weberbock	Weverboktor
Black-tip, Greenish	*Euchloe charlonia*	Grünlicher Weissling*	Groen marmerwitje
Blue, Adonis	*Polyommatus bellargus*	Himmelblauer Bläuling	Adonisblauwtje
Blue, Alcon	*Maculinea alcon*	Lungenenzian-Ameisen-Bläuling	Gentiaanblauwtje
Blue, Argus	*Plebejus argus*	Geissklee-Bläuling	Heideblauwtje
Blue, Chalk-hill	*Polyommatus coridon*	Silbergrüner Bläuling	Bleek blauwtje
Blue, Chapman's	*Polyommatus thersites*	Kleine Esparsetten-Bläuling	Esparcetteblauwtje
Blue, Eros	*Polyommatus eros*	Prächtiger Alpenbläuling	Vlaggewikkeblauwtje
Blue, Escher's	*Polyommatus escheri*	Escher-Bläuling	Groot tragantblauwtje
Blue, Forster's Furry	*Polyommatus fulgens*	Spanischer Weissdolch-Bläuling	Catalaans vachtblauwtje
Blue, Gavarnie	*Plebejus pyrenaicus*	Pyrenäen-Blauling*	Zuidelijk mansschildblauwtje
Blue, Glandon	*Plebejus glandon*	Dunkler Alpenbläuling	Noordelijk mansschildblauwtje
Blue, Green-underside	*Glaucopsyche alexis*	Himmelblauer Steinkleebläuling	Bloemenblauwtje
Blue, Large	*Maculinea arion*	Schwarzgefleckten Bläuling	Tijmblauwtje
Blue, Meleager's	*Polyommatus daphnis*	Zahnflügel-Bläuling	Getand blauwtje
Blue, Osiris	*Cupido osiris*	Kleiner Alpenbläuling	Zuidelijk dwergblauwtje
Blue, Panopte's	*Pseudophilotes panoptes*	Panoptes-Bläuling	Spaans tijmblauwtje
Blue, Rippart's Anomalous	*Polyommatus ripartii*	Südliche Esparsetten-Bläuling*	Zuidelijk esparcetteblauwtje
Blue, Silver-studded	*Plebejus argus*	Geissklee-Bläuling	Heideblauwtje

Blue, Small	*Cupido minimus*	Zwergbläuling	Dwergblauwtje
Blue, Spanish Chalk-hill	*Lysandra albicans*	Silberweisser Bläuling*	Kwartsblauwtje
Blue, Turquoise	*Polyommatus dorylas*	Wundkleebläuling	Turkooisblauwtje
Blue-eye	*Erythromma lindenii*	Pokaljungfer	Kanaaljuffer
Bluet, Common	*Enallagma cyathigerum*	Gemeine Becherjungfer	Watersnuffel
Bluet, Mediterranean	*Coenagrion caerulescens*	Südliche Azurjungfer	Zuidelijke waterjuffer
Bluet, Mercury	*Coenagrion mercuriale*	Helm-Azurjungfer	Mercuurwaterjuffer
Bluetail, Common	*Ischnura elegans*	Grosse Pechlibelle	Lantaarntje
Bluetail, Iberian	*Ischnura graellsii*	Spanische Pechlibelle	Iberische grasjuffer
Brown, Dusky Meadow	*Hyponephele lycaon*	Kleines Ochsenauge	Grauw zandoogje
Butterfly, Nettle-tree	*Libythea celtis*	Zürgelbaum-Snauzenfalter	Snuitvlinder
Cardinal	*Argynnis pandora*	Kardinal	Kardinaalsmantel
Centipede, Megarian Banded	*Scolopendra cingulata*	Riesenläufer/ Gürtelskolopender	Scolopendra*
Chaser, Broad-bodied	*Libellula depressa*	Plattbauch	Platbuik
Chaser, Four-spotted	*Libellula quadrimaculata*	Vierfleck	Viervlek
Cleopatra	*Gonepteryx cleopatra*	Mittelmeer-Zitronenfalter	Cleopatra
Clubtail, Yellow	*Gomphus simillimus*	Gelbe Keiljungfer	Gele rombout
Copper, Purple-edged	*Lycaena hippothoe*	Lilagold-Feuerfalter	Rode vuurvlinder
Copper, Purple-shot	*Lycaena alciphron*	Violetter Feuerfalter	Violette vuurvlinder
Copper, Scarce	*Lycaena virgaureae*	Dukatenfalter	Morgenrood
Copper, Sooty	*Lycaena tityrus*	Brauner Feuerfalter	Bruine vuurvlinder
Copper, Violet	*Lycaena helle*	Blauschillernder Feuerfalter	Blauwe vuurvlinder
Cricket, Steppe	*Melanogryllus desertus*	Steppengrille	Europese steppekrekel*
Damselfly, Large Red	*Pyrrhosoma nymphula*	Frühe Adonisjungfer	Vuurjuffer
Darter, Desert	*Sympetrum sinaiticum*	Blasse Heidelibelle	Woestijnheidelibel
Darter, Red-veined	*Sympetrum fonscolombii*	Frühe Heidelibelle	Zwervende Heidelibel
Demoiselle, Beautiful	*Calopteryx virgo*	Blauflügel-Prachtlibelle	Bosbeekjuffer
Demoiselle, Copper	*Calopteryx haemorrhoidalis*	Bronzene Prachtlibelle	Koperen beekjuffer
Demoiselle, Western	*Calopteryx xanthostoma*	Südwestliche Prachtlibelle	Iberische beekjuffer
Dropwing, Violet	*Trithemis annulata*	Violetter Sonnenzeiger	Purperlibel
Duke-of-Burgundy	*Hamearis lucina*	Schlüsselblumen-Würfelfalter	Sleutelbloemvlinder
Emperor, Purple	*Apatura iris*	Grosser Schillerfalter	Grote weerschijnvlinder
Featherleg, Orange	*Platycnemis acutipennis*	Orangerote Federlibelle	Oranje breedscheenjuffer
Featherleg, White	*Platycnemis latipes*	Weisse Federlibelle	Witte breedscheenjuffer
Festoon, Spanish	*Zerinthia rumina*	Spanischer Osterluzeifalter	Spaanse pijpbloemvlinder
Fritillary, Dark Green	*Argynnis aglaja*	Grosser Perlmutterfalter	Grote parelmoervlinder
Fritillary, Glanville	*Melitaea cinxia*	Wegerich-Scheckenfalter	Veldparelmoervlinder
Fritillary, Heath	*Melitaea athalia*	Gemeine Scheckenfalter	Bosparelmoervlinder
Fritillary, High Brown	*Argynnis adippe*	Feuriger Perlmutterfalter	Bosrandparelmoervlinder
Fritillary, Knapweed	*Melitaea phoebe*	Flockenblumen-Scheckenfalter	Knoopkruidparelmoervlinder
Fritillary, Lesser Marbled	*Brenthis ino*	Mädesüss-Perlmutterfalter	Purperstreepparelmoervlinder
Fritillary, Marbled	*Brenthis daphne*	Brombeer-perlmuttfalter	Braamparelmoervlinder

Fritillary, Meadow	*Melitaea parthenoides*	Westlicher Scheckenfalter	Westelijke parelmoervlinder
Fritillary, Mountain	*Boloria napaea*	Ähnlicher Perlmutterfalter	Bergparelmoervlinder
Fritillary, Niobe	*Argynnis niobe*	Stiefmütterchen-Perlmutterfalter	Duinparelmoervlinder
Fritillary, Pearl-bordered	*Boloria euphrosyne*	Frühlings-Perlmuttfalter	Zilvervlek
Fritillary, Provençal	*Mellicta deione*	Leinkraut-Scheckenfalter	Spaanse parelmoervlinder
Fritillary, Queen-of-Spain	*Issoria lathonia*	Kleiner Perlmutterfalter	Kleine parelmoervlinder
Fritillary, Shepherd's	*Boloria pales*	Hochalpen Perlmutterfalter	Herdersparelmoervlinder
Fritillary, Silver-washed	*Argynnis paphia*	Kaisermantel	Keizersmantel
Fritillary, Spotted	*Melitaea didyma*	Roter Scheckenfalter	Tweekleurige parelmoervlinder
Fritillary, Twin-spot	*Brenthis hecate*	Saumfleck-Perlmutterfalter	Dubbelstipparelmoervlinder
Fritillary, Weaver's	*Boloria dia*	Magerrasen-Perlmutterfalter	Akkerparelmoervlinder
Fritillary, Western	*Melitaea parthenoides*	Westlicher Scheckenfalter	Westelijke parelmoervlinder
Gatekeeper, Common	*Pyronia tithonus*	Rotbraunes Ochsenauge	Oranje zandoogje
Gatekeeper, Southern	*Pyronia cecilia*	Südliches Ochsenauge	Zuidelijk oranje zandoogje
Gatekeeper, Spanish	*Pyronia bathseba*	Spanischer Ochsenauge	Spaans oranje zandoogje
Goldenring, Common	*Cordulegaster boltonii*	Zweigestreifte Quelljungfer	Gewone bronlibel
Goldenring, Sombre	*Cordulegaster bidentata*	Gestreifte Quelljungfer	Zuidelijke bronlibel
Grasshopper, Long-nosed	*Acrida ungarica*	Gewöhnliche Nasenschrecke	Gewone langneussprinkhaan*
Grasshopper, Siberian	*Gomphocerus sibiricus*	Sibirische Keulenschrecke	Bergknopsprietje*
Grayling, Common	*Hipparchia semele*	Ockerbindige Samtfalter	Heivlinder
Grayling, False	*Arethusana arethusa*	Rotbindiger Samtfalter	Oranje steppevlinder
Grayling, Great Banded	*Brintesia circe*	Weisser Waldportier	Witbandzandoog
Grayling, Rock	*Hipparchia alcyone*	Kleine Waldportier	Kleine boswachter
Grayling, Striped	*Pseudotergumia fidia*	Streifen-Samtfalter*	Gestreepte heivlinder
Grayling, Tree	*Neohipparchia statilinus*	Eisenfarbiger Samtfalter	Kleine heivlinder
Grayling, Woodland	*Hipparchia fagi*	Grosser Waldportier	Grote boswachter
Hairstreak, Blue Spot	*Satyrium spini*	Kreuzdorn-Zipfelfalter	Wegedoornpage
Hairstreak, Chapman's Green	*Callophrys avis*	Erdbeerbaum Zipfelfalter*	Aardbeiboomgroentje
Hairstreak, False Ilex	*Satyrium esculi*	Südlicher Eichen-Zipfelfalter	Spaanse eikenpage
Hairstreak, Purple	*Favonius quercus*	Blauer Eichen-Zipfelfalter	Eikenpage
Hairstreak, Spanish Purple	*Laeosopis roboris*	Spanischer Blauer Zipfelfalter	Essenpage
Hawker, Blue	*Aeshna cyanea*	Blaugrüne Mosaikjungfer	Blauwe glazenmaker
Hawker, Moorland	*Aeshna juncea*	Torf-Mosaikjungfer	Venglazenmaker
Hawk-moth, Broad-bordered Bee	*Hemaris fuciformis*	Hummelschwärmer	Glasvleugelpijlstaart
Hawk-moth, Hummingbird	*Macroglossum stellatarum*	Taubenschwänzchen	Kolibrievlinder

Heath, Dusky	*Coenonympha dorus*	Dorus Wiesenvögelchen	Bleek hooibeestje
Heath, Pearly	*Coenonympha arcania*	Weissbindiges Wiesenvögelchen	Tweekleurig hooibeestje
Heath, Spanish	*Coenonympha (glycerion) iphioides*	Spanisches Rostbraunes Wiesenvögelchen*	Spaans roodstreephooibeestje
Hermit	*Chazara briseis*	Berghexe	Heremiet
Hermit, Southern	*Chazara prieuri*	Südlicher Berghexe	Bonte heremiet
Longicorn, Rosalia	*Rosalia alpina*	Alpenbock	Alpenboktor
Mantis, Praying	*Mantis religiosa*	Gottesanbeterin	Bidsprinkhaan
Moth, Great Peacock	*Saturnia pyri*	Wiener Nachtpfauenauge	Grote nachtpauwoog
Moth, Spanish Moon	*Graellsia isabellae*	Isabellaspinner	Spaanse maanvlinder
Orange-tip, Provence	*Anthocharis euphenoides*	Gelber Aurorafalter	Geel oranjetipje
Orange-tip, Sooty	*Zegris eupheme*	Dunkler Aurorafalter	Zuidelijk oranjetipje
Pasha	*Charaxes jasius*	Erdbeerbaumfalter	Aardbeiboomvlinder
Pincertail, Faded	*Onychogomphus costae*	Braune Zangenlibelle	Moorse tanglibel
Pincertail, Large	*Onychogomphus uncatus*	Grosse Zangenlibelle	Grote tanglibel
Pincertail, Small	*Onychogomphus forcipatus*	Kleine Zangenlibelle	Kleine tanglibel
Red-eye, Small	*Erythromma viridulum*	Kleines Granatauge	Kleine roodoogjuffer
Ringlet, Autumn	*Erebia neoridas*	Herbst-Mohrenfalter*	Herfsterebia
Ringlet, False Dewy	*Erebia sthennyo*	Pyrenäen Graubrauner Mohrenfalter*	Pyreneeëndauwerebia
Ringlet, Gavarnie	*Erebia gorgone*	Pyrenäen Kleiner Mohrenfalter*	Pyreneeënzijde-erebia
Ringlet, Lefebvres	*Erebia lefebvrei*	Lefebvres Mohrenfalter*	Cantabrische erebia
Ringlet, Mountain	*Erebia epiphron*	Knochs Mohrenfalter	Bergerebia
Ringlet, Piedmont	*Erebia meolans*	Gelbbindiger Mohrenfalter	Donkere erebia
Ringlet, Prunner's	*Erebia triaria*	Alpen Mohrenfalter	Zuidelijke erebia
Ringlet, Pyrenees Brassy	*Erebia rondoui*	Pyrenäen Schillernder Mohrenfalter*	Pyreneeënglanserebia
Ringlet, Western Brassy	*Erebia arvernensis*	Westlischer Schillenernder Mohrenfalter*	Westelijke glanserebia
Satyr, Black	*Satyrus actaea*	Spanische Waldportier*	Kleine saterzandoog
Satyr, Great Sooty	*Satyrus ferula*	Weisskernauge	Grote saterzandoog
Scarlet, Broad	*Crocothemis erythraea*	Feuerlibelle	Vuurlibel
Scorpion, Spanish	*Buthus ibericus*	Iberischer Skorpion*	Iberische schorpioen*
Skimmer, Keeled	*Orthetrum coerulescens*	Kleiner Blaupfeil	Beekoeverlibel
Skimmer, Southern	*Orthetrum brunneum*	Südlicher Blaupfeil	Zuidelijke oeverlibel
Skimmer, Yellow-veined	*Orthetrum nitidinerve*	Gelbader-Blaupfeil	Geeladeroeverlibel
Skipper, Alpine Grizzled	*Pyrgus andromedae*	Alpen-Würfel-Dickkopffalter	Bergspikkeldikkopje
Skipper, Cinquefoil	*Pyrgus cirsii*	Spätsommer-Würfel-Dickkopffalter	Rood spikkeldikkopje
Skipper, Large Grizzled	*Pyrgus alveus*	Sonnenröschen Würfel-Dickkopffalter	Groot spikkeldikkopje
Skipper, Lulworth	*Thymelicus acteon*	Mattscheckiger Braun-Dickkopffalter	Dwergdikkopje
Skipper, Marbled	*Carcharodus lavatherae*	Loreley Dickkopffalter	Andoorndikkopje

Skipper, Safflower	*Pyrgus carthami*	Steppenheiden-Würfel-Dickkopffalter	Witgezoomd spikkeldikkopje
Skipper, Sage	*Muschampia proto*	Brandkraut-Dickkopffalter*	Klein brandkruiddikkopje
Skipper, Silver Spotted	*Hesperia comma*	Komma-Dickkopffalter	Kommavlinder
Skipper, Southern Grizzled	*Pyrgus malvoides*	Kleiner Südlicher Würfeldickkopffalter	Zuidelijke aardbeivlinder
Spectre, Western	*Boyeria irene*	Westliche Geisterlibelle	Schemerlibel
Spider, Gravel Wolf	*Arctosa cinerea*	Flussuferwolfspinne	Grindwolfspin
Spreadwing, Common	*Lestes sponsa*	Gemeine Binsenjungfer	Gewone pantserjuffer
Swallowtail	*Papilio machaon*	Schwalbenschwanz	Koninginnenpage
Swallowtail, Scarce	*Iphiclides podalirius*	Segelfalter	Koningspage
Tiger, Cream-spot	*Arctia villica*	Schwarzer Bär	Roomvlek
Underwing, Dark Crimson	*Catocala sponsa*	Grosses Eichenkarmin	Karmozijnrood weeskind
Underwing, Light Crimson	*Catocala promissa*	Kleines Eichenkarmin	Eikenweeskind
White, Black-veined	*Aporia crataegi*	Baumweissling	Groot geaderd witje
White, Esper's Marbled	*Melanargia russiae*	Südliches Schachbrett	Zuidelijk dambordje
White, Iberian Marbled	*Melanargia lachesis*	Iberisches Schachbrett	Spaans dambordje
White, Marbled	*Melanargia galathea*	Schachbrett	Dambordje
White, Small	*Pieris rapae*	Kleiner Kohlweissling	Klein koolwitje
White, Western Dappled	*Euchloe crameri*	Westlicher Gesprenkelter Weissling	Westelijk marmerwitje
White, Western Marbled	*Melanargia occitanica*	Westliches Schachbrett	Westelijk dambordje
White, Wood	*Leptidea sinapis*	Senfweissling	Boswitje
Whiteface, Small	*Leucorrhinia dubia*	Kleine Moosjungfer	Venwitsnuitlibel
Wood Fairy	*Nemoptera bipennis*	Fadenhaft	Iberische prachtvleugel*
Yellow, Bergers Clouded	*Colias alfacariensis*	Hufeisenklee-Gelbling	Zuidelijke luzernevlinder
Yellow, Clouded	*Colias crocea*	Postillon	Oranje luzernevlinder
Yellow, Mountain Clouded	*Colias phicomone*	Alpengelbling	Bergluzernevlinder

FISH

English	**Scientific**	**German**	**Dutch**
Trout, Brown	*Salmo trutta*	Bachforelle	Beekforel

PICTURE CREDITS

In the references that follow the numbers refer to the pages and the letters to the position on the page (t=top, c=centre, b=bottom with l and r indicating left and right).

Aarts, Luc: 168 (b)
Cereza, Chema: 5 (5), 22 (c), 117 (t), 118, 129
Crossbill Guides / Cate, Bouke ten: 125, 186, 187 (b)
Crossbill Guides / Hilbers, Dirk: cover, 4 (1, 4), 5 (7,8), 10, 13 (tc, bc, b), 18 (l), 24 (t+b), 25, 29 (t+b), 30, 32, 34, 35, 36, 37, 39, 42 (t+b), 44, 46, 50, 51, 52, 55, 59, 60 (t+b), 62 (t+b), 63, 64, 65, 66 (t, c, b), 68 (t, bl, bc), 70, 71, 72 (tl, bl, br), 73 (tr, bl, br), 79, 80 (b), 88, 104, 105, 106, 109, 110, 114 (b), 117 (t), 122 (t), 123, 125 (t), 126, 128 (t+b), 130, 132, 135, 136 (t+b), 137, 139, 140, 141 (r), 145, 146, 149 (t), 152 (t+b), 155, 156 (all), 158, 159 (t+b), 160, 161, 166, 168 (t), 169, 171 (all), 172 (b), 177 (t), 178, 180 (t+b), 183, 184, 188, 192 (t+b), 192, 195 (l+r), 197, 199 (t+b), 201, 202, 205, 209 (t+b), 210, 215, 217 (t+b), 220 (l), 222 (b), 223, 224 (t+b)
Crossbill Guides / Lotterman, Kim: 4 (3), 72 (tr), 73 (tl), 191, 212, 214 (b)
Crossbill Guides / Swinkels, Constant: 144, 203
Crossbill Guides / Vliegenthart, Albert: cover, 26, 38 (b), 95 (t+b), 96, 97, 98 (b+t), 99 (b+t), 102, 102 (t,c,b), 183, 211 (b), 217 (c), 226
Grasa, Manolo: 4 (2), 54, 83 (t), 90 (t)
Hoogenboom, Dick: 82 (t)
Jaime, Chabier de: 113 (b)
Laak, Paul van der: 38 (b)
Mager, Jörg: cover, 80 (t), 84, 116 (c), 219
Martínez Arguis, Javier: cover, 87, 149 (b)
Moore, Derek: 85 (b)
Saxifraga / Dekker, Hans: 68 (br)
Saxifraga / Hoogenstein, Luc: 29 (b)
Saxifraga / Knijff, Arie de: 117 (b)
Saxifraga / Kruijsbergen, Willem van: 187 (t)
Saxifraga / Munsterman, Piet: 82 (b)
Saxifraga / Nijendijk, Jan: 208
Saxifraga / Zekhuis, Mark: 86
Sanz, Carlos: 75, 76
Uchelen, Edo van: 5 (6), 89, 91, 90 (b), 92, 94
Woutersen, Kees: cover, 13 (t), 18 (r), 19, 20, 22, 27, 38 (t), 40 (t), 43, 47, 48, 49, 74, 77, 78, 111, 113 (t), 114 (l), 115, 119, 121, 122 (b), 133, 143, 148, 150, 154, 157, 162, 167, 172 (t), 174, 175, 176, 177 (b), 181, 189, 190, 191, 193, 194, 196, 198, 207, 211, 214, 218, 220 (r)
Winkel, Edwin: 39, 85 (t), 141 (l), 222 (t), 225

All illustrations by Chris Braat, except Griffon Vulture on page 15: Horst Wolter.

ACKNOWLEDGEMENTS

The first edition of this guidebook was produced in close collaboration with TuHuesca-PRODESA, the provincial tourism organisation that operates under the slogan Huesca La Magia. Without the support of this organisation, in particular Fernando Blasco, this book would not have been possible.

This guidebook could not have been written without the help of many people – from local experts and photographers to the wide group of 'Friends of the Crossbill Guides', who often assist in the production of our books. From Huesca, we would like to thank Javier García and Alberto Campo from Inizia, who helped us bring together all the right people to produce this guidebook. Manolo Grasa from Torla provided us with a wealth of information on the Ordesa and Monte Perdido National Park. Luis Tirado from SEO/BirdLife in Aragón gave valuable details on the animal and plant life in the steppes of Monegros. Javier Mañas, from rural guesthouse Allucant, provided us with inside information on the Gallocanta lagoon. At the Instituto Pirenaico de Ecología (Jaca), we found specialised information on the flora and vegetation of the region.

Furthermore, we warmly thank the Crossbill Guides team. Henk Strijbosch gave us valuable information about reptiles and amphibians, Albert Vliegenhart on butterflies and dragonflies, and John Cantelo on birds.

In preparation for the third edition of this guidebook, we explored new areas and described new routes. From our base in Huesca – where Pilar Uriarte made us the most fabulous lunches and dinners, despite midday temperatures of almost 40 °C – we ventured into the Monegros and the Sierra de Guara.

We combined our own experiences in the field with the feedback of readers. Additionally, Niels de Haan, Gert Elbertsen and Constant Swinkels provided great support, meticulously proof-walking and proofreading parts of the text. For this third edition, we also received additional photographs from Chema Cereza, Javier Martínez Arguis and Constant Swinkels.

We thank them warmly, along with all the other photographers listed on the previous page!

Dirk Hilbers and Kees Woutersen
Crossbill Guides Foundation, September 2025